ODES AND ELEGIES

Wesleyan Poetry

ODES AND ELEGIES

Friedrich Hölderlin

Translated and edited by Nick Hoff

Wesleyan University Press
Middletown, Connecticut

Published by Wesleyan University Press, Middletown, CT 06459
www.wesleyan.edu/wespress
Wesleyan edition copyright © 2008 by Nick Hoff
Printed in the United States of America
1 3 5 4 2

Library of Congress Catalog-in-Publication Data

Hölderlin, Friedrich, 1770–1843.
[Poems. English & German. Selections]
Odes and elegies / Friedrich Hölderlin ; translated and edited
by Nick Hoff.
p. cm. — (Wesleyan poetry)
Includes bibliographical references and index.
ISBN 978-0-8195-6890-8 (cloth : alk. paper)
1. Hölderlin, Friedrich, 1770–1843—Translations into English.
I. Hoff, Nick. II. Title.
PT2359.H2A253 2008
831'.6—dc22   2008033381

This project is supported in part by an award from the National
Endowment for the Arts

NATIONAL
ENDOWMENT
FOR THE ARTS

A great nation
deserves great art.

CONTENTS

IV. Nightsongs

ACKNOWLEDGMENTS

I would like to express my deep thanks to my family, especially to my parents Linda and John, for their constant support and faith in my abilities and direction. I am also extremely grateful to the editors of the two major Hölderlin critical editions, Friedrich Beissner and D. E. Sattler, for their tremendous editorial achievements, as well as for those of Jochen Schmidt, Michael Knaupp, and Günther Mieth—this book is inconceivable without their work. I owe special thanks to Jack Hirschman and Csaba Polony, the editors at *Left Curve* who published earlier versions of some of these translations, and Russell Berman who did the same in *Telos*, for their early and invaluable encouragement. I would also like to thank Sarah Anderson, Andrew Hoff, Brian Griffey, and Jerome Hiler for their help with the introduction; John Borruso for his help formulating my ideas for the design; Clayton Carlson for his help navigating the publishing world thickets; Andrew Joron for his generous and meticulous proofreading; and Suzanna Tamminen for her enthusiasm and belief in the project. For answering my many questions on the finer points of the German language I am indebted to Stefan-Ludwig Hoffman, Tarcisius Schelbert, Hannes Schüpbach, Hans-Ulrich Gumbrecht, and Chris Hoff for their patient and helpful replies. Maia Ipp has been limitless in her support, both moral and editorial; for her overwhelming kindness and enthusiasm, and for her fine poetic sensibility, I am deeply grateful. Finally, I would like to express my deep gratitude to Richard Sieburth and Nathaniel Dorsky for their boundless generosity. Richard's support for the project and immense editorial work on the text have helped make this book a reality. Nathaniel's friendship, encouragement, and editorial ear, which have improved this book in countless ways, far surpass any thanks I can give.

INTRODUCTION

The poetry of Friedrich Hölderlin exerts an influence like the pull of a giant wayward star. So strong has been its allure that one feels compelled to ask exactly why Hölderlin's work captivates to this day so many major poets and philosophers.[1] What is it about this poet who wrote over two hundred years ago—whose translations of Sophocles were the subject of Goethe and Schiller's dismissive laughter—that speaks with such tremendous force to us today? The answer, I think, lies in Hölderlin's experience of modernity. For Hölderlin's is one of the first—and deepest—experiences that is, in its essence, our own.

As Hölderlin wrote in "The Poet's Calling," we live in a world in which "everything divine" has been "utilized" for too long, and "all the heavenly powers [. . .] thrown away." We think we can grasp the world, that we can "name all the stars in heaven," but we have lost our way to the divine.

This absence of the sacred, this deep sense of loss that underlies the unease of modern Western culture—and much of Hölderlin's work—has only intensified in the two hundred years since "The Poet's Calling" was written. Hölderlin speaks so strongly to us today because his poetry is grounded in a profound experience of this absence, of the break in tradition that in many ways defines our times. But content alone does not make lasting art. The deep pathos and strange directness of Hölderlin's poetic language are also crucial to his work's continued resonance. Hölderlin discovered his own poetic voice in his mid-twenties, in the years between 1796 and 1800 while serving as a house tutor in Frankfurt and, later, while living alone in Homburg. In the relatively short period of stability that remained to him—the six years until insanity

overwhelmed him in 1806—he produced some of the most intense
and beautiful lyric poems ever written in the German language.

Early in the summer of 1795, without telling anyone of his plans,
twenty-five-year-old Friedrich Hölderlin abruptly left Jena in east-
ern Germany and returned to his mother's home in Nürtingen,
some 275 miles to the southwest. He had been in Jena for just under
six months.

The move must have come as a surprise to his friends, for
Hölderlin, living independently for the first time in his life, was
making important contacts and beginning to establish himself as a
writer in the culturally exciting Jena. He had developed close and
friendly relationships with the philosopher Immanuel Niethammer
and the poets Christoph Martin Wieland and Friedrich Schiller,
and even Goethe and the influential philosopher Johann Gottfried
von Herder had received him kindly in nearby Weimar. At the uni-
versity in Jena, Johann Gottlieb Fichte, delivering the first of his fa-
mous lectures on his philosophical system, would occasionally ex-
change a few words with the young poet. An impressive array of
talent—the elite in German letters—was packed into those two
small Thüringen towns, and Hölderlin had personal contact with
everyone of importance.

The solicitude of his literary hero Schiller was by far the most
significant for Hölderlin. Schiller, who would later write to Goethe
that he saw much of his younger self in Hölderlin's poetry, fre-
quently invited Hölderlin to his house, gave him advice, com-
mented on his poetry, and published in his literary journals a num-
ber of Hölderlin's poems, as well as a fragment of his novel
Hyperion. Schiller had also found a publisher interested in publish-
ing the entire novel.

Hölderlin, though, often felt overwhelmed and inadequate in the
presence of Schiller and so many other "great men." In the fall of
1794 he wrote to his good friend Christian Ludwig Neuffer that

The proximity of truly great spirits [. . .] alternately strikes me down and lifts me up; I have to help myself out of this twilight and slumber; I must gently yet forcibly waken and cultivate my half-developed, half-dead energies if I'm not to take refuge, in the end, in a sad resignation, [. . .] Rather the grave than this condition! And yet I often have almost no other prospect.[2]

Hölderlin felt this inferiority most acutely in Schiller's presence. Though he wrote to his mother that a simple "visit to Schiller's [. . .] gives me more pleasure and strength than the society of anyone else,"[3] Schiller's power to unsettle Hölderlin overshadowed whatever pleasure and strength he could gain in the famous poet's presence. "Really," Hölderlin would write to Schiller two years after his flight from Jena, "you animate me too much when I am around you."[4] Hölderlin wanted desperately to earn Schiller's complete respect as a poet, and his failure to do so made it impossible to be near him. Later, in another letter to Schiller, he confessed, "I am sometimes in a secret battle with your genius that I may save my freedom from it."[5] Hölderlin's flight from Jena, seemingly so abrupt and strange, was probably born of a deep inner necessity—an attempt to save his existence as a poet.

It is not surprising, therefore, that the first time we encounter Hölderlin's own poetic voice is in a poem he wrote early in 1796, soon after this break with Jena and Schiller. Though it does not achieve the stark and strange perfection of some of his later work, it is clear that "The Oaks," the poem with which this book begins, is no longer in the realm of the abstraction and Schillerian rhymed stanzas of Hölderlin's earlier poetry, much of which seems to have been written without the conviction of experience. In contrast to this earlier work, "The Oaks" contains an imagery, meter, and syntax that exudes an urgency and longing won through hard experience and suffering. The opening dactylic rush of "Out from the gardens I'm coming to you" is something quite different from the iambic patterns that so much of Hölderlin's earlier poetry could not escape.

The content of "The Oaks," as Momme Mommsen has shown,[6] also testifies to Hölderlin's break with Schiller. The poet of "The Oaks," as we read in the poem's opening lines, cannot remain in the civilized garden where he is dependent on ("tended" by) others. The "good order" of Schiller's poetic garden will only keep the poet from being "joyful and free" in untamed nature—it will keep him from writing work authentically his own.

Schiller, for his part, seems to have thought Hölderlin's yearning for freedom and independence naïve. The last two lines of his poem "The Philosophical Egoist," published several months after Hölderlin left Jena, speak directly to Hölderlin:

Poor one, will you stand there *alone* and alone by yourself,
    When it is only by the exchange of powers that the infinite stands?

The poet of "The Oaks," explicitly replying to Schiller's poem, would indeed gladly stand by himself, if he could, like the oak trees.

Hölderlin knew that Schiller's greatness and influence would only suffocate him and never allow his own voice to develop. Two years after leaving Jena, he wrote to Schiller that

[. . .] because I feel how much a word from you can decide for me, I try sometimes to forget you in order not to become anxious while I'm working. For I'm aware that it is precisely this anxiousness and self-consciousness that are the death of art [. . .][7]

Even after Hölderlin left Jena, both Schiller and Goethe tried to influence him by steering him away from what they saw as his dangerous tendency toward a one-sided subjectivity. Schiller, for example, advised Hölderlin in a letter to "flee, where possible, philosophical subject matter [. . . and] stay near the world of the senses."[8] Hölderlin, though, resisted this pressure; the advice did not address his needs. He responded to this letter some seven months later in a willful tone highly atypical of his usually deferential correspondence with Schiller: "I have enough of my own courage and judgment," he declared, "to make myself independent of other masters and art critics and in this respect to go, with the necessary calm, my own way."[9] And although he qualifies this by writing "but my dependence on you [Schiller] is insurmountable"—a phrase that seems to contradict his willfulness—one can see in it, as Mommsen does, only a temporary mitigation of the more strident tone. For shortly after receiving Schiller's advice to "stay near the world of the senses," Hölderlin composed the following epigram, entitled "Descriptive Poetry":

> Breaking news! Apollo's now the god of newspapermen,
> And he who loyally states all the facts is his man.

As much as he admired Schiller, Hölderlin knew he could not follow his master's direction.

After leaving Jena, Hölderlin stayed in Nürtingen with his mother, who, perhaps to keep some degree of control over her son, gave Hölderlin only limited amounts of the inheritance his deceased father had left him. Hölderlin wrote to Neuffer that he felt himself "an unwanted guest" in his mother's house. Six hard months passed, and in early December an opportunity to escape finally materialized when Hölderlin received a job offer to tutor the eight-year-old son of a Frankfurt banking family.

Frankfurt am Main, a mercantile and bourgeois city, could not have been less amenable to Hölderlin's spirit. But, to gain independence from both his mother and from the Swabian Consistory that had paid for his studies,[10] he took the job without hesitation. The move was to change his life. For it was in Frankfurt, in the person of his student's mother Susette Gontard, that Hölderlin discovered love. "Dear friend," he wrote to Neuffer that summer, finally confessing his love, "there is a being in this world on whom my spirit can and will dwell for millennia [. . .]"

But the affair would prove impossible: Susette Gontard was the wife of Hölderlin's employer, the banker Jakob Friedrich Gontard. As was customary for tutors of the era, Hölderlin lived with his student's family. Jakob, though, constantly buried in his business, seemed at first to turn a blind eye to the growing intimacy between his wife and Hölderlin. After two and a half years, however, the tension in the triangle had become too much, and Hölderlin, probably on Susette's insistence, left for nearby Homburg in the fall of

1798. He and Susette exchanged letters and saw each other intermittently for two more years until Hölderlin left Homburg in June of 1800. Their last meeting was on May 8 of that year; they would never see each other again. But the experience had been decisive. In love Hölderlin discovered an intimation of the harmony and reconciliation of a unified world. But as an intimation of that unity, and not unity itself, love could only reveal a wholeness that had been lost.

The hexameters, elegiac fragments, and odes Hölderlin wrote during his four years in Frankfurt and Homburg testify to and emerge from this experience. His poetry now begins to open itself to a truly heartfelt longing and sensitivity. The directness of the opening question in "Sunset," for example, the pure loss captured by its simple, penetrating words and the intimacy of the familiar address to the sun, transports the reader into the depth of Hölderlin's world of loss and love. We experience with the poet a divine union with light and love that, like the sun, has set. Only a plaintive cry of such tender directness as the poem's opening question could reveal this absence.

> *Sunset*
> Where are you? Drunk, my soul fades
> In all your bliss; for I've just
> Listened in as the enrapturing
> Sun-boy, full of golden tones,
>
> Played the evensong upon his heavenly lyre;
> It resounded through the woods and hills.
> But he has gone, far away,
> To god-fearing peoples who revere him still.

Love is here not fulfillment but a source of longing. The sun god has fled and left us among the godless, far from the heavenly fire, and the poet, remembering the sun's bliss, sings traces of its former presence.

Remembrance of the divine is perhaps *the* key theme in Hölderlin's work. And, whether manifest in a memory of the sun gone down, or of childhood or the homeland, or of the poet's song or of ancient Greece, it is always accompanied by the acute consciousness that we—as individuals and a community—are not in harmony with the gods.[11] For only through remembrance can we recognize what we lack in the present.

In Frankfurt and Homburg Hölderlin returned repeatedly to this theme. It was then that the "absence of the gods" became one of his fundamental concerns. This theme is particularly strong in the poem "Diotima," which carries the name Hölderlin gave Susette Gontard in his poems.

Diotima

You favorite of the heavenly muse, you who once reconciled the elements,
    Come and comfort me against the chaos of our time,
Order the raging battle with the peaceful music of heaven
    Till what's cleft in two become one in the mortal heart,
Till ancient human nature, so calm, so great,
    Serenely and powerfully rise from out of our seething times.
Return to the destitute hearts of the people, O living beauty!
    Return to the banqueting table, return to the temples!
For Diotima lives, like the delicate blossoms in winter,
    And though she is rich in her spirit, she also seeks out the sun.
But the sun of the spirit, that more beautiful world, has set,
    And only the storms quarrel in frost-covered night.

Thus the remembrance of the divine, created by the poet and Diotima's love in the present, is only a trace of the gods' former presence. This trace contains the hope of the "delicate blossoms in winter," but still only "the storms quarrel in frost-covered night"— for we can no longer relate to the gods who have fled. The trace thus reveals our destitution.

Hölderlin's sense of loss and destitution was not simply due to a personal predilection for suffering, but was part of a larger cultural phenomenon that arose from powerful currents seething under the Enlightenment—an increasing alienation from nature and a growing sense of disenchantment in the face of a triumphant rationality and waning traditions and values. Hölderlin was not alone in perceiving these changes and experiencing them deeply. Hegel, for example, famously wrote of alienated consciousness, and Schiller described modern human beings as "stunted plant[s], [that] show only a feeble vestige of their nature."[12] Hölderlin, for his part, reacted to these currents with an almost overwhelming longing for lost wholeness.

Hegel, Hölderlin's roommate and friend at the Tübingen seminary, was deeply influenced by Hölderlin during the poet's Homburg period. Hegel of course turned to philosophy to understand the forces driving the momentous changes in Western culture, and Hölderlin, too, was for a time tempted by philosophy.[13] But that temptation soon passed, for after Hölderlin met Susette Gontard he no longer felt "driven into [the] abstraction" of philosophical thought. "I am in a new world," he wrote to Neuffer in July of 1796. "I thought I knew before what was beautiful and good, but now that I've seen it, I have to laugh at all my knowledge." He now enjoys, he continued, "writing poetry more than ever." If philosophy had been a possibility for him, it now no longer was: "That which is living in poetry," he wrote to Neuffer in November of 1798, "is now the chief concern of my thoughts."

It had become clear to Hölderlin in Frankfurt and Homburg, I think, that abstract, philosophical reflection could not adequately address the general and growing sense of dislocation and fragmentation in the Western world. Philosophy, in taking phenomena apart to understand their constituent pieces, could not possibly produce an experience of the whole. But since such an experience was precisely what was needed, the only possibility of achieving it lay in a creative, binding, and healing force that could make whole—or at least give an intimation of that wholeness to—our "stunted" and alienated souls. This force, Hölderlin learned in Frankfurt with Susette Gontard, was love. And poetry, because it was characterized for Hölderlin by "the constant determination [*Bestimmtheit*] of consciousness with which the poet looks at a *whole*,"[14] and because it could communicate to the people, could begin to reawaken our individual and communal longing for the unity toward which love grows.

Poetry awakens longing because it expresses a trace of the whole. And as so much of Hölderlin's poetry shows, consciousness of a trace of the whole actually implies extreme separation from it: Hölderlin's poetry from before his final breakdown in 1806 never comes to rest in a final state of calm or bliss. Perhaps it is precisely this aspect of his poetry that lets Hölderlin speak so forcefully to us today, for he does not shrink from the modern condition of separation. Filled as his poetry is with ecstatic expressions of beauty and joy, Hölderlin nevertheless always refuses to celebrate a false sense of union or feeling of oneness; he refuses to give easy salves to our sense of dislocation. Thus Hölderlin remains contemporary in our struggle to overcome our peculiarly modern alienation and distance from the world. Hölderlin discovered and nurtured this great modern theme in all its depth and poignancy during his time in Frankfurt and Homburg. It was in these four years that his work became authentically his own.

By the summer of 1800, with dwindling funds and no real job prospects, Hölderlin's existence in Homburg was in jeopardy. He had attempted to create a monthly journal that would have paid him a salary as its editor, but the interested publisher wanted famous names as contributors, and Hölderlin's appeals to Goethe, Schiller, and others came to naught. After this disappointment ("are people so completely ashamed of me?" he wrote in a letter to Susette in September of 1799), he reluctantly returned to Nürtingen in June of 1800 but then soon departed for Stuttgart, where he stayed with his friend Christian Landauer and tried to make a living giving private lessons. But this did not produce enough income, and he soon began looking for another house tutor position. By December he found one in the Swiss town of Hauptwil.

It was a lonely winter and spring, given over, perhaps, to too much self-reflection. "Is it a blessing or a curse," he wrote to Landauer in March of 1801, "this loneliness that seems destined to me by my nature." But he would have no time to situate himself in

Hauptwil. Three months later, due to a change in the situation of the family for whom he was working, Hölderlin was let go. It was back again to Nürtingen (the trip through the Alps to his home-town would serve later as the basis for the elegy "Homecoming"), where he spent the summer of 1801 at his mother's home trying to arrange for another job. These efforts bore fruit when he found a position tutoring the children of the German Consul in Bordeaux, and in December he set off on foot for the south of France—a trip that would prove harrowing. In a letter from Bordeaux, Hölderlin wrote to his mother of a mysterious experience crossing the moun-tains of the Auvergne: "I have experienced so much I can still barely speak of it. [. . .] on the snowy heights of the Auvergne, in storms and wilderness, on an ice-cold night with a loaded pistol by my rough bed—I prayed then the best prayer in my life and I will never forget it. I have made it safely—give thanks with me!"[15]

We have little insight into what happened to Hölderlin on the mountain. Nor do we know much about his stay in France in gen-eral, though some of his later hymns were marked by his experi-ences there. In any event, and for reasons unknown to us, the Bor-deaux job lasted only a matter of months, and by the early summer of 1802 Hölderlin was back in southern Germany. But he arrived there changed and shaken. According to his friend Friedrich Matthisson, Hölderlin returned to Stuttgart from France—per-haps most of the way on foot—"pale as a corpse, emaciated, his eyes hollow and wild, his hair and beard long, and dressed like a beggar." He announced himself by "murmuring in a hollow, disem-bodied tone: 'Hölderlin.'"[16]

After a brief stay in Stuttgart, the poet went back to his mother's home in Nürtingen, where his arrival there seems to have been a precursor to his final descent into madness: having sent no letters to his family for months, he suddenly appeared at his mother's home and with a confused look and frantic gestures chased everyone out of the house in a rage.[17] He didn't stay long in Nürtingen and soon returned to Stuttgart, where, we learn from a letter Landauer wrote to Hölderlin's half-brother, Hölderlin grew "gradually calmer." Several weeks later, though, he received a terrible blow in a letter from his friend Isaac Sinclair: Susette, who had been nursing her children sick with the measles, had died in June. This news was too much, and he left his friends for his mother's home once again.

In Nürtingen Hölderlin was cared for by a doctor whose son read Homer to him to soothe his nerves. In the fall, after a trip with Sinclair to Regensburg, Hölderlin felt himself to have gained a degree of calm and was able, at times, to work. For the next two years he spent most of his time in Nürtingen, alternating between periods of intense work and bouts of debilitating apathy and depression. He had been through many tribulations: the long trips on foot to and from France, the loneliness and homelessness, the mental anguish of his approaching madness. Nevertheless, this time between leaving Homburg in the summer of 1800 and spending the winter of 1803–04 in his mother's home was one of Hölderlin's most productive periods. His expressive mastery of the ode and elegy reached its zenith during these years, and his longer poems in these forms, as well as the free-verse hymns, Nightsongs, and his Pindar and Sophocles translations, all come from this time.

Did Hölderlin experience on his journey to France a fullness of such intensity—perhaps driving him to the brink of insanity—that he now saw it as too dangerous to invoke? Now, instead of simply longing for such fullness, Hölderlin's poetry acts as a mediator between the gods, who seem to have the power to grant us wholeness, and human beings. For although we may long for complete union with nature, we could not bear its intensity—the heavenly fire of this union would obliterate us as individuals. Thus the gods, that we not perish from divine fullness and might "long enjoy the light,"[18] also give us "holy sorrow."

> For they who lend us fire from heaven,
>   The gods, they grant us holy sorrow too—
>   So be it. I seem to be a son
>   Of Earth; made to love, to suffer.[19]

But we only know deep sorrow because the poets have brought their "suitable hands"[20] to "interpret the holy lore"[21] and sing us traces of the fled gods. The poets' song reminds us of the gods, of the wholeness we have lost.

By looking at the whole and interpreting its trace, the poet sings the word. For Hölderlin, this holy word is poetry's concern:

When we bless the meal, whom should I name, and when we
 Rest from the life of the day, tell me, how should I bring forth my
  thanks?
Should I then name the high one? [22]

The high one has not been named—this the poet must do that we may, through this naming, know the powers that will preserve us beholding the whole. This search for the names of the gods who have fled, which had become the task of Hölderlin's poetry as early as his time in Frankfurt, grew increasingly urgent and explicit in his work after 1800. The poems from this period, the odes and elegies composed after Hölderlin left Homburg and Susette in 1800, comprise roughly the second half of this book.

In the summer of 1804, the politically radical Sinclair arranged a position for Hölderlin as a court librarian in Homburg (Hölderlin was probably unaware that his salary was to be drawn from Sinclair's). But by then Hölderlin's health was deteriorating rapidly, and by 1806 his mind could not hold out. In January of 1805 Sinclair was put on trial for plotting against the Elector, and Hölderlin's association with his friend drew the poet into the legal proceedings as well.[23] In the end, Sinclair was released, and Hölderlin, declared insane, did not have to go on trial—he allegedly continually shouted "*Vive le roi*" and "I don't want to be a Jacobin!" and spoke, according to a Homburg doctor, a strange pidgin of German, Latin, and Greek.

But the episode had taken its toll. In August Sinclair wrote to Hölderlin's mother that she needed to fetch her son, as his ravings had so enraged the neighbors that Sinclair feared for the poet's safety. After a brief stay by the poet in a clinic in Tübingen, the carpenter Ernst Zimmer, and admirer of Hölderlin's work, and his family took care of Hölderlin and gave him a room in an old tower that used to be part of the Tübingen city wall.

For the next thirty-seven years Hölderlin continued to write poetry up in his tower, often at the specific request of visitors.[24] His writing, though, like his mind, had become a mere shadow of what it had been. He was known to spend hours some days simply pulling up grass in nearby fields, and he showed an obsequious deference to anyone who spoke to him. The Zimmer family cared for him until the end, and when Hölderlin finally died in 1843, he left behind scattered papers and notebooks containing drafts and fragments of poems from both before and after madness had overtaken him. Most of these handwritten texts were never published by Hölderlin himself.

Throughout his final lucid years, Hölderlin continuously revisited his poems, expanding, revising, and sometimes completely reworking them. Sometimes a change of even a single word or phrase, made perhaps years after the initial draft, has extraordinary implications. The second version of "The Poet's Calling," for example, where Hölderlin changed the last line of the earlier draft from

> So long as the god remains near us.

to

> [. . .] till God's absence has helped.

is astonishing in its difference. Such a far-reaching change reveals a poet who would not rest, who had to take apart and revise even the masterpiece "Bread and Wine" to bring it closer to the exacting demands of his relentless attempt to name the divine in a time marked by its absence. For this was Hölderlin's calling—to find in holy lore "the streaming word,"

> And holy memory too, to stay wakeful through the night.

NOTES

1. "Hölderlin is for us in a preeminent sense the *poet's poet*." Martin Heidegger, *Elucidations of Hölderlin's Poetry* (Amherst, N.Y., 2000), 52. Translated by Keith Hoeller. One notable forerunner to the twentieth-century recognition of Hölderlin is Nietzsche, who as a seventeen-year-old student in 1861 wrote a school essay on Hölderlin as his "favorite poet."

2. Letter to Neuffer, November 1794.

3. Letter to his mother, March 12, 1795.

4. Letter to Schiller, August 1797.

5. Letter to Schiller, June 30, 1798.

6. Momme Mommsen, "Hölderlin's Lösung von Schiller," in *Lebendige Überlieferung* (Bern, 1999). I also owe the connection between Hölderlin's "The Oaks" and Schiller's "The Philosophical Egoist" to this essay.

7. Letter to Schiller, June 20, 1797.

8. Letter to Hölderlin, November 24, 1796.

9. Letter to Schiller, June 20, 1797.

10. Hölderlin received his theological education free from the Swabian Consistory (a governing body of the church) and so would have been obliged to work for the church if he could not show he was engaged in gainful employment. Because he could not bear the idea of being sent to a village as a preacher, he was forced repeatedly to seek out house tutor positions to avoid this obligation.

11. What Hölderlin's gods are is not clear, though they are certainly not merely a simplistic reference to antiquity. Rather, as numerous passages suggest, they either are, or represent, or mediate—are in some way related to, in short—the immanence of nature's powers and our experience of wholeness in relating to those powers.

12. Friedrich Schiller, *On the Aesthetic Education of Man* (New York, 1954), 38. Translated by Reginald Snell.

13. In Jena, before he moved to Frankfurt, Hölderlin was particularly interested in how philosophy might overcome the separation of the individual from the whole. He clearly had philosophical talent. (Many scholars now believe that Hölderlin played a major role in drafting the so-called "Oldest System-Program of German Idealism," considered by many to be one of the founding documents of German Idealism; his early critique of Fichte also gives evidence of his philosophical abilities.)

Yet Hölderlin often associated philosophy with a certain dissatisfaction. We read in a letter to Schiller (September 4, 1795), for example, that "[t]he displeasure with myself and what's around me has driven me into abstraction." Or, in a letter to Neuffer (December 1795): "Recently I've taken refuge in Kant again, as I always do when I can't bear myself."

14. Friedrich Hölderlin, *Grund zum Empedokles*, *GSA*, 4:1, 156. Quoted in Jean-Luc Nancy, "The Calculation of the Poet," in Aris Fioretos, ed., *The Solid Letter* (Stanford, 1999). Translated by Simon Sparks.

15. Letter to his mother, January 28, 1802.

16. This account is taken from Wilhelm Waiblinger's 1831 "Friedrich Hölderlins Leben, Dichtung und Wahnsinn" in *Werke und Briefe* (Stuttgart, 1986), 3: 388–89. This is the first biographical account of Hölderlin.

17. Some believe that Hölderlin's mother had opened his trunk in his absence and discovered Susette's letters—she had known nothing of the affair—and confronted Hölderlin with them upon his arrival home.

18. From the second version of "Voice of the People," written in 1801.

19. From the six-stanza version of "Home," written in the summer of 1800.

20. From "Timidity," completed in 1803–04.

21. From the second version of "Voice of the People."

22. From "Homecoming," written in 1801.

23. Hölderlin may not have been the innocent bystander many have thought him to have been. He had remained a Jacobin long after many had given up on the French Revolution, and his letters and poetry often express his hopes for revolutionary change in Germany. Though not a mainstream view, the French critic Pierre Bertaux does claim, citing the steel metaphor in Hölderlin's ode "To Eduard" (not translated here), that Höldelin was prepared, at least intellectually, to commit tyrranicide. This poem was, according to Bertaux, a "reference to a plan to assassinate the Elector [of Württenburg], which Sinclair and Hölderlin would have executed together" had the opportunity arisen (quoted in Helen Fehervary, *Hölderlin and the Left* [Heidelberg, 1977]).

24. The writer J. G. Fischer visited Hölderlin in his tower toward the end of the poet's life and asked Hölderlin for a few lines. "As your holiness commands," he reports Hölderlin saying, "shall they be verses on Greece, Spring, or on the Spirit of the Times?" (Translated by David Constantine in *Hölderlin* [Oxford, 1988], 305.) Hölderlin then wrote a short poem and signed it "Scardanelli, 24 May 1748."

ABOUT THIS BOOK

The poems in this book are selected from the odes, elegies, and hexameters Hölderlin wrote during the decade between 1796 and 1806. The focus on these forms is unique among Hölderlin books in English and provides, together with the notes and translated variants, a thorough overview of Hölderlin's development as a mature poet in metrical forms.

The first half of the book, up to about "Rousseau" (the dating of many poems is uncertain), corresponds to Hölderlin's important time in Frankfurt and Homburg; the second half corresponds to the difficult period, between 1800 and 1806, in which Hölderlin wrote some of his most memorable poems but was tormented by a perpetual search for stable employment, separation from the woman he loved, and the onrush of madness.

Although not a complete collection of his work in the ode, elegy, and hexameter, the comprehensive selection offered here includes nearly all of Hölderlin's major Alcaic and Asclepiadic odes, three of his major long elegies ("Stuttgart," "Bread and Wine," and "Homecoming"), the attempted revision of "Bread and Wine" (translated into English here for the first time), most of the elegiac fragments, and all of his hexameters and hexameter fragments (excluding only the early "Kanton Schweiz" and "An den Früling," and the long and often-translated "Der Archipelagus").[1] Except for the three shorter "Nightsongs" that end the book, I have not included any of Hölderlin's later free-verse work, most of which, written between 1803 and 1806, has been excellently translated by Richard Sieburth. Because philosophers and literary critics tend to concentrate on these later free-verse texts, Hölderlin's mature metrical work is often relegated to a diminished status within his oeuvre. My hope is that this book will give voice to the intense presence of these "lesser" poems' unique beauty and depth.

The poems are arranged chronologically in order of their composition, so far as they can be dated accurately. As far as I can tell, thirteen of the poems have never been translated in their entirety or at all into English,[2] and at least four of them—"The Oaks," "To the Aether," "Leisure," and the revised version of "Bread and Wine"—are extraordinary achievements and of major importance for understanding Hölderlin's development. The thirteen previously untranslated poems, in roughly chronological order, are:

The Oaks
To the Aether
[and, smiling, the sovereigns . . .]
To Neuffer (included in Appendix C)
Leisure
The Battle (included in Appendix C)
To the Universally Known (included in Appendix C)
The Lovers
Voice of the People (two stanzas)
Achilles
Dying for the Fatherland
The Walk in the Country
Bread and Wine (revised version)

The messy state of Hölderlin's manuscripts, with their numerous incomplete drafts, revisions, and cross-outs, makes it next to impossible to determine Hölderlin's final intentions for the poems he did not himself see into print. This difficulty has given rise to competing editorial constructions and presentations of the texts. The two major historical-critical editions (discussed in more detail in Appendix A) thus often differ in their construction of the "final" text of a poem.

I have tried to reflect in my translations the unfinished nature of many of Hölderlin's texts by translating incomplete poems (which in some cases end in a comma or contain spaces for planned but unfinished lines), different versions of poems, interesting fragments of earlier drafts, and alternative reconstructions of the texts by the critical editions. Many of these translated variants and drafts are included in Appendix C and have never been translated before into English.

The strange familiarity of the direct depth and longing in Hölderlin's lines can be revelatory. My primary concern as a translator has been to try to render this quality of Hölderlin's verse. I have attempted this through simplicity of expression and a certain selective literalness that I hope renders some of the striking quality of Hölderlin's at times strange and forceful syntax. The lack of gender and inflected cases in English, however, has made simplification in the English word order an unfortunately all-too-frequent occurrence.

Though I have not ignored completely the formal metrical properties of the poems, I have always opted for force of expression over strict adherence to form, since reproducing Hölderlin's precise meters proved highly problematic. The meters of Hölderlin's odes and elegies[3] have no history in English-language poetry similar to their history in the German tradition, in which they were already well domesticated by Klopstock in the mid-eighteenth century. In English there have been a smattering of isolated attempts at the Alcaic ode, but nothing has really taken hold. An English Alcaic ode thus comes across as just plain odd, since our ears and language have not been trained for it. But in addition to this difference in traditions, the inherent difficulty in translating formal elements, even in the case of metrical elements between stressed languages as similar as German and English, makes retention of meter that much more problematic. In the case of Hölderlin, I have found that although metrical imitations are possible, achieving the proper syllabic count and placement of stress must often be founded upon a less fortunate word choice, contorted English syntax, antiquated expressions, or even the addition of superfluous words. I have therefore opted for a relatively free treatment of meter—but I have still attempted to save traces of the original meter as best I could. For example, because the Alcaic ode never has two stressed syllables back to back, I have tried not to let this occur in the English, though I have made exceptions, as in the first line of "Sunset"; I have also tried in the Alcaic odes, for example, to place a dactylic foot near the beginning of the fourth line of each verse to give some sense of the falling nature of that line. My hope is that such echoes of the original meter provide at least some sense of the poems' difference from the overwhelming iambic tendency of English verse, and introduce some sense of regularity to distinguish the poems from free verse. In the end, though, directness and forcefulness were my guiding principles.

The etymological reverberations present in Hölderlin's poems present another vexing problem for the translator. As Rolf Zuberbühler has convincingly argued,[4] Hölderlin's language is self-consciously aware of its origins and makes use of them by playing on etymological roots. In most cases, such word play is impossible to reproduce, but some lucky coincidences have been possible. For example, the German *hold* is a particularly difficult word to translate as it can mean dear, lovely, sweet, fair, graceful, charming, fond, gracious, and even merciful (an older meaning that described a master's relationship to his servant). But Hölderlin adds another level of difficulty to the word, as he hears in *hold* the echo of *helden* (to incline or lean) and *Halde* (slope or hillside). Thus in "Heidelberg" he describes bushes blossoming down into the valley as "*An den Hügel gelehnt, oder dem Ufer hold,*" which literally would run something like "Leaning [*gelehnt*] against the hill, or fond of/dear /lovely/inclined to [*hold*] the riverbank"). Where appropriate, I have tried to amplify the trace of incline or slope in *hold*, which has a lucky echo in the English use of "inclination" or "incline" to indicate preference. In one particularly fortuitous instance, my English version of

> Doch minder nicht sind jene den Menschen hold,
> Sie lieben wieder, so wie geliebt sie sind,

is able to connect a more literal meaning of the German *hold* (dear) with its etymological root *helden* (to incline) via its English homonym (hold) to produce its specific meaning in this passage (to be fond of or well disposed toward):

> Yet they aren't less inclined to hold man dear,
> They love us back as they are loved

Lucky too is the repeated "love" in the following line, which echoes the alternate "lovely" for "dear."

Such success is often offset by the all-too-frequent impossibilities. *Geist,* for example, inadequately but necessarily rendered as "spirit" or "mind," carries within its German roots *Gest* and *Gischt* (a fermenting foam created in the making of wine), as Zuberbühler observes, which is an animating, upward-striving element.[5] "Spirit," because of its Latin root *spiritus* (breathing, breath), feels closer to the effervescence of *Geist* than does "mind" and its the Old English root *gemynd* (memory), but it still does not capture enough of the ferment. Zuberbühler's book is filled with instances like these that are not possible to reproduce in translation. I have noted significant occurrences of such etymological play in the notes to the poems.

NOTES

1. The few odes and elegies I've excluded are to my mind simply not as strong as the others in the book, or they repeated, in a less interesting way, another poem already included.

2. The second version of "The Poet's Courage" has been translated by Stanley Corngold for his translation of the Walter Benjamin essay on Hölderlin. It has not, though, been included in a book of English Hölderlin translations.

3. The Alcaic and Asclepiadic odes and the elegiac distich. See Appendix B for an explanation of these terms.

4. Rolf Zuberbühler, *Hölderlins Erneuerung der Sprache* (Berlin, 1969). I owe my awareness of Hölderlin's use of etymological roots to this monograph.

5. That this valence, lost to us in translation, is intended by Hölderlin is evidenced by his use of the word *Geist* in connection with *Wein* (wine) in the odic draft "Buonaparte":

> Heilige Gefäße sind die Dichter,
>> Worinn des Lebens Wein, der Geist
>>> Der Helden, sich aufbewahrt, [...]

> The poets are holy vessels
>> In which the wine of life, the spirit
>>> Of heroes, is kept [...]

CHRONOLOGY*

1770   Born in Lauffen, Swabia, on March 20.

1772   Father dies.

1774   Mother moves to Nürtingen and remarries.

1779   Stepfather dies.

1784   Enters the Klosterschule in Denkendorf; writes first poems.

1786   Enters the Klosterschule in Maulbronn.

1788   Enters the Tübinger Stift; meets Hegel and Neuffer.

1790   Breaks off relations with Louise Nast, whom he had intended to marry. Reads Kant.

1792   Begins work on the novel *Hyperion*. First poems published in G. F. Stäudlin's *Musenalmanach*.

1793   Meets Sinclair. Meets Schiller toward the end of September. On the recommendation of Schiller, finds a house tutor position with the von Kalb family in Walterhausen.

1794   Befriends Wilhelmine Kirms, a friend of Charlotte von Kalb. Fragment of *Hyperion* published by Schiller in *Thalia*. Meets Goethe at Schiller's.

1795   Moves to Jena with money from Charlotte von Kalb. Attends Fichte's lectures. Meets often with Schiller. Leaves Jena at the end of May and returns to Nürtingen, where he writes that he's "freezing in the winter that surrounds me." Louise Agnese, a child Hölderlin fathers with Wilhelmine Kirms, is born. Meets Landauer.

1796   In Frankfurt as tutor for the Gontard family. First meets Susette Gontard. Works on *Hyperion*; writes "The Oaks"

*This chronology is based on David Constantine's *Hölderlin* (Oxford, 1988) and Adolf Beck's *Hölderlin: Eine Chronik in Text und Bild* (Frankfurt, 1970).

and "To the Aether." Death of Louise Agnese in September. Letter from Schiller advising Hölderlin to "flee philosophical subject matter." Arranges a job for Hegel in Frankfurt.

1797   First volume of *Hyperion* published. Visits Goethe in Frankfurt in July. Works on second volume of *Hyperion*, begins planning the tragedy *Empedocles.* Writes shorter odes.

1798   Difficult and lonely time in Frankfurt. Separates from Susette and moves to Homburg, but they arrange secret meetings. Attends the Rastatter Congress with Sinclair.

1799   Translates Sophocles. Second volume of *Hyperion* published.

1800   Last meeting with Susette on May 8. Leaves Homburg. Stays with Gustav Landauer in his Stuttgart home. Begins writing elegies.

1801   Works as a house tutor in Hauptwil, which only lasts until April. Returns to Nürtingen. Writes several free-verse hymns. In December leaves on foot for house tutor job in Bordeaux.

1802   Arrives in Bordeaux on January 28. Leaves France in late May or early June. Sussette dies on June 22. Arrives in Stuttgart at the end of June. First conceives the Nightsongs. Visits Sinclair in Regensburg. Lives in Nürtingen.

1804   Sophocles translations published. Sinclair brings Hölderlin to Homburg, where he arranges a position for him as a court librarian.

1805   Sinclair put on trial for conspiracy; Hölderlin is drawn into the proceedings but does not have to stand trial because he is declared insane. Nightsongs published. Works on Pindar.

1806   Sinclair asks Hölderlin's mother to fetch her son, and Hölderlin is brought to a clinic in Tübingen.

1807   Hölderlin given over to Ernst Zimmer, whose family cares for him until his death.

1843   Hölderlin dies on June 7.

I

Poems from the
Early Frankfurt Period

Die Eichbäume.

Aus den Gärten komm' ich zu euch, ihr Söhne des Berges!
Aus den Gärten, da lebt die Natur geduldig und häuslich,
Pflegend und wieder gepflegt mit den fleißigen Menschen zusammen.
Aber ihr, ihr Herrlichen! steht, wie ein Volk von Titanen
In der zahmeren Welt und gehört nur euch und dem Himmel,
Der euch nährt' und erzog und der Erde, die euch geboren.
Keiner von euch ist noch in die Schule der Menschen gegangen,
Und ihr drängt euch fröhlich und frei, aus der kräftigen Wurzel,
Unter einander herauf und ergreift, wie der Adler die Beute,
Mit gewaltigem Arme den Raum, und gegen die Wolken
Ist euch heiter und groß die sonnige Krone gerichtet.
Eine Welt ist jeder von euch, wie die Sterne des Himmels
Lebt ihr, jeder ein Gott, in freiem Bunde zusammen.
Könnt' ich die Knechtschaft nur erdulden, ich neidete nimmer
Diesen Wald und schmiegte mich gern ans gesellige Leben.
Fesselte nur nicht mehr ans gesellige Leben das Herz mich,
Das von Liebe nicht läßt, wie gern würd' ich unter euch wohnen!

An den Aether.

Treu und freundlich, wie du, erzog der Götter und Menschen
Keiner, o Vater Aether! mich auf; noch ehe die Mutter
In die Arme mich nahm, und ihre Brüste mich tränkten,
Faßtest du zärtlich mich an und gossest himmlischen Trank mir,
Mir den heiligen Othem zuerst in den keimenden Busen.

Nicht von irdischer Kost gedeihen einzig die Wesen,
Aber du nährst sie all' mit deinem Nektar, o Vater!
Und es dringt sich und rinnt aus deiner ewigen Fülle
Die beseelende Luft durch alle Röhren des Lebens.
Darum lieben die Wesen dich auch und bliken und streben
Unaufhörlich hinauf nach dir im freudigen Wachstum.

The Oaks

Out from the gardens I'm coming to you, sons of the mountain!
Out from the gardens where Nature patiently lives in good order,
Tending to hard-working men and tended by them in turn.
But you, glorious ones! You stand like a race of Titans
In the tamer world, belong only to yourselves and to heaven
Who nourished and raised you, and to the earth who bore you.
None of you has attended the school of men,
And upward you press from your powerful roots so joyful and free
There among yourselves, and your mighty arms seize at space
As the eagle grips its prey, and your sunny crowns,
Serene and great, are raised up toward the clouds.
Each of you is a world, you live as the stars in heaven,
Each one a god, bound together in freedom.
If I could only bear slavery I'd no longer envy
These woods, I'd gladly embrace a life of easy companions,
If only my heart weren't so chained to this life of easy companions,
Or so set on love, how gladly I'd dwell there among you!

To the Aether

Loyally and kindly you've raised me, O Father Aether,
Like no other god or man; even before my mother had
Taken me into her arms and given me drink from her breasts,
You tenderly touched me and poured me a heavenly drink,
You, the first to give holy breath to my burgeoning breast.

Not from earthly fare alone do creatures flourish,
But you nourish them all with your nectar, O Father,
And the enlivening air, it pushes and flows
From out of your fullness, eternal, through all of the hollows of life.
Thus do the creatures love you and gaze and strive
Ceaselessly upward toward you, joyful in growth.

Himmlischer! sucht nicht dich mit ihren Augen die Pflanze,
Strekt nach dir die schüchternen Arme der niedrige Strauch nicht?
Daß er dich finde, zerbricht der gefangene Saame die Hülse,
Daß er belebt von dir in deiner Wooge sich bade,
Schüttelt der Wald den Schnee, wie ein überlästig Gewand ab.
Auch die Fische kommen herauf und hüpfen verlangend
Über die glänzende Fläche des Stroms, als begehrten auch diese
Aus der Wooge zu dir; auch den edeln Thieren der Erde
Wird zum Fluge der Schritt, wenn oft das gewaltige Sehnen
Die geheime Liebe zu dir sie ergreift, sie hinaufzieht.
Es verachtet den Boden das Roß, wie gebogener Stahl strebt
In die Höhe sein Hals, mit der Hufe berührt es den Sand kaum.
Wie zum Scherze, berührt der Fuß der Hirsche den Grashalm,
Hüpft, wie ein Zephyr, über den Bach, der reißend hinabschäumt,
Hin und wieder und schweift kaum sichtbar durch die Gebüsche.

Aber des Aethers Lieblinge, sie, die glüklichen Vögel
Wohnen und spielen vergnügt in der ewigen Halle des Vaters.
Raums genug ist für alle. Der Pfad ist keinem bezeichnet,
Und es regen sich frei im Haußse die Großen und Kleinen.
Über dem Haupte frolokken sie mir und es sehnt sich auch mein Herz
Wunderbar zu ihnen hinauf; wie die freundliche Heimath,
Winkt es von oben herab, und auf die Gipfel der Alpen
Möcht' ich wandern und rufen von da dem eilenden Adler,
Daß er, wie einst in die Arme des Zeus den seeligen Knaben,
Aus der Gefangenschaft in des Aethers Halle mich trage.

Thöricht treiben wir uns umher; wie die irrende Rebe,
Wenn ihr der Stab gebricht, woran zum Himmel sie aufwächst,
Breiten wir über dem Boden uns aus, und suchen und wandern
Durch die Zonen der Erd', o Vater Aether! vergebens,
Denn es treibt uns die Lust, in deinen Gärten zu wandeln.
In die Meersfluth werfen wir uns, in den freieren Ebnen
Uns zu sättigen, und es umspielt die unendliche Wooge
Unsern Kiel und es freut sich das Herz an den Kräften des Meergotts.

Heavenly one! Doesn't the plant search you out with its eyes,
Doesn't the lowliest bush reach meekly to you with its arms?
The entrapped seed breaks its shell that it might find you,
The forest shakes off the snow like a burdensome robe
That, enlivened by you, it might bathe in your waves.
The fish too, yearning they rise to the surface and jump
Through the shimmering plane of the stream, as if they desired
To reach you from out of the waves; and the noble animals of Earth,
All their steps turn to flight when that powerful longing,
That secret love for you seizes them, draws them up high.
The steed scoffs at the ground, his neck arching upward
Like steel in the air, his hooves barely touching the sand.
The deer glances the grass with his hoof and toys with the blades
As he bounds like a zephyr over the raging and down-foaming stream,
And he ranges through the woods, barely visible through the leaves.

But the Aether's favorites, the happy birds,
They joyously live and play in the Father's eternal halls.
There's room enough for all. No path is forbidden:
Creatures large and small range free throughout his house,
They're exulting above me, and my heart fills with singular
Longing to join them; the sky above beckons
As friendly as home, I'd like to wander the Alpine peaks
And call to the rushing eagle who once bore
The blessèd boy into the arms of Zeus, that he
Might free me from this prison and take me into Aether's halls.

Foolishly we run about; like the errant tendril
With no stake on which to grow toward heaven,
We spread ourselves throughout the world and search and wander
The earthly lands, O Father Aether, and all in vain,
For the desire to walk in your gardens is driving us on.
We throw ourselves in the ocean current to sate ourselves
On freer plains, and the unending waves, they play round our keel,
And our heart delights in the sea god's powers.

Dennoch genügt uns nie, denn der tiefere Ocean reizt uns
Wo die leichtere Wooge sich regt—o wer an die goldnen
Küsten dort oben das wandernde Schiff zu treiben vermöchte!

Aber indeß ich hinauf in die dämmernde Ferne mich sehne,
Wo du die fremden Ufer umfängst mit der bläulichen Wooge
Kömmst du säuselnd herab von des Fruchtbaums blühenden Wipfeln,
Vater Aether! und sänftigest selbst das strebende Herz mir,
Und ich lebe nun gerne, wie sonst, mit den Blumen der Erde.

[und die ewigen Bahnen . . .]

               und die ewigen Bahnen
        Lächelnd über uns hin zögen die Herrscher der Welt,
Sonne und Mond und Sterne, und auch die Blize der Wolken
        Spielten, des Augenbliks feurige Kinder, um uns,
Aber in unsrem Innern, ein Bild der Fürsten des Himmels,
        Wandelte neidlos der Gott unserer Liebe dahin,
Und er mischte den Duft, die reine, heilige Seele,
        Die, von des Frühlinges silberner Stunde genährt,
Oft überströmte, hinaus in's glänzende Meer des Tages,
        Und in das Abendroth und in die Woogen der Nacht,
Ach! wir lebten so frei im innig unendlichen Leben,
        Unbekümmert und still, selber ein seeliger Traum,
Jezt uns selber genug und jezt in's Weite verfliegend,
        Aber im Innersten doch immer lebendig und eins.
Glüklicher Baum! wie lange, wie lange könnt' ich noch singen
        Und vergehen im Blik auf dein erbebendes Haupt,
Aber siehe! dort regt sich's, es wandeln in Schleiern die Jungfrau'n
        Und wer weiß es, vieleicht wäre mein Mädchen dabei;
Laß mich, laß mich, ich muß—lebewohl! es reißt mich in's Leben,
        Daß ich im kindischen Gang folge der lieblichen Spur,
Aber du Guter, dich will, dich will ich nimmer vergessen,
        Ewig bist du und bleibst meiner Geliebtesten Bild.

But we're never content, for the deeper ocean attracts us
Where the gentler waves roll—O who could
Drive the wandering ship up there on the golden coasts!

But as I long for the heights of the twilit distance
Where you embrace the foreign shores with your blue-tinted waves,
You come whispering down from the top of the fruit tree in bloom,
Father Aether, and soften even my striving heart;
And I'll dwell now gladly, just as before, with the flowers of the earth.

[and, smiling, the sovereigns . . .]

                              and, smiling, the sovereigns
    Of the world drift on timeless paths above,
Sun and moon and stars and the flashing of the clouds,
    The moment's fiery children, all played around us,
But in our innermost depths is an image of the princes of heaven,
    And there without envy strolled the god of our love,
And he mixed the sweet air, the pure and holy soul
    That, nurtured by springtime's silver hour,
Overflowed often in the shimmering sea of the day
    And into the red of the evening and waves of the night;
Ah, we lived so freely in inwardly infinite life,
    Unconcerned and in silence, a blessèd dream ourselves,
Now sufficient unto ourselves, now flying into the vastness,
    But always alive and at one in our innermost core.
Happy tree! How long, how long I could still sing
    And lose myself in the sight of your trembling crown.
But look! Something's afoot, the virgins in veils are strolling,
    And, who knows, my girl may be among them;
Let me go, let me go, I've got to—farewell! I'm thrown into life
    That with childlike steps I might follow the charming trace,
But you, benevolent one, you I'll—you I'll never forget;
    You're eternal, the image of my most beloved.

Und käm' einmal ein Tag, wo sie die meinige wäre
O! dann ruht' ich mit ihr, unter dir, Freundlicher, aus
Und du zürnetest nicht, du gössest Schatten und Düfte
Und ein rauschendes Lied über die Glüklichen aus.

An Diotima.

Schönes Leben! du lebst, wie die zarten Blüthen im Winter,
In der gealterten Welt blühst du verschlossen, allein.
Liebend strebst du hinaus, dich zu sonnen am Lichte des Frühlings,
Zu erwarmen an ihr suchst du die Jugend der Welt.
Deine Sonne, die schönere Zeit, ist untergegangen
Und in frostiger Nacht zanken Orkane sich nun.

Diotima.

Komm und besänftige mir, die du einst Elemente versöhntest
Wonne der himmlischen Muse das Chaos der Zeit,
Ordne den tobenden Kampf mit Friedenstönen des Himmels
Bis in der sterblichen Brust sich das entzweite vereint,
Bis der Menschen alte Natur die ruhige große,
Aus der gährenden Zeit, mächtig und heiter sich hebt.
Kehr' in die dürftigen Herzen des Volks, lebendige Schönheit!
Kehr an den gastlichen Tisch, kehr in die Tempel zurük!
Denn Diotima lebt, wie die zarten Blüthen im Winter,
Reich an eigenem Geist sucht sie die Sonne doch auch.
Aber die Sonne des Geists, die schönere Welt ist hinunter
Und in frostiger Nacht zanken Orkane sich nur.

And if the day should come when she would be mine,
O friendly one, then I'd find my rest with her under you,
And you wouldn't be angry, you'd pour shade and sweet
Breath, and a rustling song, over this happy pair's bliss.

To Diotima

Beautiful creature! You live like the tender blossoms in winter,
In a world grown old you bloom withdrawn and alone.
You lovingly strive to bathe in the sunlight of springtime,
To warm yourself there you search for the youth of the world.
But your sun, the more beautiful age, has gone down,
And now the storms quarrel in frost-covered night.

Diotima

You favorite of the heavenly muse, you who once reconciled the
    elements,
Come and comfort me against the chaos of our time,
Order the raging battle with the peaceful music of heaven
Till what's cleft in two become one in the mortal heart,
Till ancient human nature, so calm, so great,
Serenely and powerfully rise from out of our seething times.
Return to the destitute hearts of the people, O living beauty!
Return to the banqueting table, return to the temples!
For Diotima lives, like the delicate blossoms in winter,
And though she is rich in her spirit, she also seeks out the sun.
But the sun of the spirit, that more beautiful world, has set,
And only the storms quarrel in frost-covered night.

Die Muße.

Sorglos schlummert die Brust und es ruhn die strengen Gedanken.
Auf die Wiese geh' ich hinaus, wo das Gras aus der Wurzel
Frisch, wie die Quelle mir keimt, wo die liebliche Lippe der Blume
Mir sich öffnet und stum mit süßem Othem mich anhaucht.
Und an tausend Zweigen des Hains, wie an brennenden Kerzen
Mir das Flämchen des Lebens glänzt, die röthliche Blüthe,
Wo im sonnigen Quell die zufriednen Fische sich regen,
Wo die Schwalbe das Nest mit den thörigen Jungen umflattert,
Und die Schmetterlinge sich freun und die Bienen da wandl' ich
Mitten in ihrer Lust; ich steh im friedlichen Felde
Wie ein liebender Ulmbaum da, und wie Reben und Trauben
Schlingen sich rund um mich die süßen Spiele des Lebens.

Oder schau ich hinauf zum Berge, der mit Gewölken
Sich die Scheitel umkränzt und die düstern Loken im Winde
Schüttelt, und wenn er mich trägt auf seiner kräftigen Schulter,
Wenn die leichtere Luft mir alle Sinne bezaubert
Und das unendliche Thal, wie eine farbige Wolke
Unter mir liegt, da werd' ich zum Adler, und ledig des Bodens
Wechselt mein Leben im All der Natur wie Nomaden den Wohnort.
Und nun führt mich der Pfad zurück ins Leben der Menschen,
Fernher dämmert die Stadt, wie eine eherne Rüstung
Gegen die Macht des Gewittergotts und der Menschen geschmiedet
Majestätisch herauf, und ringsum ruhen die Dörfchen;
Und die Dächer umhüllt, vom Abendlichte geröthet
Freundlich der häußliche Rauch; es ruhn die sorglich umzäunten
Gärten, es schlummert der Pflug auf den gesonderten Feldern.

Aber ins Mondlicht steigen herauf die zerbrochenen Säulen
Und die Tempelthore, die einst der Furchtbare traf, der geheime
Geist der Unruh, der in der Brust der Erd' und der Menschen
Zürnet und gährt, der Unbezwungne, der alte Eroberer
Der die Städte, wie Lämmer, zerreißt, der einst den Olympus
Stürmte, der in den Bergen sich regt, und Flammen herauswirft.

Leisure

My breast slumbers without worry and demanding thoughts are quiet.
I wander through the meadow where the grass grows up to meet me
Fresh from its roots like a spring, where the delicate lips of flowers
Open and sweetly blow their breath in silence over me.
And on a thousand woodland branches, as on burning candles,
The flame of life shines at me, blossoming red,
Where the fish swim about content in the sunlit spring,
Where the swallow flits around its nest and foolish young,
And the butterflies rejoice and the bees—I stroll there
In the midst of their joy; I stand there in the peaceful field
Like a loving elm tree, and like the vines and the grapes
The sweet game of life is winding itself all around me.

Or I look to the mountain that crowns its head
With clouds and whose darkened curls shake in the wind,
And when it carries me up on its powerful shoulder,
When the lighter breeze bewitches my senses,
And, like a colorful cloud, the unending valley
Lies far below—then I'm an eagle, and free of the earth
My life changes in Nature's All like nomads moving on,
And the path now leads me back to the life of men,
The town in the distance majestically glows in the twilight of dusk,
Like a bronze suit of armor to protect 'gainst the might
Of the storm god and men, and the villages lie at rest;
The smoke from the houses, reddened by the evening light,
Gently envelops the rooves; the gardens, carefully
Fenced, lie at rest, the plow slumbers on separated fields.

But into the moonlight rise broken-down columns
And the gates of the temples once struck by the Dreadful, the secret
Spirit of Unrest, who rages and seethes in the breasts of the earth
And of men—the unvanquished, the conqueror of old
Who rips apart cities like lambs, who once stormed Olympus,
Who rumbles in mountains and shoots forth his flames,

Der die Wälder entwurzelt und durch den Ozean hinfährt
Und die Schiffe zerschlägt und doch in der ewigen Ordnung
Niemals irre dich macht, auf der Tafel deiner Geseze
Keine Sylbe verwischt, der auch dein Sohn, o Natur, ist
Mit dem Geiste der Ruh' aus Einem Schoose geboren.—

Hab' ich zu Hauße dann, wo die Bäume das Fenster umsäuseln
Und die Luft mit dem Lichte mir spielt, von menschlichem Leben
Ein erzählendes Blatt zu gutem Ende gelesen:
Leben! Leben der Welt! du liegst wie ein heiliger W
Sprech ich dann und es nehme die Axt, wer will dich zu ebnen,
Glüklich wohn' ich in dir,

[Die Völker schwiegen, schlummerten . . .]

Die Völker schwiegen, schlummerten, da sahe
Das Schiksaal, daß sie nicht entschliefen und es kam
Der unerbittliche, der furchtbare Sohn
Der Natur, der alte Geist der Unruh
Der regte sich, wie Feuer, das im Herzen
Der Erde gährt, das wie den reifen Obstbaum
Die alten Städte schüttelt, das die Berge
Zerreißt, und die Eichen hinabschlingt und die Felsen.

Und Heere tobten, wie die kochende See.
Und wie ein Meergott, herrscht' und waltete
Manch großer Geist im kochenden Getümmel.
Manch feurig Blut zerran im Todesfeld
Und jeder Wunsch und jede Menschenkraft
Vertobt auf Einer da, auf ungeheurer Wahlstat
Wo von dem blauen Rheine bis zur Tyber
Die unaufhaltsame die jahrelange Schlacht

He who uproots the forests and courses through oceans
And smashes up ships and yet never in all of eternity
Will lead you astray, nor erase one letter
From your tables of laws, who is also, O Nature, your son,
Who was born from *one* womb with the Spirit of Calm.—

At home, then, where the trees are rustling around my window,
And the breezes play with the light, with pleasure I read
To the end a storied page of human life:
Life! Life of the world! You lie there like some holy *w*
I said then, and if someone would take an axe to level you down,
I'd still happily live in you,

[The nations were silent, they slumbered . . .]

The nations were silent, they slumbered, but Fate
Made sure that they not fall asleep,
And the unrelenting one, the terrible son
Of Nature came, the ancient Spirit of Unrest,
And he stirred like the fire that seethes in the heart
Of the earth and shakes the ancient cities
Like trees of ripened fruit, and tears down
The mountains and swallows up oaks and the rocks.

And the hosts raged like the boiling sea.
And like a sea god many great spirits
Ruled and prevailed in the furious fray.
The killing field flowed with fiery blood,
And every desire, and every human effort,
Raged there on one enormous battleground,
Where from the blue Rhine to the Tiber
The unstoppable fight flew

In wilder Ordnung sich umherbewegte,
Es spielt' ein kühnes Spiel in dieser Zeit
Mit allen Sterblichen das mächtge Schiksaal.

Und blinken goldne Früchte wieder dir
Wie heitre holde Sterne, durch die kühle Nacht
Der Pomeranzenwälder in Italien.

All around in savage array, year after year,
Powerful fate played a bold game
With all of the mortals back then.

And the golden fruits sparkle again for you
Like shining, lovely stars through the cool night
Of the orange groves in Italy.

An Diotima.

Komm und siehe die Freude um uns; in kühlenden Lüften
    Fliegen die Zweige des Hains,
Wie die Loken im Tanz'; und wie auf tönender Leier
    Ein erfreulicher Geist
Spielt mit Reegen und Sonnenschein auf der Erde der Himmel
    Wie in liebendem Streit
Über dem Saitenspiel' ein tausendfältig Gewimmel
    Flüchtiger Töne sich regt,
Wandelt Schatten und Licht in süßmelodischem Wechsel
    Über die Berge dahin.
Leise berührte der Himmel zuvor mit der silbernen Tropfe
    Seinen Bruder den Strom
Nah ist er nun, nun schüttet er ganz, die köstliche Fülle
    Die er am Herzen trug
Über den Hain und den Strom, und

Und das Grünen des Hains, und des Himmels Bild in dem Strome
    Dämmert und schwindet vor uns
Und des einsamen Berges Haupt mit den Hütten und Felsen
    Die er im Schoose verbirgt,
Und die Hügel, die um ihn her, wie Lämmer, gelagert
    Und in blühend Gesträuch
Wie in zarte Wolle gehüllt, sich nähren von klaren
    Kühlenden Quellen des Bergs,
Und das dampfende Thal mit seinen Saaten und Blumen,
    Und der Garten vor uns
Nah und fernes entweicht, verliert sich in froher Verwirrung
    Und die Sonne verlischt.
Aber vorübergerauscht sind nun die Fluthen des Himmels
    Und geläutert, verjüngt
Geht mit den seeligen Kindern hervor die Erd' aus dem Bade.
    Froher lebendiger
Glänzt im Haine das Grün, und goldner funkeln die Blumen,

Weiß, wie die Heerde, die in den Strom der Schäfer geworfen,

To Diotima

Come and look at the joy all around us; in cooling breezes
        The branches of trees
Sway like curls at a dance; and, like a spirit of joy
        Strumming a lyre,
The sky plays over Earth with the sunshine and rain;
        And as in loving quarrel
A thousandfold tumult of tones moves fleetingly
        Over the strings,
So shadow and light play, melodically tumbling,
        Over the hills.
Moments earlier the sky gently grazed his brother, the stream,
        With silvery drops;
Now he is near, now spilling the wonderful fullness
        He bore in his heart
Over the grove and the stream, and

And the green of the woods, and the image of sky in the stream now
        Fades, disappears from sight,
And the mountain with its lonely peak, with its huts and its cliffs
        That are hidden in folds,
And the hills all around rest like lambs and are covered
        With bushes in bloom,
Soft as if wool, nourished on clear cooling
        Springs of the mountain,
And the steaming valley with its seeds and its flowers
        And the garden before us,
What's near and what's far flee away, lost in joyful confusion,
        And the sun goes out.
But the heavenly downpour now has rushed past,
        And with blessèd children
The earth emerges from its bath rejuvenated and pure.
        The forest's green
Shines with renewed joy and life, the flowers gleam brighter with gold,

White like the flock that the shepherd has herded into the stream,

II

The Shorter Odes

Das Unverzeihliche.

Wenn ihr Freunde vergeßt, wenn ihr den Künstler höhnt,
    Und den tieferen Geist klein und gemein versteht,
        Gott vergiebt es, doch stört nur
            Nie den Frieden der Liebenden.

Ehmals und jezt.

In jüngern Tagen war ich des Morgens froh,
    Des Abends weint' ich; jezt, da ich älter bin,
        Beginn ich zweifelnd meinen Tag, doch
            Heilig und heiter ist mir sein Ende.

Die Liebenden.

Trennen wollten wir uns, wähnten es gut und klug;
    Da wir's thaten, warum schrökt' uns, wie Mord, die That?
        Ach! wir kennen uns wenig,
            Denn es waltet ein Gott in uns.

The Unpardonable

If you forget all your friends, if you scoff at the artists
    And toward nobler spirits are petty and vile,
        God will forgive you. Only never
           Upset the peace lovers have.

Then and Now

In my younger days the mornings were a joy
    And I wept in the evenings; now that I'm older
        I start my day doubting but
           Find its end holy, serene.

The Lovers

We wanted to go our separate ways, thought it well and good,
    But once it was done the act scared us like murder—why?
        Ah, we barely know ourselves,
           For inside us a god is at work.

An die Deutschen.

Spottet ja nicht des Kinds, wenn es mit Peitsch' und Sporn
  Auf dem Rosse von Holz muthig und groß sich dünkt,
    Denn, ihr Deutschen, auch ihr seyd
      Thatenarm und gedankenvoll.

Oder kömt, wie der Stral aus dem Gewölke kömt,
  Aus Gedanken die That? Leben die Bücher bald?
    O ihr Lieben, so nimmt mich,
      Daß ich büße die Lästerung.

Ihre Genesung.

Deine Freundin, Natur! leidet und schläft und du
  Allbelebende, säumst? ach! und ihr heilt sie nicht
    Mächt'ge Lüfte des Aethers,
      Nicht ihr Quellen des Sonnenlichts?

Alle Blumen der Erd', alle die fröhlichen,
  Schönen Früchte des Hains, heitern sie alle nicht
    Dieses Leben, o Götter!
      Das ihr selber in Lieb' erzogt?—

Ach! schon athmet und tönt heilige Lebenslust
  Ihr im reizenden Wort wieder wie sonst und schon
    Glänzt das Auge des Lieblings
      Freundlichoffen, Natur! dich an.

To the Germans

Don't mock the child when with his spurs and whip
   He thinks himself so big and brave sitting on his wooden horse,
      For, you Germans, you too are
         Poor in deed and rich in thought.

Or will the deed emerge from thought like a flash
   From the clouds? Will books soon come to life?
      O dear friends, seize me so I'll
         Pay for these blasphemous words.

Her Recovery

Your friend, O Nature, is suffering and sleeping while you,
   Giver of life, just stand by? Ah, and you don't heal her,
      Powerful breezes of Aether,
         Nor you, sources of sunlight?

All the flowers of Earth, all the joyous,
   Beautiful fruits of the grove, why don't they
      Brighten her life, O gods,
         A life you yourselves raised in love?—

Ah, the holy desire for life breathes already and rings
   Again through her words, charming as ever before,
      And already the eyes of your darling,
         O Nature, open and gleam with affection for you.

An die jungen Dichter.

Lieben Brüder! es reift unsere Kunst vieleicht
 Da, dem Jünglinge gleich, lange sie schon gegährt,
  Bald zur Stille der Schönheit;
   Seid nur fromm, wie der Grieche war!

Liebt die Götter und denkt freundlich der Sterblichen!
 Haßt den Rausch, wie den Frost! lehrt und beschreibet nichts!
  Wenn der Meister euch ängstigt,
   Fragt die große Natur um Rath.

Lebenslauf.

Hoch auf strebte mein Geist, aber die Liebe zog
 Schön ihn nieder; das Laid beugt ihn gewaltiger;
  So durchlauf ich des Lebens
   Bogen und kehre, woher ich kam.

An Ihren Genius.

Send' ihr Blumen und Frücht' aus nieversiegender Fülle,
 Send' ihr, freundlicher Geist, ewige Jugend herab!
Hüll' in deine Wonnen sie ein und laß sie die Zeit nicht
 Sehn, wo einsam und fremd sie, die Athenerin, lebt,
Bis sie im Lande der Seeligen einst die fröhlichen Schwestern,
 Die zu Phidias Zeit herrschten und liebten, umfängt.

To the Young Poets

Dear brothers! Perhaps our art,
    Which like the grapes of youth has long fermented,
      Will ripen soon to the stillness of beauty;
        Just be devout like the ancient Greeks were!

Love the gods and think kindly of mortals,
    Detest intoxication like frost! Don't describe or teach!
      And if your master frightens you,
        Ask awesome Nature for advice.

The Course of Life

High my spirit soared, love though dragged it
    Down; suffering bends it still lower;
      So I run through life's arc
        And return to where I began.

To Her Genius

Send her the flowers and fruit of your unending fullness,
    Send her, kind spirit, eternal youth from above!
Wrap your bliss all around her and let her not see the times
    In which, lonely and estranged, she, the Athenian, lives;
Not till she takes, in the land of the blest, the joyful sisters,
    They who loved and ruled in Phidias' times, in her arms.

Die Kürze.

„Warum bist du so kurz? liebst du, wie vormals, denn
   „Nun nicht mehr den Gesang? fandst du, als Jüngling, doch,
      „In den Tagen der Hoffnung,
         „Wenn du sangest, das Ende nie!

Wie mein Glük, ist mein Lied.—Willst du im Abendroth
   Froh dich baden? hinweg ists! und die Erd' ist kalt,
      Und der Vogel der Nacht schwirrt
         Unbequem vor das Auge dir.

An die Parzen.

Nur Einen Sommer gönnt, ihr Gewaltigen!
   Und einen Herbst zu reifem Gesange mir,
      Daß williger mein Herz, vom süßen
         Spiele gesättiget, dann mir sterbe.

Die Seele, der im Leben ihr göttlich Recht
   Nicht ward, sie ruht auch drunten im Orkus nicht;
      Doch ist mir einst das Heil'ge, das am
         Herzen mir liegt, das Gedicht gelungen,

Willkommen dann, o Stille der Schattenwelt!
   Zufrieden bin ich, wenn auch mein Saitenspiel
      Mich nicht hinab geleitet; Einmal
         Lebt ich, wie Götter, und mehr bedarfs nicht.

Brevity

"Why then are you so curt? You no longer love
　　Your song as before? When you were young,
　　　　In those days filled with hope,
　　　　　　Your singing never did end!"

My song is like my happiness.—Would you joyfully bathe
　　In the sunset's red glow? It's gone!
　　　　And the earth is cold, and the nightbird
　　　　　　Vexingly flits by your eyes.

To the Fates

Grant me but one summer, O powerful gods!
　　And one autumn too of ripened song,
　　　　That my heart, sated on such sweet play,
　　　　　　Might all the more willingly die.

A soul, not receiving its divine right
　　In life, does not repose down Orcus' way;
　　　　But if what's holy, the poem close to my heart,
　　　　　　Might just for once meet with success—

Then welcome, O silence of the world of shades!
　　I'll then be content if my song does not descend
　　　　There with me, for I'll have
　　　　　　Lived for once like the gods, and need of nothing more.

Abbitte.

Heilig Wesen! gestört hab' ich die goldene
    Götterruhe dir oft, und der geheimeren,
        Tiefern Schmerzen des Lebens
           Hast du manche gelernt von mir.

O vergiß es, vergieb! gleich dem Gewölke dort
    Vor dem friedlichen Mond, geh' ich dahin und du
        Ruhst und glänzest in deiner
           Schöne wieder, du süßes Licht!

Der gute Glaube.

Schönes Leben! du liegst krank, und das Herz ist mir
    Müd vom Weinen und schon dämmert die Furcht in mir,
        Doch, doch kann ich nicht glauben,
           Daß du sterbest, so lang du liebst.

Diotima.

Du schweigst und duldest, und sie verstehn dich nicht,
    Du heilig Leben! welkest hinweg und schweigst,
        Denn ach, vergebens bei Barbaren
           Suchst du die Deinen im Sonnenlichte,

Die zärtlichgroßen Seelen, die nimmer sind!
    Doch eilt die Zeit. Noch siehet mein sterblich Lied
        Den Tag, der, Diotima! nächst den
           Göttern mit Helden dich nennt, und dir gleicht.

Apology

Holy being! I've often disturbed
  Your divine and golden repose;
    And you've heard much of life's
      Deeper, more secret pains from me.

Forget it, forgive me! Like the clouds drifting
  By the peaceful moon, I too pass away,
    And you rest, radiant once more
      In all your beauty, O sweet sweet light!

Good Faith

Beautiful life! You lie sick, and my heart is tired
  From weeping, and fear is already dawning in me—
    No, no, I just can't believe
      That you're dying as long as you love.

Diotima

You fall silent and suffer, and no one understands you,
  O holy being! You're wilting away and fall silent,
    For you look in vain among the barbarians
      To find your kin in the sunlight,

Those great and tender souls who are no more!
  But time steals by. My mortal song will yet see
    The day, Diotima, that in your likeness
      Names you among all the heroes and gods.

Die Heimath.

Froh kehrt der Schiffer heim an den stillen Strom
   Von fernen Inseln, wo er geerndtet hat;
      Wohl möcht' auch ich zur Heimath wieder;
         Aber was hab' ich, wie Laid, geerndtet?——

Ihr holden Ufer, die ihr mich auferzogt,
   Stillt ihr der Liebe Leiden? ach! gebt ihr mir,
      Ihr Wälder meiner Kindheit, wann ich
         Komme, die Ruhe noch Einmal wieder?

Menschenbeifall.

Ist nicht heilig mein Herz, schöneren Lebens voll,
   Seit ich liebe? warum achtetet ihr mich mehr,
      Da ich stolzer und wilder,
         Wortereicher und leerer war?

Ach! der Menge gefällt, was auf den Marktplaz taugt,
   Und es ehret der Knecht nur den Gewaltsamen;
      An das Göttliche glauben
         Die allein, die es selber sind.

Home

Gladly the boatman turns home to the river's calm
    From his harvest on faraway isles;
        If only I too were homeward bound;
            Yet what harvest have I but sorrow?—

O blessèd riverbanks that raised me,
    Can you ease the sorrows of love? Ah, when I come
        To you, woods of my youth, will you
            Grant me peace once again?

Human Applause

Isn't my heart holy, full of higher, more beautiful life,
    Now that I love? Why did you respect me more
        When I was prouder and wilder,
            More full of words and more vacuous?

Ah, the crowd enjoys whatever sells in the marketplace,
    And the slave respects only the masters;
        Only those who are themselves
            Like gods believe in the divine.

Die scheinheiligen Dichter.

Ihr kalten Heuchler, sprecht von den Göttern nicht!
　　Ihr habt Verstand! ihr glaubt nicht an Helios,
　　　　Noch an den Donnerer und Meergott;
　　　　　　Todt ist die Erde, wer mag ihr danken?—

Getrost, ihr Götter! zieret ihr doch das Lied,
　　Wenn schon aus euren Nahmen die Seele schwand,
　　　　Und ist ein großes Wort vonnöthen,
　　　　　　Mutter Natur! so gedenkt man deiner.

Sokrates und Alcibiades.

„Warum huldigest du, heiliger Sokrates,
　　„Diesem Jünglinge stets? kennest du Größers nicht?
　　　　„Warum siehet mit Liebe,
　　　　　　„Wie auf Götter, dein Aug' auf ihn?

Wer das Tiefste gedacht, liebt das Lebendigste,
　　Hohe Jugend versteht, wer in die Welt geblikt
　　　　Und es neigen die Weisen
　　　　　　Oft am Ende zu Schönem sich.

The Sanctimonious Poets

You cold hypocrites, don't speak of the gods!
　　You're rational! You don't believe in Helios,
　　　　Nor in the Thunderer or the Sea God;
　　　　　　The earth is dead, who's there to thank her?—

Take comfort, O gods! For you still grace the song
　　Though the soul be faded from your names;
　　　　And should a big-time word be needed,
　　　　　　Mother Nature, then they pay you heed.

Socrates and Alcibiades

"Why, holy Socrates, do you worship
　　This youth without cease? Do you know nothing greater?
　　　　Why do you linger on him with your eyes
　　　　　　Full of love that's reserved for the gods?"

Those who've thought most deeply love what's most alive,
　　Those who've looked into the world know youth's noble light,
　　　　And, in the end, the wise
　　　　　　Often bow down to beauty.

An unsre großen Dichter.

Des Ganges Ufer hörten des Freudengotts
   Triumph, als allerobernd vom Indus her
     Der junge Bacchus kam, mit heilgem
       Weine vom Schlafe die Völker wekend.

O wekt, ihr Dichter! wekt sie vom Schlummer auch,
   Die jezt noch schlafen, gebt die Geseze, gebt
     Uns Leben, siegt, Heroën! ihr nur
       Habt der Eroberung Recht, wie Bacchus.

Dem Sonnengott.

Wo bist du? trunken dämmert die Seele mir
   Von aller deiner Wonne; denn eben ists,
     Daß ich gesehn, wie, müde seiner
       Fahrt der entzükende Götterjüngling

Die jungen Loken badet' im Goldgewölk';
   Und jezt noch blikt mein Auge von selbst nach ihm;
     Doch fern ist er zu frommen Völkern,
       Die ihn noch ehren, hinweggegangen.

Dich lieb' ich, Erde! trauerst du doch mit mir!
   Und unsre Trauer wandelt, wie Kinderschmerz,
     In Schlummer sich, und wie die Winde
       Flattern und flüstern im Saitenspiele,

Bis ihm des Meisters Finger den schönern Ton
   Entlokt, so spielen Nebel und Träum' um uns,
     Bis der Geliebte wiederkömt und
       Leben und Geist sich in uns entzündet.

To Our Great Poets

The banks of the Ganges heard the triumph
   Of the god of joy when the all-conquering youthful
      Bacchus went forth from Indus, his holy
         Wine waking the nations from sleep.

Wake them, O poets! Wake them from their slumbers,
   Those still asleep, hand down the laws,
      Give us life, O heroes, and be triumphant, only you,
         Like Bacchus, possess the right to conquer.

To the Sun God

Where are you? Drunk, my soul fades
   In all your bliss; for I've just
      Seen, tired from his journey,
         The young and enrapturing god

Bathe his youthful locks in golden clouds;
   And my eyes are still drawn to him;
      But he has gone, far away,
         To god-fearing peoples who revere him still.

I love you, Earth, for you share my grief!
   And like a child's pain our mourning turns
      To slumber, and as the winds
         Flutter and whisper in the lyre

Until the master's fingers lure out a finer
   Song, so do mists and dreams play around us
      Until our loved one returns
         And ignites our life and spirit.

Sonnenuntergang.

Wo bist du? trunken dämmert die Seele mir
Von aller deiner Wonne; denn eben ists,
    Daß ich gelauscht, wie, goldner Töne
      Voll, der entzükende Sonnenjüngling

Sein Abendlied auf himmlischer Leier spielt';
Es tönten rings die Wälder und Hügel nach.
    Doch fern ist er zu frommen Völkern,
      Die ihn noch ehren, hinweggegangen.

Stimme des Volks.

Du seiest Gottes Stimme, so ahndet' ich
In heil'ger Jugend; ja, und ich sag' es noch.—
    Um meine Weisheit unbekümmert
      Rauschen die Wasser doch auch, und dennoch

Hör' ich sie gern, und öfters bewegen sie
Und stärken mir das Herz, die gewaltigen;
    Und meine Bahn nicht, aber richtig
      Wandeln in's Meer sie die Bahn hinunter.

Sunset

Where are you? Drunk, my soul fades
   In all your bliss; for I've just
      Listened in as the enrapturing
         Sun-boy, full of golden tones,

Played the evensong upon his heavenly lyre;
   It resounded through the woods and hills.
      But he has gone, far away,
         To god-fearing peoples who revere him still.

Voice of the People

You were the voice of god, so I used to think
   In my holy youth; yes, and I maintain this still.—
      But the waters also rush onward
         Unconcerned with my wisdom, and yet

Gladly I hear them, and often they move
   And strengthen my heart, those powerful ones;
      They don't follow my course but
         Unfailingly flow toward the sea.

III

Later Odes;
Elegies and Elegiac Fragments

[Da ich ein Knabe war . . .]

Da ich ein Knabe war,
　Rettet' ein Gott mich oft
　　Vom Geschrei und der Ruthe der Menschen,
　Da spielt' ich sicher und gut
　　Mit den Blumen des Hains,
　　　Und die Lüftchen des Himmels
　　　Spielten mit mir.

Und wie du das Herz
Der Pflanzen erfreust,
Wenn sie entgegen dir
Die zarten Arme streken,

So hast du mein Herz erfreut
Vater Helios! und, wie Endymion,
War ich dein Liebling,
Heilige Luna!

O all ihr treuen
Freundlichen Götter!
Daß ihr wüßtet,
Wie euch meine Seele geliebt!

Zwar damals rieff ich noch nicht
Euch mit Nahmen, auch ihr
Nanntet mich nie, wie die Menschen sich nennen
Als kennten sie sich.

Doch kannt' ich euch besser,
Als ich je die Menschen gekannt,
Ich verstand die Stille des Aethers
Der Menschen Worte verstand ich nie.

[When I was a boy . . .]

When I was a boy
   A god often spared me
      From the screams and rods of men;
         Then I played safely and well
           With the forest's flowers,
              And the breezes of heaven
              Played with me.

And, as you delight
The hearts of plants
When they stretch their
Tender arms toward you,

So have you cheered my heart,
Father Helios! And, like Endymion,
I was your lover,
Holy Luna!

O all you loyal
Friendly gods,
If you only knew
How my soul has loved you!

True, I didn't call you
By name then, but neither did you
Name me the way men name themselves—
As if they knew each other.

Yes, I knew you better
Than I ever knew a human being,
I understood the silence of the Aether;
Human words I never understood.

Mich erzog der Wohllaut
Des säuselnden Hains
Und lieben lernt' ich
Unter den Blumen.

Im Arme der Götter wuchs ich groß.

[*Hyperions Schiksaalslied*]

Ihr wandelt droben im Licht
　　Auf weichem Boden, seelige Genien!
　　Glänzende Götterlüfte
　　　Rühren euch leicht,
　　　　Wie die Finger der Künstlerin
　　　Heilige Saiten.

Schiksaallos, wie der schlafende
　　Säugling, athmen die Himmlischen;
　　Keusch bewahrt
　　In bescheidener Knospe,
　　　Blühet ewig
　　　　Ihnen der Geist,
　　　　　Und die seeligen Augen
　　　　Bliken in stiller
　　　　　Ewiger Klarheit.

Doch uns ist gegeben,
　　Auf keiner Stätte zu ruhn,
　　Es schwinden, es fallen
　　Die leidenden Menschen
　　Blindlings von einer
　　　Stunde zur andern,
　　　　Wie Wasser von Klippe
　　　　Zu Klippe geworfen,
　　　　　Jahr lang ins Ungewisse hinab.

I was raised by the melody
Of the whispering grove
And learned to love
Among the flowers.

I grew tall in the arms of gods.

[Hyperion's Song of Fate]

You walk on soft ground
  High up in the light, O blessèd spirits!
    The gods' shining breezes
      Touch you gently,
        As the musician's fingers
          Pluck her holy strings.

Fateless, the heavenly ones breathe
  Like the sleeping infant;
    Chastely kept
      In modest bud
        The spirit blooms
          For them eternal,
            And their blessèd eyes
              Gaze forth in still,
                Eternal clarity.

Yet it's our lot
  To wander homeless;
    Suffering men fade away,
      Fall blindly
        From one hour to the next,
          Like water thrown
            Year after year,
              From rock to rock,
                Down into the great unknown.

Achill.

Herrlicher Göttersohn! da du die Geliebte verloren,
  Giengst du ans Meergestaad, weintest hinaus in die Fluth,
Weheklagend, hinab verlangt in den heiligen Abgrund
  In die Stille dein Herz, wo, von der Schiffe Gelärm
Fern, tief unter den Woogen, in friedlicher Grotte die blaue
  Thetis wohnte, die dich schüzte, die Göttin des Meers.
Mutter war dem Jünglinge sie, die mächtige Göttin,
  Hatte den Knaben einst liebend, am Felsengestaad
Seiner Insel, gesäugt, mit dem kräftigen Liede der Welle
  Und im stärkenden Bad' ihn zum Heroën genährt.
Und die Mutter vernahm die Weheklage des Jünglings,
  Stieg vom Grunde der See, trauernd, wie Wölkchen, herauf,
Stillte mit zärtlichem Umfangen die Schmerzen des Lieblings,
  Und er hörte, wie sie schmeichelnd zu helfen versprach.

Göttersohn! o wär ich, wie du, so könnt' ich vertraulich
  Einem der Himmlischen klagen mein heimliches Laid.
Sehen soll ich es nicht, soll tragen die Schmach, als gehört ich
  Nimmer zu ihr, die doch meiner mit Thränen gedenkt
Gute Götter! doch hört ihr jegliches Flehen des Menschen,
  Ach! und innig und fromm liebt' ich dich heiliges Licht,
Seit ich lebe, dich Erd' und deine Quellen und Wälder,
  Vater Aether und dich fühlte zu sehnend und rein
Dieses Herz—o sänftiget mir, ihr Guten, mein Laiden,
  Daß die Seele mir nicht allzufrühe verstummt,

Achilles

Glorious son of gods! When you lost your belovèd
    You went to the seashore and wept in the tide,
Your heart, lamenting, longed in the depths that are holy,
    Into the silence where far from the din
Of the ships, deep under the waters, blue Thetis lived
    In her grotto in peace, the sea goddess who protected you.
The powerful goddess was the youth's mother,
    And on her island's rocky shore she once suckled him
With love, with the powerful song of the waves
    And strength-giving baths she nurtured a hero.
And the mother heard the youth's lament,
    And mourning like mist she rose from the floor of the sea
And stilled all the pains of her darling with tender embraces,
    And he heard, as she clung to him, her promise of aid.

Son of Olympus! If I were like you I could, lamenting,
    Confide my secret pain to one of the gods.
But I won't see that day, I must bear this my burden of shame
    As if I had never been hers, even though her tears are for me.
Kind gods! You *do* hear supplications of men—
    Ah, and deeply, devoutly I've loved you, holy light,
All my life, and you, Earth, with all of your forests and springs,
    And this heart, too wracked with longing, too pure, has felt you,
Father Aether—O you kind ones, soothe my pain
    That my soul not fade into silence too soon,

[Götter wandelten einst . . .]

Götter wandelten einst bei Menschen, die herrlichen Musen
    Und der Jüngling, Apoll, heilend, begeisternd wie du.
Und du bist mir, wie sie, als hätte der Seeligen Einer
    Mich ins Leben gesandt, geh ich, es wandelt das Bild
Meiner Heldin mit mir, wo ich duld' und bilde, mit Liebe
    Bis in den Tod, denn diß lernt' ich und hab' ich von ihr.

4.

Laß uns leben, o du mit der ich leide, mit der ich
    Innig und glaubig und treu ringe nach schönerer Zeit.
Sind doch wirs! und wüßten sie noch in kommenden
    Von uns beiden, wenn einst wieder der Genius gilt,
Sprächen sie: ihr schuffet euch einst ihr Einsamen liebend
    Nur von Göttern gekannt eure geheimere Welt.
Ihr Verwaisten, so lebtet ihr fromm in genügsamer Stille

Denn die Sterbliches nur besorgt, es empfängt sie die Erde
    Aber näher zum Licht wandern, zum Aether zurük
Sie, die inniger Liebe treu, und göttlichem Geiste
    Hoffend und duldend und still über das Schiksaal gesiegt.

[*Time was the gods walked with men . . .*]

Time was the gods walked with men, the glorious muses
    And the youthful Apollo, healing and inspiring like you.
And to me you are like the gods, as if one of the blest
    Had sent me into life I venture forth, and my heroine's
Image accompanies me where I endure and create with love
    Unto death, for this I've learned and received from her.

4.

Let us live, O you with whom I suffer, with whom I struggle
    For better times so ardently, so faithful and true.
This is *us!* And if they should come to know us
    In future   when genius is revered once more,
They would say: there was a time when you, O lonely ones,
    Created in love a more secret world, known only to the gods.
You orphaned ones, you lived devoutly in silence that suffices

Those who care for only mortal things—the earth shall take them;
    But they who wander nearer the light, back to the Aether
And true to the most tender love and the spirit of gods,
    Hoping and patient and still they have triumphed over fate.

Der Mensch.

Kaum sproßten aus den Wassern, o Erde, dir
  Der jungen Berge Gipfel und dufteten
    Lustathmend, immergrüner Haine
      Voll, in des Oceans grauer Wildniß

Die ersten holden Inseln; und freudig sah
  Des Sonnengottes Auge die Neulinge
    Die Pflanzen, seiner ew'gen Jugend
      Lächelnde Kinder, aus dir geboren.

Da auf der Inseln schönster, wo immerhin
  Den Hain in zarter Ruhe die Luft umfloß,
    Lag unter Trauben einst, nach lauer
      Nacht, in der dämmernden Morgenstunde

Geboren, Mutter Erde! dein schönstes Kind;—
  Und auf zum Vater Helios sieht bekannt
    Der Knab', und wacht und wählt die süßen
      Beere versuchend, die heil'ge Rebe

Zur Amme sich; und bald ist er groß; ihn scheun
  Die Thiere, denn ein anderer ist, wie sie
    Der Mensch; nicht dir und nicht dem Vater
      Gleicht er, denn kühn ist in ihm und einzig

Des Vaters hohe Seele mit deiner Lust,
  O Erd'! und deiner Trauer von je vereint;
    Der Göttermutter, der Natur, der
      Allesumfassenden möcht' er gleichen!

Ach! darum treibt ihn, Erde! vom Herzen dir
  Sein Übermuth, und deine Geschenke sind
    Umsonst und deine zarten Bande;
      Sucht er ein Besseres doch, der Wilde!

Man

Scarcely had they surged from your waters, O Earth,
  The first inclining, lovely isles in the gray ocean wastes,
    Sprouting youthful mountain peaks
      And evergreen woods full of the fragrant

Breath of joy, when the sun god's eye
  Gladly gazed upon the smiling children
    Of his timeless youth,
      The plants newly born from your soil.

Then on the loveliest isle where the air
  Still flowed round the grove in gentle calm,
    Lay, O Mother Earth, your loveliest
      Child, born under the grapevine

As the morning hour broke on gentle night;—
  And the boy looks up to Father Helios
    With familiar eyes and wakes, and tasting
      Sweet berries takes the holy vine

For his nurse; and soon he is grown; the animals
  Shun him, for man is different than they;
    He's not like you or his father,
      O Earth, for your joys and your sorrows

And the Father's high soul are forever
  Uniquely and boldly united in him;
    He'd like to equal Nature,
      The mother of gods, the all-embracing one!

Ah, Earth, that's why presumption drives
  Him from your heart, and you bestow all your gifts
    And your gentle bonds in vain;
      The savage one is looking for a better deal!

Von seines Ufers duftender Wiese muß
  Ins blüthenlose Wasser hinaus der Mensch,
    Und glänzt auch, wie die Sternenacht, von
      Goldenen Früchten sein Hain, doch gräbt er

Sich Höhlen in den Bergen und späht im Schacht
  Von seines Vaters heiterem Lichte fern,
    Dem Sonnengott auch ungetreu, der
      Knechte nicht liebt und der Sorge spottet.

Denn freier athmen Vögel des Walds, wenn schon
  Des Menschen Brust sich herrlicher hebt, und der
    Die dunkle Zukunft sieht, er muß auch
      Sehen den Tod und allein ihn fürchten.

Und Waffen wider alle, die athmen, trägt
  In ewigbangem Stolze der Mensch; im Zwist
    Verzehrt er sich und seines Friedens
      Blume, die zärtliche, blüht nicht lange.

Ist er von allen Lebensgenossen nicht
  Der seeligste? Doch tiefer und reißender
    Ergreift das Schiksaal, allausgleichend,
      Auch die entzündbare Brust dem Starken.

Man must embark over flowerless water
    From his shores where the fragrant meadows lie,
        And, full of golden fruit, his grove gleams too
            Like the starry night, yet he hollows out

Caves in mountains and peers down their shafts,
    Far from the cheerful light of his father
        And disloyal to the sun god too, who
            Loves no slave and scorns his servile cares.

For birds of the forest breathe more freely,
    And though man's heart might rise to more splendid heights,
        He who sees the dark future must also
            See death and fear it alone.

Man carries arms in constant and fearful pride
    Against all who breathe; he consumes himself
        In quarrel, and his tender
            Flower of peace doesn't bloom very long.

Isn't he the most blessèd of all his
    Fellow creatures? Yet Fate, leveling all,
        Far more deeply and more enraged,
            Seizes the fiery, quick-tempered heart of the strong.

Die Launischen.

Hör' ich ferne nur her, wenn ich für mich geklagt,
    Saitenspiel und Gesang, schweigt mir das Herz doch gleich;
        Bald auch bin ich verwandelt,
           Blinkst du, purpurner Wein! mich an

Unter Schatten des Walds, wo die gewaltige
    Mittagssonne mir sanft über dem Laube glänzt;
        Ruhig siz' ich dasselbst, wenn
           Zürnend schwerer Belaidigung

Ich im Felde geirrt—Zürnen zu gerne doch
    Deine Dichter, Natur! trauern und weinen leicht,
        Die Beglükten; wie Kinder,
           Die zu zärtlich die Mutter hält,

Sind sie mürrisch und voll herrischen Eigensinns;
    Wandeln still sie des Wegs, irret Geringes doch
        Bald sie wieder; sie reißen
           Aus dem Gleise sich sträubend dir.

Doch du rührest sie kaum, Liebende! freundlich an,
    Sind sie friedlich und fromm; fröhlich gehorchen sie;
        Du lenkst, Meisterinn! sie mit
           Weichem Zügel, wohin du willst.

The Temperamental Ones

If, when bemoaning my lot, I hear the music of strings
    And of song from afar, my heart falls silent at once;
        And I'm quickly transformed
           When you, purple wine, sparkle at me

In the shade of the woods, where the strong
    Noontime sun softly glimmers in leaves;
        I sit there calmly after
           Roaming through fields

In anger at some gross offense—yes, Nature, your poets
    Have too short a temper, they're too quick to grieve,
        These lucky ones; like children held
           By their mother in pampered embrace

They're moody and haughtily stubborn;
    Calmly walking a path, a trifle
        Throws them off; bristling at you
           They jump off the track.

Yet, O loving one, with your softest of touches and kindness
    They become peaceful, devout; they gladly obey;
        With the gentlest of reins, O mistress,
           You guide them wherever you please.

Der Tod fürs Vaterland.

Du kömmst, o Schlacht! schon woogen die Jünglinge
    Hinab von ihren Hügeln, hinab ins Thal,
        Wo kek herauf die Würger dringen,
           Sicher der Kunst und des Arms, doch sichrer

Kömmt über sie die Seele der Jünglinge,
    Denn die Gerechten schlagen, wie Zauberer,
        Und ihre Vaterlandsgesänge
           Lähmen die Kniee den Ehrelosen.

O nimmt mich, nimmt mich mit in die Reihen auf,
    Damit ich einst nicht sterbe gemeinen Tods!
        Umsonst zu sterben, lieb' ich nicht, doch
           Lieb' ich, zu fallen am Opferhügel

Fürs Vaterland, zu bluten des Herzens Blut
    Fürs Vaterland—und bald ists geschehn! Zu euch
        Ihr Theuern! komm' ich, die mich leben
           Lehrten und sterben, zu euch hinunter!

Wie oft im Lichte dürstet' ich euch zu sehn,
    Ihr Helden und ihr Dichter aus alter Zeit!
        Nun grüßt ihr freundlich den geringen
           Fremdling und brüderlich ists hier unten;

Und Siegesboten kommen herab: Die Schlacht
    Ist unser! Lebe droben, o Vaterland,
        Und zähle nicht die Todten! dir ist,
           Liebes, nicht Einer zu viel gefallen.

Dying for the Fatherland

You've come, O battle! The youths are already flowing
    Down from their hills and into the valley
        Where the cut-throat foe is boldly poised,
            Sure of its art and its arms, but the surer

Souls of the youths descend down upon them,
    For the righteous slay as if in a spell,
        And the songs of their fatherland
            Weaken the knees of those without honor.

O enlist me, enlist me in the ranks
    So I won't die some paltry death!
        I don't want to die in vain,
            I'd rather fall on the field, a sacrifice

For the fatherland, to bleed my heart's
    Blood for the fatherland—and now it will happen!
        I'm coming down to you, my dear friends, down to you
            Who taught me how to live and die!

How often I longed to see you in the light,
    O heroes and poets of ancient times!
        Now you kindly welcome this lowly
            Stranger into the brotherhood down here;

And messages of victory arrive: The battle's
    Ours! Live, O Fatherland, remain there on high
        And don't count the dead! O my belovèd,
            Not one too many has died for you.

Der Zeitgeist.

Zu lang schon waltest über dem Haupte mir
   Du in der dunkeln Wolke, du Gott der Zeit!
     Zu wild, zu bang ist's ringsum, und es
       Trümmert und wankt ja, wohin ich blike.

Ach! wie ein Knabe, seh' ich zu Boden oft,
   Such' in der Höhle Rettung vor dir, und möcht'
     Ich Blöder, eine Stelle finden,
       Alleserschütt'rer! wo du nicht wärest.

Lass' endlich, Vater! offenen Aug's mich dir
   Begegnen! hast denn du nicht zuerst den Geist
     Mit deinem Stral aus mir gewekt? mich
       Herrlich an's Leben gebracht, o Vater!—

Wohl keimt aus jungen Reben uns heil'ge Kraft;
   In milder Luft begegnet den Sterblichen,
     Und wenn sie still im Haine wandeln,
       Heiternd ein Gott; doch allmächt'ger wekst du

Die reine Seele Jünglingen auf, und lehrst
   Die Alten weise Künste; der Schlimme nur
     Wird schlimmer, daß er bälder ende,
       Wenn du, Erschütterer! ihn ergreiffest.

The Time-Spirit

You've ruled over me too long,
   O god of the dark clouds, O god of time!
      Everything's too fearful and desolate around me,
         And everywhere I look it crumbles and falls.

Ah, like a boy I often gaze at the ground,
   I look in caves for deliverance from you,
      And I timidly search for places
         Where you, Earth-shaker, wouldn't be.

Father, let me finally confront you
   With open eyes! For weren't you the first
      To wake my spirit with your ray, and didn't you,
         O Father, bring me gloriously to life?

Young vines enliven us with holy strength;
   Walking through the grove in silence,
      Mortals are confronted in the mild breeze with a god
         Who brings them clear skies; but you, more almighty,

Rouse the pure souls of youths and teach
   Wise arts to the old; the bad man alone
      Slides further down so that his end will come sooner
         When you, almighty shaker, seize his life.

Abendphantasie.

Vor seiner Hütte ruhig im Schatten sizt
   Der Pflüger, dem Genügsamen raucht sein Heerd.
     Gastfreundlich tönt dem Wanderer im
       Friedlichen Dorfe die Abendgloke.

Wohl kehren izt die Schiffer zum Hafen auch,
   In fernen Städten, fröhlich verrauscht des Markts
     Geschäfft'ger Lärm; in stiller Laube
       Glänzt das gesellige Mahl den Freunden.

Wohin denn ich? Es leben die Sterblichen
   Von Lohn und Arbeit; wechselnd in Müh' und Ruh'
     Ist alles freudig; warum schläft denn
       Nimmer nur mir in der Brust der Stachel?

Am Abendhimmel blühet ein Frühling auf;
   Unzählig blühn die Rosen und ruhig scheint
     Die goldne Welt; o dorthin nimmt mich
       Purpurne Wolken! und möge droben

In Licht und Luft zerrinnen mir Lieb' und Laid!—
   Doch, wie verscheucht von thöriger Bitte, flieht
     Der Zauber; dunkel wirds und einsam
       Unter dem Himmel, wie immer, bin ich—

Komm du nun, sanfter Schlummer! zu viel begehrt
   Das Herz; doch endlich, Jugend! verglühst du ja,
     Du ruhelose, träumerische!
       Friedlich und heiter ist dann das Alter.

Evening Fantasy

The plowman calmly sits beside his shaded
  Hut; smoke rises from his modest hearth.
    The peaceful village sounds its evening
      Bell to the wanderer in welcome tones.

The boatmen, too, are returning to the harbor,
  The busy noise of the market cheerfully
    Subsides in distant towns; in a quiet arbor
      A hearty meal is shining for friends.

But where should I go? Mortals live
  From work and wage; rest upon toil
    Makes everything a joy; why then does
      This breast-bound thorn never grant me repose?

In the evening sky a springtime blooms;
  Countless roses blossom, the golden world
    Seems calm; carry me there,
      O crimson clouds! And up there let

My love and pain dissolve in the light and air!—
  Yes, the spell is breaking, as if frightened away
    By foolish pleas; it's getting dark, and,
      As always, I'm alone under heaven—

Come then now, you gentle slumber! My heart desires
  Too much; but youth, O restless one, you dreamer,
    You'll finally burn away!
      And issue in old age, peaceful and serene.

Des Morgens.

Vom Thaue glänzt der Rasen; beweglicher
   Eilt schon die wache Quelle; die Buche neigt
     Ihr schwankes Haupt und im Geblätter
       Rauscht es und schimmert; und um die grauen

Gewölke streifen röthliche Flammen dort,
   Verkündende, sie wallen geräuschlos auf;
     Wie Fluthen am Gestade, woogen
       Höher und höher die Wandelbaren.

Komm nun, o komm, und eile mir nicht zu schnell,
   Du goldner Tag, zum Gipfel des Himmels fort!
     Denn offner fliegt, vertrauter dir mein
       Auge, du Freudiger! zu, so lang du

In deiner Schöne jugendlich blikst und noch
   Zu herrlich nicht, zu stolz mir geworden bist;
     Du möchtest immer eilen, könnt ich,
       Göttlicher Wandrer, mit dir!—doch lächelst

Des frohen Übermüthigen du, daß er
   Dir gleichen möchte; seegne mir lieber dann
     Mein sterblich Thun und heitre wieder
       Gütiger! heute den stillen Pfad mir.

In the Morning

Dew glistens on the grass; the wakened stream
    Rushes faster; the beech tree
        Bends its supple crown, a rustle
            And shimmer of leaves; and reddish

Flames streak forth among the clouds of gray,
    Prophetically ascend without a sound;
        Ever-changing, like waves upon the shore,
        They billow always higher.

Come now, O come, O golden day, and don't
    Hasten up to heaven's peak too soon!
        For my eyes rise up to you more open
            And familiar, O joyful one, as long as

You gaze on in youthful beauty and haven't
    Grown too resplendent, too proud for me;
        And I'll let you always rush onward, godly wanderer,
        If only I could go with you!—But you smile

At this joyful presumption of one who'd be
    Like you; bless instead, then,
        My mortal deeds today and brighten again,
        O kindly one, this my quiet path.

Der Main.

Wohl manches Land der lebenden Erde möcht'
    Ich sehn, und öfters über die Berg' enteilt
        Das Herz mir, und die Wünsche wandern
            Über das Meer, zu den Ufern, die mir

Vor andern, so ich kenne, gepriesen sind;
    Doch lieb ist in der Ferne nicht Eines mir,
        Wie jenes, wo die Göttersöhne
            Schlafen, das trauernde Land der Griechen.

Ach! einmal dort an Suniums Küste möcht'
    Ich landen, deine Säulen, Olympion!
        Erfragen, dort, noch eh der Nordsturm
            Hin in den Schutt der Athenertempel

Und ihrer Götterbilder auch dich begräbt;
    Denn lang schon einsam stehst du, o Stolz der Welt,
        Die nicht mehr ist!—und o ihr schönen
            Inseln Ioniens, wo die Lüfte

Vom Meere kühl an warme Gestade wehn,
    Wenn unter kräft'ger Sonne die Traube reift,
        Ach! wo ein goldner Herbst dem armen
            Volk in Gesänge die Seufzer wandelt,

Wenn die Betrübten izt ihr Limonenwald
    Und ihr Granatbaum, purpurner Aepfel voll
        Und süßer Wein und Pauk' und Zithar
            Zum labyrintischen Tanze ladet—

Zu euch vieleicht, ihr Inseln! geräth noch einst
    Ein heimathloser Sänger; denn wandern muß
        Von Fremden er zu Fremden, und die
            Erde, die freie, sie muß ja leider!

The Main

Yes I'd like to see many a land
  On this living earth, and often my heart
    Rushes over the mountains, and my wishes roam
    Over the sea to the shores that are

Praised above those that I know;
  And nothing is dearer to me in the distance
    Than that place where the sons of gods
    Are sleeping, the mournful land of the Greeks.

Ah, just for once I'd like to set shore
  On Sunium's coast and ask the way
    To your columns, Olympieion! There before
    The northern storm buries you too in the ruins

Of Athens' temples and their images of gods;
  For you've stood there alone so long, O pride
    Of that vanished world!—And O you
    Beautiful Ionian isles, where the breezes

Of the sea blow cool against the calid shores,
  Where the grape grows ripe in the powerful sun,
    Ah, where a golden autumn turns
    The poor people's sighs into song,

When their lemon groves and their pomegranate
  Trees full of purple fruit, and sweet wine
    And drum and zither invite the saddened ones
    Into labyrinthine dance—

To you, perhaps, O islands, a homeless
  Singer might one day come; for he must
    Wander from stranger to stranger, and the
    Earth, so wide and free, must serve him

Statt Vaterlands ihm dienen, so lang er lebt,
  Und wenn er stirbt—doch nimmer vergeß ich dich,
    So fern ich wandre, schöner Main! und
      Deine Gestade, die vielbeglükten.

Gastfreundlich nahmst du Stolzer! bei dir mich auf
  Und heitertest das Auge dem Fremdlinge,
    Und still hingleitende Gesänge
      Lehrtest du mich und geräuschlos Leben.

O ruhig mit den Sternen, du Glüklicher!
  Wallst du von deinem Morgen zum Abend fort,
    Dem Bruder zu, dem Rhein; und dann mit
      Ihm in den Ocean freudig nieder!

Alas as home in place of his country
    While he lives. And when he dies—yet I'll never forget you
        As far as I roam, O lovely Main, with
            Your shores blest and blest again.

Openhearted, O proud one, you welcomed me
    And brightened the eyes of this stranger,
        And you taught me silently flowing
            Songs and how to live without a sound.

As silent as the stars, O happy one,
    You course from your morning to evening
        Toward your brother, the Rhine, and then
            Down to the Ocean with him in joy!

FÜNF EPIGRAMME

Προς εαυτον

Lern im Leben die Kunst, im Kunstwerk lerne das Leben,
  Siehst du das Eine recht, siehst du das andere auch.

Sophokles

Viele versuchten umsonst das Freudigste freudig zu sagen
  Hier spricht endlich es mir, hier in der Trauer sich aus.

[Der zürnende Dichter]

Fürchtet den Dichter nicht, wenn er edel zürnet, sein Buchstab
  Tödtet, aber es macht Geister lebendig der Geist.

[Die Scherzhaften]

Immer spielt ihr und scherzt? ihr m ü ß t ! o Freunde! mir geht diß
  In die Seele, denn diß müssen Verzweifelte nur.

Wurzel alles Übels.

Einig zu seyn, ist göttlich und gut; woher ist die Sucht denn
  Unter den Menschen, daß nur Einer und Eines nur sei?

FIVE EPIGRAMS

Προς εαυτον

Learn about art from your life, and learn about life from your art.
    If you see one correctly, you'll see the other one too.

Sophocles

Many have tried in vain to express the most joyful with joy;
    Here it speaks finally to me, expressing itself in deep sorrow.

[The Angry Poet]

Don't fear the poet in noble rage; his letter
    Kills, but his spirit brings spirits to life.

[The Jokers]

You always play around and joke? You *must!* O friends,
    This pierces my soul, for those who must joke are caught in despair.

Root of All Evil

To be at one is godly and good; but where does this come from,
    This human obsession that there be only one and one only?

Mein Eigentum.

In seiner Fülle ruhet der Herbsttag nun,
　Geläutert ist die Traub und der Hain ist roth
　　Vom Obst, wenn schon der holden Blüthen
　　　Manche der Erde zum Danke fielen.

Und rings im Felde, wo ich den Pfad hinaus
　Den stillen wandle, ist den Zufriedenen
　　Ihr Gut gereift, und viel der frohen
　　　Mühe gewähret der Reichtum ihnen.

Vom Himmel bliket zu den Geschäfftigen
　Durch ihre Bäume milde das Licht herab,
　　Die Freude theilend, denn es wuchs durch
　　　Hände der Menschen allein die Frucht nicht.

Und leuchtest du, o Goldnes, auch mir, und wehst
　Auch du mir wieder Lüftchen, als seegnetest
　　Du eine Freude mir, wie einst, und
　　　Irrst, wie um Glükliche, mir am Busen?

Einst war ichs, doch wie Rosen, vergänglich war
　Das fromme Leben, ach und es mahnen noch
　　Die blühend mir geblieben sind, die
　　　Holden Gestirne zu oft mich dessen.

Beglükt, wer, ruhig liebend ein frommes Weib,
　Am eignen Heerd in rühmlicher Heimath lebt,
　　Es leuchtet über vestem Boden
　　　Schöner dem sicheren Mann sein Himmel.

Denn, wie die Pflanze, wurzelt auf eignem Grund
　Sie nicht, verglüht die Seele des Sterblichen
　　Der mit dem Tageslichte nur, ein
　　　Armer auf heiliger Erde wandelt.

What Is Mine

The autumn day rests now in fullness,
    The clear grapes are pressed, and the orchard is red
        With fruit, though many lovely
            Blossoms have fallen to Earth in thanks.

And all over the fields, where I wander
    The quiet path, the crops have ripened
        For contented men and women, and abundance
            Grants them so much of joyful work.

The light from the heavens softly filters
    Through trees on everyone busy at work
        And shares in their joy, for the fruits didn't
            Grow by human hands alone.

And will you shine, O golden one, for me too,
    And you too, O breeze, will you blow against me and bless
        Me with joy as before, and float
            About my breast as you do for happy men?

I was once, but, like roses, my god-fearing
    Life was fleeting; ah, and the lovely
        Constellations that still bloom for me
            Remind me all too often of this.

He is happy who quietly loves a gentle wife
    And has his own hearth in an honored land,
        Heaven shines more beautifully above
            The solid ground for a man this secure.

For, like a plant not rooted in its ground,
    A mortal soul will fade away
        If it only wanders with the daylight,
            A pauper, over holy Earth.

Zu mächtig ach! ihr himmlischen Höhen zieht
    Ihr mich empor; bei Stürmen, am heitern Tag
        Fühl ich verzehrend euch im Busen
            Wechseln, ihr wandelnden Götterkräfte.

Doch heute laß mich stille den trauten Pfad
    Zum Haine gehn dem golden die Wipfel schmükt
        Sein sterbend Laub, und kränzt auch mir die
            Stirne, ihr holden Erinnerungen!

Und daß auch mir zu retten mein sterblich Herz
    Wie andern eine bleibende Stätte sei
        Und heimathlos die Seele mir nicht
            Über das Leben hinweg sich sehne

Sei du, Gesang, mein freundlich Asyl! sei du
    Beglükender! mit sorgender Liebe mir
        Gepflegt, der Garten, wo ich, wandelnd
            Unter den Blüthen, den immerjungen

In sichrer Einfalt wohne, wenn draußen mir
    Mit ihren Wellen alle die mächtge Zeit
        Die Wandelbare fern rauscht und die
            Stillere Sonne mein Wirken fördert.

Ihr seegnet gütig über den Sterblichen
    Ihr Himmelskräfte! jedem sein Eigentum,
        O seegnet meines auch und daß zu
            Frühe die Parze den Traum nicht ende.

Ah, O heavenly heights, you pull me up
    With too much force; in storms or on a sunny
        Day I feel you changing,
            Consuming in my breast, O mutable godly powers.

Today, then, let me walk the path I know
    In silence, to the grove whose dying leaves grace
        The tops of trees with gold, and ring my brow
            As well, O lovely memories!

And that my mortal heart too be saved
    And provide, as others' do, a lasting resting place,
        And that my homeless soul not
            Long for more than what this life contains,

May you, O song, be my friendly refuge! May you,
    O bringer of joy, be tended with caring love by me,
        And be the garden where, strolling
            Among the ever-young blossoms

I live in secure simplicity, when outside, far away,
    Mighty time rolls its changes
        In wave upon wave, and the
            Quieter sun looks after my work.

O heavenly powers! You kindly bless
    What belongs to each mortal;
        O bless what I own too, lest Fate
            Cut down my dreaming life too soon.

[Wohl geh' ich täglich . . .]

Wohl geh' ich täglich andere Pfade, bald
  Ins grüne im Walde, zur Quelle bald,
    Zum Felsen, wo die Rosen blühen,
      Blike vom Hügel ins Land, doch nirgend

Du Holde, nirgend find ich im Lichte dich
  Und in die Lüfte schwinden die Worte mir
    Die frommen, die bei dir ich ehmals

Ja ferne bist du, seeliges Angesicht!
  Und deines Lebens Wohllaut verhallt von mir
    Nicht mehr belauscht, und ach! wo seid ihr
      Zaubergesänge, die einst das Herz mir

Besänftiget mit Ruhe der Himmlischen?
  Wie lang ist's! o wie lange! der Jüngling ist
    Gealtert, selbst die Erde, die mir
      Damals gelächelt, ist anders worden.

Leb immer wohl! es scheidet und kehrt zu dir
  Die Seele jeden Tag und es weint um dich
    Das Auge, daß es helle wieder
      Dort wo du säumest, hinüberblike.

[*Each day I walk . . .*]

Each day I walk a different path, now through
 The forest's green, now to the spring,
  To the cliffs where roses bloom,
   I look from the hill to the vale, but nowhere,

My love, I find you nowhere in the light,
 And my words disappear in the breezes,
  God-fearing words that once with you I

Yes, you are far away, O blissful face!
 And the harmony of your life dies away from me,
  No longer heard, and where are you,
   Magical songs, who once soothed my

Heart with the calm of the gods?
 It's been so long, O so long! That youth has
  Grown old, and even Earth, who once
   Smiled on me, now is changed.

Fare thee well! My soul departs and returns to you
 Each day, and my eyes weep for you
  That I might clearly gaze again
   To the distance in which you linger.

[Geh unter, schöne Sonne . . .]

Geh unter, schöne Sonne, sie achteten
   Nur wenig dein, sie kannten dich, heilge, nicht,
      Denn mühelos und stille bist du
         Über den mühsamen aufgegangen.

Mir gehst du freundlich unter und auf, o Licht!
   Und wohl erkennt mein Auge dich, herrliches!
      Denn göttlich stille ehren lernt' ich
         Da Diotima den Sinn mir heilte.

O du des Himmels Botin! wie lauscht ich dir!
   Dir, Diotima! Liebe! wie sah von dir
      Zum goldnen Tage dieses Auge
         Glänzend und dankend empor. Da rauschten

Lebendiger die Quellen, es athmeten
   Der dunkeln Erde Blüthen mich liebend an,
      Und lächelnd über Silberwolken
         Neigte sich seegnend herab der Aether.

[Go now and set, O beautiful sun . . .]

Go now and set, O beautiful sun, they had little
    Respect for you; they didn't know you, O holy one,
        For in effortless calm you
            Silently rose above laboring men.

To me you rise and set so kindly!
    And my eyes recognize you well, O glorious light!
        For I've learned to honor in godly calm
            Since Diotima has healed my mind.

O messenger from heaven, how I listened to you!
    To you, Diotima! Love! How these eyes,
        Shining and thankful, looked up from you
            To the golden day. Then the springs

Murmured livelier, the blossoms of dark Earth
    Breathed more sweetly on me,
        And Aether, smiling above the silver clouds,
            Bowed down bestowing his blessing.

Die Götter.

Du stiller Aether! immer bewahrst du schön
   Die Seele mir im Schmerz, und es adelt sich
      Zur Tapferkeit vor deinen Stralen,
         Helios! oft die empörte Brust mir.

Ihr guten Götter! arm ist, wer euch nicht kennt,
   Im rohen Busen ruhet der Zwist ihm nie,
      Und Nacht ist ihm die Welt und keine
         Freude gedeihet und kein Gesang ihm.

Nur ihr, mit eurer ewigen Jugend, nährt
   In Herzen die euch lieben, den Kindersinn,
      Und laßt in Sorgen und in Irren
         Nimmer den Genius sich vertrauern.

Heidelberg.

Lange lieb ich dich schon, möchte dich, mir zur Lust,
   Mutter nennen und dir schenken ein kunstlos Lied,
      Du der Vaterlandsstädte
         Ländlichschönste, so viel ich sah.

Wie der Vogel des Walds über die Gipfel fliegt,
   Schwingt sich über den Strom, wo er vorbei dir glänzt
      Leicht und kräftig die Brüke
         Die von Wagen und Menschen tönt.

Wie von Göttern gesandt, fesselt' ein Zauber einst
   Auf die Brüke mich an, da ich vorüber gieng
      Und herein in die Berge
         Mir die reizende Ferne schien,

The Gods

O silent Aether! You preserve the beauty always
    Of my soul in pain, and my heart, often
        Enraged, grows noble in your rays,
            O Helios, finding its courage there.

O kindly gods! He's poor who doesn't know you,
    The discord in his savage breast will never grow still,
        The world is night to him,
            And for him no joy will flourish and no song.

Only you, eternally young, can nourish
    The innocent mind within the hearts that love you,
        And never let the genius grieve its time away
            In mournful confusion and cares.

Heidelberg

Long have I loved you, and if I could I'd call you mother
    For my own delight, and give you an artless song,
        You, the most rustically beautiful town
            Of all those I've seen in my land.

As the birds of the forest fly over the trees,
    So does the bridge lightly soar and vault strongly,
        Spanning the river that flows by you gleaming,
            Resounding with wagons and men.

Once, as if sent by gods, a spell gripped
    Me fast on that bridge as I crossed,
        And right through the mountains
            The enthralling distance shone,

Und der Jüngling der Strom fort in die Ebne zog
 Traurigfroh, wie das Herz, wenn es, sich selbst zu schön
  Liebend unterzugehen
   In die Fluthen der Zeit sich wirft.

Quellen hattest du ihm, hattest dem Flüchtigen
 Kühle Schatten geschenkt, und die Gestade sahn
  All ihm nach, und es bebte
   Aus den Wellen ihr lieblich Bild.

Aber schwer in das Thal hieng die gigantische
 Schiksaalskundige Burg nieder bis auf den Grund
  Von den Wettern zerrissen;
   Doch die ewige Sonne goß

Ihr verjüngendes Licht über das alternde
 Riesenbild, und umher grünte lebendiger
  Epheu; freundliche Wälder
   Rauschten über die Burg herab.

Sträuche blühten herab, bis wo im heitern Thal,
 An den Hügel gelehnt, oder dem Ufer hold,
  Deine fröhlichen Gassen
   Unter duftenden Gärten ruhn.

And that youth, the river, floated away to the plain
   Sadly joyous, like the heart too full of beauty
      That throws itself to the tides of time
         So that, loving, it may perish going down.

You'd bestowed sources on him,
   Given cool shade to the fugitive,
      And the shores gazed upon him
         And their form quivered lightly from out of the waves.

But, fate-met and lorn, the gigantic castle
   Hung heavily into the vale, ripped down
      By storms to the ground;
         Yet the eternal sun poured

Its youth-giving light on this scene
   Of giant decay, and around it grew ivy
      Lively in green; mild pleasing woods
         Rustled down over the stones.

Bushes bloomed down till the point in the bright serene
   Valley where, hugging the hill or fondly inclined
      To the shore, your alleys and streets
         Joyfully rest below gardens in bloom.

Der Nekar.

In deinen Thälern wachte mein Herz mir auf
Zum Leben, deine Wellen umspielten mich,
Und all der holden Hügel, die dich
Wanderer! kennen, ist keiner fremd mir.

Auf ihren Gipfeln löste des Himmels Luft
Mir oft der Knechtschaft Schmerzen; und aus dem Thal,
Wie Leben aus dem Freudebecher,
Glänzte die bläuliche Silberwelle.

Der Berge Quellen eilten hinab zu dir,
Mit ihnen auch mein Herz und du nahmst uns mit,
Zum stillerhabnen Rhein, zu seinen
Städten hinunter und lustgen Inseln.

Noch dünkt die Welt mir schön, und das Aug entflieht
Verlangend nach den Reizen der Erde mir,
Zum goldenen Pactol, zu Smirnas
Ufer, zu Ilions Wald. Auch möcht ich

Bei Sunium oft landen, den stummen Pfad
Nach deinen Säulen fragen, Olympion!
Noch eh der Sturmwind und das Alter
Hin in den Schutt der Athenertempel

Und ihrer Gottesbilder auch dich begräbt,
Denn lang schon einsam stehst du, o Stolz der Welt,
Die nicht mehr ist. Und o ihr schönen
Inseln Ioniens! wo die Meerluft

Die heißen Ufer kühlt und den Lorbeerwald
Durchsäuselt, wenn die Sonne den Weinstok wärmt,
Ach! wo ein goldner Herbst dem armen
Volk in Gesänge die Seufzer wandelt,

The Neckar

In your valleys my heart woke to life,
   Your waves played around me, and of all the graceful hills
      That know you, wanderer, inclined to you
         And dear, not one is a stranger to me.

Upon their peaks the air of heaven
   Often released me from slavish pain; and like
      Life poured from a cup of gladness, the bluish,
         Silvery waves glistened in the valley below.

The springs of the mountain hurried down to you,
   With them my heart as well, and you took us both
      To the calm and lordly Rhine, to its
         Towns below and pleasing islands.

The world seems still beautiful to me, and my longing
   Eyes flee to the wonders of the earth,
      To golden Pactolus, to Smyrna's
         Shores, to Ilium's woods. And I've often

Desired to set shore at Sunium and ask the silent
   Path the way to your columns, Olympieion!
      Before the storm winds and age
         Bury you too in the ruins

Of Athens' temples and their images of god,
   For you've stood there alone so long, O pride
      Of that vanished world. And O you
         Beautiful Ionian isles, where the seabreezes

Cool the blazing shores and whisper through
   The laurel woods, where the sun warms the grapevine,
      Ah, where a golden autumn turns
         The poor people's sighs into song,

Wenn sein Granatbaum reift, wenn aus grüner Nacht
Die Pomeranze blinkt, und der Mastyxbaum
Von Harze träuft und Pauk und Cymbel
Zum labyrintischen Tanze klingen.

Zu euch, ihr Inseln! bringt mich vielleicht, zu euch
Mein Schuzgott einst; doch weicht mir aus treuem Sinn
Auch da mein Nekar nicht mit seinen
Lieblichen Wiesen und Uferweiden.

Empedokles.

Das Leben suchst du, suchst und es quillt und glänzt
Ein göttlich Feuer tief aus der Erde dir,
Und du in schauderndem Verlangen
Wirfst dich hinab, in des Aetna Flammen.

So schmelzt' im Weine Perlen der Übermuth
Der Königin; und mochte sie doch! hättst du
Nur deinen Reichtum nicht, o Dichter
Hin in den gährenden Kelch geopfert!

Doch heilig bist du mir, wie der Erde Macht,
Die dich hinwegnahm, kühner Getödteter!
Und folgen möcht' ich in die Tiefe,
Hielte die Liebe mich nicht, dem Helden.

When the pomegranate ripens, when the orange grove
   Gleams in the green of the night and the mastic tree
      Drips its resin, and drum and cymbal
         Sound the labyrinthine dance.

To you, O islands! To you perhaps my guardian
   God will bring me one time; but even then
      My loyal thoughts will not forget my
         Neckar, with its lovely fields and willowed shores.

Empedocles

You search for life, you search, and a divine fire
   Gleams and wells from deep within Earth to you,
      And with a shuddering urge you
         Hurl yourself down into Aetna's flames.

Thus the whim of the queen once melted
   Pearls in wine—and well she should have! If only
      You, O poet, hadn't sacrificed
         Your wealth to the fermenting cup!

But you're holy to me, like the powers of Earth
   That seized you away, the boldly killed!
      And if love no longer held me in its grasp,
         I'd gladly follow this hero down into the depths.

An die Deutschen.

Spottet nimmer des Kinds, wenn noch das alberne
  Auf dem Rosse von Holz herrlich und groß sich dünkt,
    O ihr Guten! auch wir sind
      Thatenarm und gedankenvoll!

Aber komt, wie der Stral aus dem Gewölke komt,
  Aus Gedanken vieleicht, geistig und reif die That?
    Folgt die Frucht, wie des Haines
      Dunklem Blatte, der stillen Schrift?

Und das Schweigen im Volk, ist es die Feier schon
  Vor dem Feste? die Furcht, welche den Gott ansagt?
    O dann nimmt mich, ihr Lieben!
      Daß ich büße die Lästerung.

Schon zu lange, zu lang irr ich, dem Laien gleich,
  In des bildenden Geists werdender Werkstatt hier,
    Nur was blühet, erkenn ich,
      Was er sinnet, erkenn ich nicht.

Und zu Ahnen ist süß, aber ein Leiden auch,
  Und schon Jahre genug leb' ich in sterblicher
    Unverständiger Liebe
      Zweifelnd, immer bewegt vor ihm

Der das stetige Werk immer aus liebender
  Seele näher mir bringt, lächelnd dem Sterblichen
    Wo ich zage, des Lebens
      Reine Tiefe zu Reife bringt.

Schöpferischer, o wann, Genius unsers Volks,
  Wann erscheinest du ganz, Seele des Vaterlands
    Daß ich tiefer mich beuge
      Daß die leiseste Saite selbst

To the Germans

Never mock the child when the silly creature
    Thinks himself so glorious and big sitting on his wooden horse,
        O my good friends, we too are
            Poor in deed and rich in thought!

But will the deed perhaps emerge from thought,
    Fully fledged and inspirited, like a flash from the clouds?
        Does the fruit follow the quiet written word
            As it follows dark leaves of the grove?

And the people's silence, is it celebration
    Before the feast? The fear that announces the god?
        O seize me, dear friends, so I'll
            Pay for these blasphemous words.

Too long, too long I've strayed like a layman
    In this emerging workshop of the sculpting spirit,
        Only what blooms do I see,
            What he's planning I don't.

And it's sweet to guess at this, yet a sorrow as well,
    And I've spent too many years already
        Lost in mortal, senseless love,
            Doubting, always moved in his presence,

He who from his loving soul always brings
    His constant work nearer to me, smiles
        At this mortal man where I lose heart,
            And ripens the pure depth of life.

O Creator, O when, genius of our people,
    When will you wholly appear, soul of the fatherland,
        That I might bow more deeply,
            That my quietest string

Mir verstumme vor dir, daß ich beschämt
  Eine Blume der Nacht, himmlischer Tag, vor dir
    Enden möge mit Freuden
      Wenn sie alle, mit denen ich

Vormals trauerte, wenn unsere Städte nun
  Hell und offen und wach, reineren Feuers voll
    Und die Berge des deutschen
      Landes Berge der Musen sind,

Wie die herrlichen einst, Pindos und Helikon,
  Und Parnassos, und rings unter des Vaterlands
    Goldnem Himmel die freie,
      Klare geistige Freude glänzt.

Wohl ist enge begränzt unsere Lebenszeit,
  Unserer Jahre Zahl sehen und zählen wir,
    Doch die Jahre der Völker
      Sah ein sterbliches Auge sie?

Wenn die Seele dir auch über die eigne Zeit
  Sich die sehnende schwingt, trauernd verweilest du
    Dann am kalten Gestade,
      Bei den Deinen und kennst sie nie,

Und die Künftigen auch, sie, die Verheißenen
  Wo wo siehest du sie, daß du an Freundeshand
    Einmal wieder erwarmest,
      Einer Seele vernehmlich seist?

Klanglos,   ists in der Halle längst,
  Armer Seher! bei dir, sehnend verlischt dein Aug
    Und du schlummerst hinunter,
      Ohne Nahmen und unbeweint.

Aber ihr!
                        Richterin,
  Wenn er ihn sah,

Might fall silent before you, that I, ashamed,
    A flower of night, O heavenly day, might
        End before you in joy,
            When all of them with whom

I used to mourn, when our cities grow
    Bright and open, awake, full of purer fire,
        And the mountains of the German
            Lands become the mountains of the Muses

As the glorious ones once were, Pindus and Helicon,
    And Parnassus, and under
        The fatherland's golden sky the spiritual joy
            Gleams free and clear all around.

All too limited is the time of our life,
    We observe and count out our number of years,
        But has a mortal eye
            Observed the years of a nation?

When your soul, ever-longing, soars
    Beyond its time, you linger in grief
        On freezing shores
            With your own and don't know them,

And as for the future ones, the promised ones,
    Where, where do you glimpse them that you might once
        Again find a warm and friendly hand
            And be heard by a single simple soul?

The halls, poor seer, have given   no echo
    For years, longing your eyes grow dim
        And you slump down in sleep,
            Nameless, unwept.

But you!
                        judge,
    When he saw him,

Rousseau.

Wie eng begränzt ist unsere Tageszeit.
  Du warst und sahst und stauntest, schon Abend ists.
    Nun schlafe, wo unendlich ferne
      Ziehen vorüber die Völkerjahre.

Und mancher siehet über die eigne Zeit
  Ihm zeigt ein Gott ins Freie, doch sehnend stehst
    Am Ufer du, ein Aergerniß den
      Deinen, ein Schatten, und liebst sie nimmer,

Und jene, die du nennst, die Verheißenen,
  Wo sind die Neuen, daß du an Freundeshand
    Erwarmst, wo nahn sie, daß du einmal
      Einsame Rede, vernehmlich seiest?

Klanglos ists, armer Mann, in der Halle dir,
  Und gleich den Unbegrabenen, irrest du
    Unstät und suchest Ruh und niemand
      Weiß den beschiedenen Weg zu weisen.

Sei denn zufrieden!   der Baum entwächst
  Dem heimathlichen Boden, aber es sinken ihm
    Die liebenden, die jugendlichen
      Arme, und trauernd neigt er sein Haupt.

Des Lebens Überfluß, das Unendliche,
  Das um ihn   und dämmert, er faßt es nie.
    Doch lebts in ihm und gegenwärtig,
      Wärmend und wirkend, die Frucht entquillt ihm.

Du hast gelebt! ge   auch dir, auch dir
  Erfreut die ferne Sonne dein Haupt,
    Und Stralen aus der schönern Zeit, es
      Haben die Boten dein Herz gefunden.

Rousseau

How limited the time of our day.
 You were and saw and marveled, it's evening already.
  So sleep now, where infinitely far
   The years of the nations drift overhead.

And some see past their own time,
 A god has shown them the open, but longing
  You stand on the shore, a scandal to your kin,
   A shade, and you no longer love them,

And those you name, the new and promised ones,
 Where are they to warm you with their
  Friendly hands, and where do they approach so that you,
   Lonely speech, might one day be heard?

The halls, poor man, give no echo,
 And like the unburied dead you wander
  Unsettled and look for rest, and no one can
   Show you the determined path.

So content yourself with this!   the tree outgrows
 Its native soil, but its loving,
  Youthful boughs droop down,
   And it bows its crown in mourning.

The overflow of life, the infinite,
 That   around him, dawning, he never grasps it.
  Yet it lives in him, and, all the while,
   Warming and effective, the fruit springs forth from him.

You have lived! The distant sun   ed you too
 And gladdens too your head,
  And rays from a better time,
   The messengers have found your heart.

Vernommen hast du sie verstanden die Sprache der Fremdlinge,
  Gedeutet ihre Seele! Dem Sehnenden war
    Genug der Wink, und Winke sind
      Von Alters her die Sprache der Götter.

Und wunderbar, als hätte von Anbeginn
  Des Menschen Geist, das Werden und Wirken all,
    Des Lebens alte Weise schon erfahren

Kennt er im ersten Zeichen Vollendetes schon,
  Und fliegt, der kühne Geist, wie Adler den
    Gewittern, weissagend seinen
      Kommenden Göttern, voraus,

Die Heimath.

Froh kehrt der Schiffer heim an den stillen Strom,
  Von Inseln fernher, wenn er geerndtet hat;
    So käm' auch ich zur Heimath, hätt' ich
      Güter so viele, wie Laid, geerndtet.

Ihr theuren Ufer, die mich erzogen einst,
  Stillt ihr der Liebe Leiden, versprecht ihr mir,
    Ihr Wälder meiner Jugend, wenn ich
      Komme, die Ruhe noch einmal wieder?

Am kühlen Bache, wo ich der Wellen Spiel,
  Am Strome, wo ich gleiten die Schiffe sah,
    Dort bin ich bald; euch traute Berge,
      Die mich behüteten einst, der Heimath

Verehrte sichre Grenzen, der Mutter Haus
  Und liebender Geschwister Umarmungen
    Begrüß' ich bald und ihr umschließt mich,
      Daß, wie in Banden, das Herz mir heile,

You perceived, you understood the language of strangers,
  Interpreted their soul! The hint sufficed
    The longing one, and hints have long
      Been the language of gods.

And wondrous, as if from the outset the human spirit
  Had experienced all that would be born and made manifest,
    The ancient way of life

In the first signs he sees their completion
  And, emboldened with this insight, flying like an eagle
    Ahead of the storm, he prophesies
      The coming of his gods,

Home

Gladly the boatman turns home to the river's calm
  From his harvest on faraway isles;
    I too would come home if only
      My harvest of goods had equaled my sorrow.

O dear riverbanks that raised me,
  Can you ease the sorrows of love? If I came to you,
    O woods of my youth, could you
      Promise me peace once again?

On the cool stream where I saw the play
  Of waves, and on the river where ships glide by,
    I'll be there soon; O trusted mountains
      Who protected me once, my homeland's

Secure and honored borders, I'll greet you soon,
  And you too, my mother's house, and siblings
    In loving embrace—you'll all surround me,
      Healing my heart in your bands of love,

Ihr treugebliebnen! aber ich weiß, ich weiß
  Der Liebe Laid, diß heilet so bald mir nicht,
    Diß singt kein Wiegensang, den tröstend
      Sterbliche singen, mir aus dem Busen.

Denn sie, die uns das himmlische Feuer leihn,
  Die Götter schenken heiliges Laid uns auch,
    Drum bleibe diß. Ein Sohn der Erde
      Schein' ich; zu lieben gemacht, zu leiden.

Die Liebe.

Wenn ihr Freunde vergeßt, wenn ihr die Euern all
  O ihr Dankbaren, sie, euere Dichter schmäht,
    Gott vergeb' es, doch ehret
      Nur die Seele der Liebenden.

Denn o saget, wo lebt menschliches Leben sonst
  Da die knechtische jezt alles, die Sorge zwingt?
    Darum wandelt der Gott auch
      Sorglos über dem Haupt uns längst.

Doch, wie immer das Jahr kalt und gesanglos ist
  Zur beschiedenen Zeit, aber aus weißem Feld
    Grüne Halme doch sprossen
      Oft ein einsamer Vogel singt,

Wenn sich mälig der Wald dehnet, der Strom sich regt,
  Schon die mildere Luft leise von Mittag weht
    Zur erlesenen Stunde,
      So ein Zeichen der schönern Zeit,

O you ever-loyal ones! But I know, I know
 The sorrow of love won't soon heal for me,
  No lullaby that mortals sing for comfort
   Will sing away the sorrow from my heart.

For they who lend us fire from heaven,
 The gods, they grant us holy sorrow too—
  So be it. I seem to be a son
   Of Earth; made to love, to suffer.

Love

If you forget all your friends, if you revile,
 O grateful ones, all your own poets,
  May god forgive you; but
   Always honor the lovers' soul.

So tell me, where else does human life live
 Now that we're slaves to our cares?
  That's why even the god has walked
   So long above our heads, uncaring.

Yes, as always the year is songless and cold
 At the determined time, but from the white field
  The green grass sprouts forth,
   Often a lonely bird sings

As the woods expand slowly and the river stirs,
 Already a milder noontime breeze blows
  Calmly at the chosen hour,
   And thus, a sign of the better times

Die wir glauben, erwächst einziggenügsam noch,
 Einzig edel und fromm über dem ehernen,
  Wilden Boden die Liebe,
   Gottes Tochter, von ihm allein.

Sei geseegnet, o sei, himmlische Pflanze, mir
 Mit Gesange gepflegt, wenn des ätherischen
  Nektars Kräfte dich nähren,
   Und der schöpfrische Stral dich reift.

Wachs und werde zum Wald! eine beseeltere,
 Vollentblühende Welt! Sprache der Liebenden
  Sei die Sprache des Landes,
   Ihre Seele der Laut des Volks!

Lebenslauf.

Größers wolltest auch du, aber die Liebe zwingt
 All uns nieder, das Laid beuget gewaltiger,
  Doch es kehret umsonst nicht
   Unser Bogen, woher er kommt.

Aufwärts oder hinab! herrschet in heil'ger Nacht,
 Wo die stumme Natur werdende Tage sinnt,
  Herrscht im schiefesten Orkus
   Nicht ein Grades, ein Recht noch auch?

Diß erfuhr ich. Denn nie, sterblichen Meistern gleich,
 Habt ihr Himmlischen, ihr Alleserhaltenden,
  Daß ich wüßte, mit Vorsicht,
   Mich des ebenen Pfads geführt.

Alles prüfe der Mensch, sagen die Himmlischen,
 Daß er, kräftig genährt, danken für Alles lern',
  Und verstehe die Freiheit,
   Aufzubrechen, wohin er will.

In which we believe, uniquely content, uniquely
    Noble and reverent, God's daughter,
        Love, she grows above the iron, virgin ground
            And comes from him alone.

Be blessèd, heavenly plant, tended
    By my song when the powers
        Of Aether's nectar nourish you,
            And the life-giving ray makes you ripe.

Grow and become a forest, more full of soul,
    A fully blooming world! May the language of lovers
        Be the language of the country,
            Let their soul be the people's voice!

The Course of Life

You too wanted greater things, but love forces
    All of us down, and suffering bends us still lower;
        Yet our arc does not return
            To where it began in vain.

Upward or down! Doesn't a straightness,
    A law, prevail in the holy night
        Where mute Nature imagines the coming days,
            Down in the crookedest bend of hell?

This I learned. For you heavenly ones, who maintain all,
    Have never, as far as I know,
        Led me with caution, as mortal
            Masters do, along the level path.

The gods say: let man test everything
    So that, powerfully nourished, he'll learn to be thankful
        For all and realize his freedom
            To set out wheresoever he choose.

Ihre Genesung.

Sieh! dein Liebstes, Natur, leidet und schläft und du
   Allesheilende, säumst? oder ihr seids nicht mehr,
     Zarte Lüfte des Aethers,
       Und ihr Quellen des Morgenlichts?

Alle Blumen der Erd, alle die goldenen
   Frohen Früchte des Hains, alle sie heilen nicht
     Dieses Leben, ihr Götter,
       Das ihr selber doch euch erzogt?

Ach! schon athmet und tönt heilige Lebenslust
   Ihr im reizenden Wort wieder, wie sonst und schon
     Glänzt in zärtlicher Jugend
       Deine Blume wie sonst, dich an,

Heilge Natur, o du, welche zu oft, zu oft,
   Wenn ich trauernd versank lächelnd das zweifelnde
     Haupt mit Gaaben umkränzte
       Jugendliche, nun auch, wie sonst!

Wenn ich alte dereinst, siehe so geb ich dir
   Die mich täglich verjüngt Allesverwandelnde
     Deiner Flamme die Schlaken,
       Und ein anderes leb ich auf.

Her Recovery

Look, Nature, your favorite is suffering and sleeping while you,
    All-healing one, just stand by? Or is your strength gone,
        Gentle breezes of Aether,
            And you, sources of morning light?

All the flowers of Earth, all the golden,
    Joyful fruits of the grove, why don't they
        Heal her life, O gods,
            A life that you yourselves raised?

Ah, the holy desire for life breathes already and rings
    Again through her words, charming as ever before,
        And already, tender in youth, your
            Flower gleams to you as before,

Holy Nature, O you who too often, too often
    When I sank in myself in mourning, you wreathed
        My doubting head with your smiles
            And gifts, O youthful one, now too as before!

Look, one day when I'm old I shall give you,
    You who transform all and renew my youth
        Each day, I shall give my cinders to your flame,
            And rise up another man.

Diotima.

Du schweigst und duldest, denn sie verstehn dich nicht,
  Du edles Leben! siehest zur Erd' und schweigst
    Am schönen Tag, denn ach! umsonst nur
      Suchst du die Deinen im Sonnenlichte,

Die Königlichen, welche, wie Brüder doch,
  Wie eines Hains gesellige Gipfel sonst
    Der Lieb' und Heimath sich und ihres
      Immerumfangenden Himmels freuten,

Des Ursprungs noch in tönender Brust gedenk;
  Die Dankbarn, sie, sie mein' ich, die einzigtreu
    Bis in den Tartarus hinab die Freude
      Brachten, die Freien, die Göttermenschen,

Die zärtlichgroßen Seelen, die nimmer sind;
  Denn sie beweint, so lange das Trauerjahr
    Schon dauert, von den vor'gen Sternen
      Täglich gemahnet, das Herz noch immer

Und diese Todtenklage, sie ruht nicht aus.
  Die Zeit doch heilt. Die Himmlischen sind jezt stark,
    Sind schnell. Nimmt denn nicht schon ihr altes
      Freudiges Recht die Natur sich wieder?

Sieh! eh noch unser Hügel, o Liebe, sinkt,
  Geschiehts, und ja! noch siehet mein sterblich Lied
    Den Tag, der, Diotima! nächst den
      Göttern mit Helden dich nennt, und dir gleicht.

Diotima

You fall silent and suffer, for no one understands you,
   O noble being! You gaze to the earth and fall silent
      On the beautiful day, for you look in vain
         For your kin in the sunlight,

Those royal ones who, yes, like brothers,
   Who like companioned treetops of a grove,
      Rejoiced once in love and homeland
         And their ever-embracing heaven,

Remembering still their source in resounding hearts;
   Those thankful ones, I mean those uniquely faithful ones
      Who brought joy down to Tartarus,
         Those free ones, the men born of gods,

Those great and tender souls who are no more;
   For, reminded by the stars of that time,
      The heart still and always weeps for them,
         So long the year of mourning has lasted.

And this dirge, it finds no rest.
   But time heals. The heavenly are now strong,
      Are fast. Hasn't Nature already
         Claimed its ancient, joyful right again?

Look, O my love, before our hill sinks down
   It will happen, and my mortal song will yet see
      The day, Diotima, that in your likeness
         Names you among all the heroes and gods.

Rükkehr in die Heimath.

Ihr milden Lüfte! Boten Italiens!
   Und du mit deinen Pappeln, geliebter Strom!
    Ihr woogenden Gebirg! o all ihr
      Sonnigen Gipfel, so seid ihrs wieder?

Du stiller Ort! in Träumen erschienst du fern
   Nach hoffnungslosem Tage dem Sehnenden,
    Und du mein Haus, und ihr Gespielen,
      Bäume des Hügels, ihr wohlbekannten!

Wie lang ists, o wie lange! des Kindes Ruh
   Ist hin, und hin ist Jugend und Lieb' und Lust;
    Doch du, mein Vaterland! du heilig-
      Duldendes! siehe, du bist geblieben.

Und darum, daß sie dulden mit dir, mit dir
   Sich freun, erziehst du, theures! die deinen auch
    Und mahnst in Träumen, wenn sie ferne
      Schweifen und irren, die Ungetreuen.

Und wenn im heißen Busen dem Jünglinge
   Die eigenmächt'gen Wünsche besänftiget
    Und stille vor dem Schiksaal sind, dann
      Giebt der Geläuterte dir sich lieber.

Lebt wohl dann, Jugendtage, du Rosenpfad
   Der Lieb', und all' ihr Pfade des Wanderers,
    Lebt wohl! und nimm und seegne du mein
      Leben, o Himmel der Heimath, wieder!

Return to the Homeland

You gentle breezes, messengers of Italy,
    And you with your poplars, belovèd stream!
      You surging mountains, O all you
        Sunny peaks, is it really you again?

You silent site, after hopeless days
    You appeared distant in dreams to me as I longed,
      And you my house, and you childhood friends,
        Trees on the hill, I know you so well!

How long it's been, O how long! The peace of childhood
    Is gone, and gone is my youth, love, and joy,
      Yet you, my fatherland, you holy
        Suffering one, look how you have remained.

And that's why, dear one, so they'll suffer
    And delight with you, you raise your kin
      And warn them in dreams, the unfaithful ones,
        When they roam far away in confusion.

And when capricious desires
    Are stilled in youth's passionate heart
      And grow calm before fate,
        Purified then he'll give himself gladly to you.

Farewell, then, days of my youth, you rose path
    Of love and all you paths of the wanderer,
      Farewell! Take now and bless my life,
        O you heaven of the homeland, once again!

Dichterberuf.

Des Ganges Ufer hörten des Freudengotts
    Triumph, als alleroberñd vom Indus her
        Der junge Bacchus kam, mit heilgem
            Weine vom Schlafe die Völker wekend.

Und du, des Tages Engel! erwekst sie nicht,
    Die jezt noch schlafen? gieb die Geseze, gieb
        Uns Leben, siege, Meister, du nur
            Hast der Eroberung Recht, wie Bacchus.

Nicht, was wohl sonst des Menschen Geschik und Sorg'
    Im Haus und unter offenem Himmel ist,
        Wenn edler, denn das Wild, der Mann sich
            Wehret und nährt! denn es gilt ein anders,

Zu Sorg' und Dienst den Dichtenden anvertraut!
    Der Höchste, der ists, dem wir geeignet sind
        Daß näher, immerneu besungen
            Ihn die befreundete Brust vernehme.

Und dennoch, o ihr Himmlischen all, und all
    Ihr Quellen und ihr Ufer und Hain' und Höhn,
        Wo wunderbar zuerst, als du die
            Loken ergriffen, und unvergeßlich

Der unverhoffte Genius über uns
    Der schöpferische, göttliche kam, daß stumm
        Der Sinn uns ward und, wie vom
            Strale gerührt das Gebein erbebte,

Ihr ruhelosen Thaten in weiter Welt!
    Ihr Schiksaalstag', ihr reißenden, wenn der Gott
        Stillsinnend lenkt, wohin zorntrunken
            Ihn die gigantischen Rosse bringen,

The Poet's Calling

The banks of the Ganges heard the triumph
    Of the god of joy when the all-conquering youthful
        Bacchus went forth from Indus, his holy
            Wine waking the nations from sleep.

And you, O Angel of Day, you don't wake them,
    Those still asleep? Hand down the laws,
        Give us life, O master, and be triumphant—only you,
            Like Bacchus, possess the right to conquer.

The familiar domain of human beings, the care
    And skill they show in their homes and under the open sky,
        And even though they nourish themselves and work
            More nobly than the beasts—it's not this

But something else that's entrusted to the poets' serving care!
    We're meant to serve the highest one
        So that, ever newly sung, he might be
            More closely heard by friendly hearts.

And yet, O all you heavenly ones, and all you
    Springs and banks and groves and heights
        Where wondrously at first when you
            Seized us by our locks and the unhoped-for

Genius, the divine Creator, unforgettably
    Came over us, and our minds
        Became dumbfounded, and as if
            Struck by a flash all our bones were shaken,

O restless deeds across the world!
    O fateful days roaring down, when the god,
        Steering his gigantic horses drunk with rage,
            Calmly considers whither they shall bring him,

Euch sollten wir verschweigen, und wenn in uns
　　Vom stetigstillen Jahre der Wohllaut tönt,
　　　　So sollt' es klingen, gleich als hätte
　　　　　　Muthig und müßig ein Kind des Meisters

Geweihte, reine Saiten im Scherz gerührt?
　　Und darum hast du, Dichter! des Orients
　　　　Propheten und den Griechensang und
　　　　　　Neulich die Donner gehört, damit du

Den Geist zu Diensten brauchst und die Gegenwart
　　Des Guten übereilest, in Spott, und den Albernen
　　　　Verläugnest, herzlos, und zum Spiele
　　　　　　Feil, wie gefangenes Wild, ihn treibest.

Bis aufgereizt vom Stachel im Grimme der
　　Des Ursprungs sich erinnert und ruft, daß selbst
　　　　Der Meister kommt, dann unter heißen
　　　　　　Todesgeschossen entseelt dich lässet.

Zu lang ist alles Göttliche dienstbar schon
　　Und alle Himmelskräfte verscherzt, verbraucht
　　　　Die Gütigen, zur Lust, danklos, ein
　　　　　　Schlaues Geschlecht und zu kennen wähnt es

Wenn ihnen der Erhabne den Aker baut,
　　Das Tagslicht und den Donnerer, und es späht
　　　　Das Sehrohr wohl sie all und zählt und
　　　　　　Nennet mit Nahmen des Himmels Sterne;

Der Vater aber deket mit heilger Nacht,
　　Damit wir bleiben mögen, die Augen zu.
　　　　Nicht liebt er Wildes! doch es zwinget
　　　　　　Nimmer die weite Gewalt den Himmel.

Should we keep quiet about you, and if the ever-silent
    Year sounds its melody inside us,
        Should it ring as if an impudent
            Idle child had plucked

The master's pure and hallowed strings in jest?
    And, O poet, is that why you heard
        The Eastern prophets and Grecian
            Song, and recently the thunder, that you

Might use the spirit for your ends and rush
    Upon the presence of the good, and heartlessly mock and deny
        The simple one, forcing him,
            Like some captive beast, into performance for pay?

Until, enraged and incited by that goad,
    He remembers his origin and calls out
        For the master himself to come and cut
            Down your life in a blaze of lethal shots.

For too long has everything divine been utilized,
    And all the heavenly powers, the kindly ones, thrown away,
        Consumed for kicks by thankless,
            Cunning men, who, when the exalted

One works in their fields, think they
    Know the daylight and the Thunderer,
        And their telescope might see them all and
            Count and name all the stars in heaven;

But the Father covers our eyes with holy
    Night so we might remain.
        He loves no wildness! Our expanding
            Power will never force heaven.

Noch ists auch gut, zu weise zu seyn. Ihn kennt
   Der Dank. Doch nicht behält er es leicht allein,
      Und gern gesellt, damit verstehn sie
         Helfen, zu anderen sich ein Dichter.

Furchtlos bleibt aber, so er es muß, der Mann
   Einsam vor Gott, es schüzet die Einfalt ihn,
      Und keiner Waffen brauchts und keiner
         Listen, so lange, bis Gottes Fehl hilft.

Stimme des Volks.

[Zweite Fassung]

Du seiest Gottes Stimme, so glaubt' ich sonst
   In heil'ger Jugend; ja, und ich sag' es noch!
      Um unsre Weisheit unbekümmert
         Rauschen die Ströme doch auch, und dennoch,

Wer liebt sie nicht? und immer bewegen sie
   Das Herz mir, hör' ich ferne die Schwindenden,
      Die Ahnungsvollen meine Bahn nicht,
         Aber gewisser ins Meer hin eilen.

Denn selbstvergessen, allzubereit den Wunsch
   Der Götter zu erfüllen, ergreifft zu gern
      Was sterblich ist, wenn offnen Augs auf
         Eigenen Pfaden es einmal wandelt,

Ins All zurük die kürzeste Bahn; so stürzt
   Der Strom hinab, er suchet die Ruh, es reißt,
      Er ziehet wider Willen ihn, von
         Klippe zu Klippe den Steuerlosen

Nor is it good to be too wise. Gratitude
　　Knows him. Yet a poet can't so easily keep it himself,
　　　　And so he joins gladly with others
　　　　　　So they will help him to understand.

Fearless though, if he must, the man remains
　　Alone before God, and simplicity protects him,
　　　　And he needs no weapon and no
　　　　　　Guile till God's absence has helped.

Voice of the People

[second version]

You were the voice of God, so I believed
　　In my holy youth; yes, and I maintain this still!
　　　　But the rivers also rush onward
　　　　　　Unconcerned with our wisdom, and yet

Who doesn't love them? And they always move
　　My heart when I hear those fleeting ones far away
　　　　So full of foreboding, they don't follow my course
　　　　　　But rush down more surely into the sea.

For mortal beings forget themselves, and once they've
　　Wandered their allotted paths with open eyes,
　　　　They're all too ready to do what the gods
　　　　　　Wish for them, and too eagerly

They take the shortest way back to the All; thus do
　　Rivers plunge, searching for peace and rushing,
　　　　The wondrous longing for depths
　　　　　　Drives them down against their will

Das wunderbare Sehnen dem Abgrund zu;
  Das Ungebundne reizet und Völker auch
    Ergreifft die Todeslust und kühne
      Städte, nachdem sie versucht das Beste,

Von Jahr zu Jahr forttreibend das Werk, sie hat
  Ein heilig Ende troffen; die Erde grünt
    Und stille vor den Sternen liegt, den
      Betenden gleich, in den Sand geworfen

Freiwillig überwunden die lange Kunst
  Vor jenen Unnachahmbaren da; er selbst,
    Der Mensch, mit eigner Hand zerbrach, die
      Hohen zu ehren, sein Werk der Künstler.

Doch minder nicht sind jene den Menschen hold,
  Sie lieben wieder, so wie geliebt sie sind,
    Und hemmen öfters, daß er lang im
      Lichte sich freue, die Bahn des Menschen.

Und, nicht des Adlers Jungen allein, sie wirft
  Der Vater aus dem Neste, damit sie nicht
    Zu lang' ihm bleiben, uns auch treibt mit
      Richtigem Stachel hinaus der Herrscher.

Wohl jenen, die zur Ruhe gegangen sind,
  Und vor der Zeit gefallen, auch die, auch die
    Geopfert, gleich den Erstlingen der
      Erndte, sie haben ein Theil gefunden.

Am Xanthos lag, in griechischer Zeit, die Stadt,
  Jezt aber, gleich den größeren die dort ruhn
    Ist durch ein Schiksaal sie dem heilgen
      Lichte des Tages hinweggekommen.

From rock to rock, utterly blind;
    The unbound depths seduce, and lust for death
        Might seize whole peoples too,
            And a holy end strikes bold towns

That have given their best, year after year
    Pursuing their work; the earth grows green,
        And art that's long lies under stars
            In silence, like a man in prayer

On his knees in the sand, willingly vanquished
    Before that matchless one; man himself,
        The artist, he smashed his work
            With his own two hands to honor the high ones.

Yet they aren't less inclined to hold man dear,
    They love us back as they are loved
        And often block man's course
            That he might long enjoy the light.

And not only does the eagle throw
    His young from the nest so they won't stay
        With him too long; he who rules
            Drives us out too with a fitting prod.

Praise be to those who went to rest
    And fell before their time, for even they,
        Sacrificed like first-fruits
            Of the harvest, even they have found their lot.

The town lay on the Xanthus' shores in Grecian times,
    But now, like the more glorious ones who rest there,
        Fate has snuffed out
            That town's holy light of day.

Sie kamen aber nicht in der offnen Schlacht
    Durch eigne Hand um. Fürchterlich ist davon,
        Was dort geschehn, die wunderbare
            Sage von Osten zu uns gelanget.

Es reizte sie die Güte von Brutus. Denn
    Als Feuer ausgegangen, so bot er sich
        Zu helfen ihnen, ob er gleich, als Feldherr,
            Stand in Belagerung vor den Thoren.

Doch von den Mauern warfen die Diener sie
    Die er gesandt. Lebendiger ward darauf
        Das Feuer und sie freuten sich und ihnen
            Streket' entgegen die Hände Brutus

Und alle waren außer sich selbst. Geschrei
    Entstand und Jauchzen. Drauf in die Flamme warf
        Sich Mann und Weib, von Knaben stürzt' auch
            Der von dem Dach, in der Väter Schwerdt der.

Nicht räthlich ist es, Helden zu trozen. Längst
    Wars aber vorbereitet. Die Väter auch
        Da sie ergriffen waren, einst, und
            Heftig die persischen Feinde drängten,

Entzündeten, ergreiffend des Stromes Rohr,
    Daß sie das Freie fänden, die Stadt. Und Haus
        Und Tempel nahm, zum heilgen Aether
            Fliegend und Menschen hinweg die Flamme.

So hatten es die Kinder gehört, und wohl
    Sind gut die Sagen, denn ein Gedächtniß sind
        Dem Höchsten sie, doch auch bedarf es
            Eines, die heiligen auszulegen.

The people of Xanthus didn't die in open battle
    But by their own hand. And as the wondrous legend,
        Reaching us from the East, describes,
            What happened there was dreadful beyond measure.

The kindness of Brutus incensed them. For
    When the fire had broken out, he, though leading
        His troops in a siege of the gates,
            Offered aid to the town,

Yet the servants he sent were thrown
    From the walls. The fire flamed
        Higher and the Xanthians rejoiced,
            And Brutus stretched his hand to them,

And they were beside themselves. Hue and cry
    Arose and rejoicing. The men and their wives then
        Threw themselves on the flames, and boys
            Plunged from the rooftops or on their fathers' swords.

It's not wise to defy heroes. But
    It was prepared long ago. The town's forefathers,
        When they were once besieged,
            And the Persian foe pressed hard upon the city walls,

They too grabbed river reeds and set the town
    Ablaze so the Persians would find mere open land instead of town.
        And the flames that flew to holy Aether
            Took house and temple away, and the people too were taken up.

The children had heard all this, and doubtless such
    Legends are good, for they remind us
        Of the highest, yet still we stand in need
            Of one to interpret the holy lore.

Dichtermuth.

[Zweite Fassung]

Sind denn dir nicht verwandt alle Lebendigen,
    Nährt die Parze denn nicht selber im Dienste dich?
        Drum, so wandle nur wehrlos
           Fort durchs Leben, und fürchte nichts!

Was geschiehet, es sei alles geseegnet dir,
    Sei zur Freude gewandt! oder was könnte denn
        Dich belaidigen, Herz! was
           Da begegnen, wohin du sollst?

Denn, seitdem der Gesang sterblichen Lippen sich
    Friedenathmend entwand, frommend in Laid und Glük
        Unsre Weise der Menschen
           Herz erfreute, so waren auch

Wir, die Sänger des Volks, gerne bei Lebenden
    Wo sich vieles gesellt, freudig und jedem hold,
        Jedem offen; so ist ja
           Unser Ahne, der Sonnengott,

Der den fröhlichen Tag Armen und Reichen gönnt,
    Der in flüchtiger Zeit uns, die Vergänglichen,
        Aufgerichtet an goldnen
           Gängelbanden, wie Kinder, hält.

Ihn erwartet, auch ihn nimmt, wo die Stunde kömmt,
    Seine purpurne Fluth; sieh! und das edle Licht
        Gehet, kundig des Wandels,
           Gleichgesinnet hinab den Pfad.

So vergehe denn auch, wenn es die Zeit einst ist
    Und dem Geiste sein Recht nirgend gebricht, so sterb'
        Einst im Ernste des Lebens
           Unsre Freude, doch schönen Tod!

The Poet's Courage

[second version]

Aren't all living creatures kin to you?
    Doesn't fate herself raise you to serve her ends?
      So then wander defenseless
        Through life and fear nothing!

Whatever happens, may it all be a blessing to you,
    Be well-versed in joy! Or what could
      Offend you, heart, what could
        Affront you there on your way?

For ever since the song freed itself from mortal
    Lips in breaths of peace, our melody, helpful
      In sorrow and fortune, brought joy
        To human hearts, so too were

We, the singers of the people, glad to find ourselves among the living
    Where many companions are gathered in joy, fondly inclined to all,
      Open to all; thus indeed is
        Our forefather the sun god,

Who grants the joyful day to poor and to rich,
    Who holds us upright in fleeting time,
      Us transient ones, on golden
        Leading strings, like children.

His flood of crimson light awaits him and takes him too
    When the hour comes; look! And with equable mind
      The noble light descends on its path,
        So well does it know of this change.

May it pass away like that too when the time at last comes,
    And the spirit lacks nowhere its right, so may
      Our joy die one day in the earnestness
        Of life, but a beautiful death!

Der gefesselte Strom.

Was schläfst und träumst du, Jüngling, gehüllt in dich,
   Und säumst am kalten Ufer, Geduldiger,
      Und achtest nicht des Ursprungs, du, des
         Oceans Sohn, des Titanenfreundes!

Die Liebesboten, welche der Vater schikt,
   Kennst du die lebenathmenden Lüfte nicht?
      Und trift das Wort dich nicht, das hell von
         Oben der wachende Gott dir sendet?

Schon tönt, schon tönt es ihm in der Brust, es quillt,
   Wie, da er noch im Schoose der Felsen spielt',
      Ihm auf, und nun gedenkt er seiner
         Kraft, der Gewaltige, nun, nun eilt er,

Der Zauderer, er spottet der Fesseln nun,
   Und nimmt und bricht und wirft die Zerbrochenen
      Im Zorne, spielend, da und dort zum
         Schallenden Ufer und an der Stimme

Des Göttersohns erwachen die Berge rings,
   Es regen sich die Wälder, es hört die Kluft
      Den Herold fern und schaudernd regt im
         Busen der Erde sich Freude wieder.

Der Frühling komt; es dämmert das neue Grün;
   Er aber wandelt hin zu Unsterblichen;
      Denn nirgend darf er bleiben, als wo
         Ihn in die Arme der Vater aufnimmt.

The Fettered River

Why, youthful one, O patient one, are you sleeping and dreaming,
  Wrapped in yourself and lingering cold on the banks,
    And you don't heed the origin, you
      Son of the Ocean, the friend to the Titans!

The messengers of love your father sends—
  Don't you know the life-breathing breezes?
    And does the word not strike you, sent so
      Bright by the waking god above?

Already sounding, it already resounds in his breast
  As when he played in the laps of rocks,
    And it surges up, and now he recalls his strength,
      The powerful one, now, he hastens now,

The idler, he mocks his fetters now
  And takes and breaks and throws the broken pieces down
    In playful anger, this way and that
      On resounding banks, and the voice

Of this son of gods wakes the mountains around him,
  The forests stir and the gorges hear
    The distant herald, and in the bosom
      Of Earth joy shudders again.

Spring is coming; the green is dawning anew;
  But he wanders off to immortals;
    For he may only stay where
      The arms of his father receive him.

Der blinde Sänger.

Ελυσεν αινον αχος απ' ομματων Αρης.
—Sophokles.

Wo bist du, Jugendliches! das immer mich
　　Zur Stunde wekt des Morgens, wo bist du, Licht!
　　　　Das Herz ist wach, doch bannt und hält in
　　　　　　Heiligem Zauber die Nacht mich immer.

Sonst lauscht' ich um die Dämmerung gern, sonst harrt'
　　Ich gerne dein am Hügel, und nie umsonst!
　　　　Nie täuschten mich, du Holdes, deine
　　　　　　Boten, die Lüfte, denn immer kamst du,

Kamst allbeseeligend den gewohnten Pfad
　　Herein in deiner Schöne, wo bist du, Licht!
　　　　Das Herz ist wieder wach, doch bannt und
　　　　　　Hemmt die unendliche Nacht mich immer.

Mir grünten sonst die Lauben; es leuchteten
　　Die Blumen, wie die eigenen Augen, mir;
　　　　Nicht ferne war das Angesicht der
　　　　　　Meinen und leuchtete mir und droben

Und um die Wälder sah ich die Fittige
　　Des Himmels wandern da ich ein Jüngling war;
　　　　Nun siz ich still allein, von einer
　　　　　　Stunde zur anderen und Gestalten

Aus Lieb und Laid der helleren Tage schafft
　　Zur eignen Freude nun mein Gedanke sich,
　　　　Und ferne lausch' ich hin, ob nicht ein
　　　　　　Freundlicher Retter vieleicht mir komme.

The Blind Singer

Ελυσεν αινον αχος απ' ομματων Αρης.
—Sophocles

Where are you, O youthful one, who always woke
   Me at daybreak, where are you, light?
      My heart's awake but night enthralls and
         Always holds me under its holy spell.

I used to listen gladly at dawn, I used to gladly wait
   Upon the hill for you, I never waited in vain!
      Your heralding breezes never
         Deceived me, dear one, for you always came,

You came down the usual path in your
   Beauty inspiring all—where are you, light?
      My heart's awake again, but
         The unending night always enthralls and hinders me.

The leaves of trees once greened for me;
   Flowers glowed like my own eyes;
      Faces of those I loved were near
         And glowed for me, and high above

And round the woods I saw the wings
   Of heaven fly when I was young;
      Now I sit alone in silence from one
         Hour to the next, and for their own

Delight my thoughts spin shapes
   From the love and pain of brighter days,
      And I strain my hearing harder, for perhaps a
         Kindly savior is approaching.

Dann hör ich oft die Stimme des Donnerers
    Am Mittag, wenn der eherne nahe kommt,
        Wenn ihm das Haus bebt und der Boden
            Unter ihm dröhnt und der Berg es nachhallt.

Den Retter hör' ich dann in der Nacht, ich hör'
    Ihn tödtend, den Befreier, belebend ihn,
        Den Donnerer vom Untergang zum
            Orient eilen und ihm nach tönt ihr

Ihm nach, ihr meine Saiten! es lebt mit ihm
    Mein Lied und wie die Quelle dem Strome folgt,
        Wohin er denkt, so muß ich fort und
            Folge dem Sicheren auf der Irrbahn.

Wohin? wohin? ich höre dich da und dort
    Du Herrlicher! und rings um die Erde tönts.
        Wo endest du? und was, was ist es
            Über den Wolken und o wie wird mir?

Tag! Tag! du über stürzenden Wolken! sei
    Willkommen mir! es blühet mein Auge dir.
        O Jugendlicht! o Glük! das alte
            Wieder! doch geistiger rinnst du nieder

Du goldner Quell aus heiligem Kelch! und du,
    Du grüner Boden, friedliche Wieg'! und du,
        Haus meiner Väter! und ihr Lieben,
            Die mir begegneten einst, o nahet,

O kommt, daß euer, euer die Freude sei,
    Ihr alle, daß euch seegne der Sehende!
        O nimmt, daß ich's ertrage, mir das
            Leben, das Göttliche mir vom Herzen.

I often hear the Thunderer's voice at noon
   When the brazen one draws near,
      When his house quakes and under him
         The floor rumbles and echoes in the hills.

I hear the savior then in the night, I hear
   Him killing, the liberator, enlivening,
      The Thunderer rushing from the sunset
         To the East, and you, you echo

Him, my strings! My song is alive with him,
   And as the spring flows down to the river,
      So must I go wherever his thinking leads me,
         I must follow the certain one through confusing ways.

Where to? Where to? I hear you everywhere,
   Glorious one, and all the earth resounds.
      Where do you end? And what, what is
         Above in the clouds, and O what will become of me?

Day! Day! You above the toppling clouds, I
   Welcome you! My eyes are abloom for you.
      O light of youth! O Joy! Once
         More as you were! More full of spirit,

You golden source, you stream from the holy cup,
   And you, O green ground, O peaceful cradle,
      And you, my forefathers' home, and you, dear friends,
         Who used to gather with me, O come nearer,

O come that what is yours might be joyous,
   That this one who sees might bless you!
      O, that I might bear this burden, O take
         The life, take the divine out of my heart.

Stutgard.

An Siegfried Schmidt.

1.

Wieder ein Glük ist erlebt. Die gefährliche Dürre geneset,
  Und die Schärfe des Lichts senget die Blüthe nicht mehr.
Offen steht jezt wieder ein Saal, und gesund ist der Garten,
  Und von Reegen erfrischt rauschet das glänzende Thal,
Hoch von Gewächsen, es schwellen die Bäch' und alle gebundnen
  Fittige wagen sich wieder ins Reich des Gesangs.
Voll ist die Luft von Fröhlichen jezt und die Stadt und der Hain ist
  Rings von zufriedenen Kindern des Himmels erfüllt.
Gerne begegnen sie sich, und irren untereinander,
  Sorgenlos, und es scheint keines zu wenig, zu viel.
Denn so ordnet das Herz es an, und zu athmen die Anmuth,
  Sie, die geschikliche, schenkt ihnen ein göttlicher Geist.
Aber die Wanderer auch sind wohlgeleitet und haben
  Kränze genug und Gesang, haben den heiligen Stab
Vollgeschmükt mit Trauben und Laub bei sich und der Fichte
  Schatten; von Dorfe zu Dorf jauchzt es, von Tage zu Tag,
Und wie Wagen, bespannt mit freiem Wilde, so ziehn die
  Berge voran und so träget und eilet der Pfad.

2.

Aber meinest du nun, es haben die Thore vergebens
  Aufgethan und den Weg freudig die Götter gemacht?
Und es schenken umsonst zu des Gastmahls Fülle die Guten
  Nebst dem Weine noch auch Beeren und Honig und Obst?
Schenken das purpurne Licht zu Festgesängen und kühl und
  Ruhig zu tieferem Freundesgespräche die Nacht?
Hält ein Ernsteres dich, so spars dem Winter und willst du

Stuttgart

To Siegfried Schmidt

1.

Joy is experienced again. The ground recovers from dangerous dryness,
    And the harshness of sun sears the blossom no more.
A hall stands open again, the garden is healthy,
    And, refreshed by the rain, streams in the valley are gleaming;
Growth teems and brooks swell, and all the bound wings
    Dare to fly now again in the high realm of song.
The air is filled with the joyful ones now, and the town and the grove
    Are full, filled with the satisfied children of sky.
They love to encounter each other and wheel in confusion,
    They fly without care, there's not a single one too many or few.
For thus the heart orders the world, and the divine spirit bestows on them
    Grace, that which is proper, so they may breathe it as they fly.
But the wanderers too are well-led and have enough
    Garlands and song, and they carry their holy staffs
Well-adorned with the grapevine and leaves, and the shade of the fir
    Always near; their exultation flows through the towns and the days,
And, like wagons hitched to wild beasts, the mountains
    Surge on ahead, and thus does the path both tarry and rush.

2.

But do you think then the gods have opened
    The doors and made the way joyful in vain?
That for nothing the kind ones have bestowed on the banquet's
    Great fullness not only wine, but berries and honey and fruit?
And given the red-purple light to the songs of the feast,
    And the night cool and calm for deeper conversing with friends?
If you ponder more serious things, save them for winter,

Freien, habe Gedult, Freier beglüket der Mai.
Jezt ist Anderes Noth, jezt komm' und feire des Herbstes
    Alte Sitte, noch jezt blühet die Edle mit uns.
Eins nur gilt für den Tag, das Vaterland und des Opfers
    Festlicher Flamme wirft jeder sein Eigenes zu.
Darum kränzt der gemeinsame Gott umsäuselnd das Haar uns,
    Und den eigenen Sinn schmelzet, wie Perlen, der Wein.
Diß bedeutet der Tisch, der geehrte, wenn, wie die Bienen,
    Rund um den Eichbaum, wir sizen und singen um ihn,
Diß der Pokale Klang, und darum zwinget die wilden
    Seelen der streitenden Männer zusammen der Chor.

3.

Aber damit uns nicht, gleich Allzuklugen, entfliehe
    Diese neigende Zeit, komm' ich entgegen sogleich,
Bis an die Grenze des Lands, wo mir den lieben Geburtsort
    Und die Insel des Stroms blaues Gewässer umfließt.
Heilig ist mir der Ort, an beiden Ufern, der Fels auch,
    Der mit Garten und Haus grün aus den Wellen sich hebt.
Dort begegnen wir uns; o gütiges Licht! wo zuerst mich
    Deiner gefühlteren Stralen mich einer betraf.
Dort begann und beginnt das liebe Leben von neuem;
    Aber des Vaters Grab seh' ich und weine dir schon?
Wein' und halt' und habe den Freund und höre das Wort, das
    Einst mir in himmlischer Kunst Leiden der Liebe geheilt.
Andres erwacht! ich muß die Landesheroën ihm nennen,
    Barbarossa! dich auch, gütiger Kristoph, und dich,
Konradin! wie du fielst, so fallen Starke, der Epheu
    Grünt am Fels und die Burg dekt das bacchantische Laub,
Doch Vergangenes ist, wie Künftiges heilig den Sängern,
    Und in Tagen des Herbsts sühnen die Schatten wir uns.

And if you're looking to marry, be patient, for May will bring lovers
    their day.
Now, though, we need something different, come now and honor
    The fall's ancient rite, since the noble one still blooms with us.
For today only one thing's important, the fatherland,
    And everyone offers the festival flame what is his.
That's why, like a garland, the communal god blows through our hair,
    And the wine melts our minds as if they were pearls.
This is the table's great meaning, thus honored when, like bees,
    We sit by the oak singing around it,
This is the cups' ringing out, and that's why the choir
    Forces together the wild souls of arguing men.

3.

But, so this fading season not escape us and flee,
    As it does from the cleverest men, I approach it at once
Toward the edge of our country, where the river's blue water
    Flows around my dear birthplace and the island there.
This site is holy to me, both of its shores, and the rock,
    With its garden and house, that rises up green from the waves.
We'll meet there, O kindly light, the place
    Where one of your rays, more strongly felt, first hit its mark.
Dear life began there and begins now anew;
    But now, on seeing my father's grave, I'm already weeping to you?
Weep then and hold and keep the friend and hear the word
    That with its heavenly sound once healed me of suffering love.
Other things waken! I must name the native heroes to him:
    Barbarossa and you, good Christoph, and you,
Conradin! Strong ones fall as you did, the ivy
    Grows green on the rock and the leaves of the wine god cover the keep,
Yet the past like the future is holy to singers,
    And on days in the fall we atone for the shades.

4.

So der Gewaltgen gedenk und des herzerhebenden Schiksaals,
    Thatlos selber, und leicht, aber vom Aether doch auch
Angeschauet und fromm, wie die Alten, die göttlicherzognen
    Freudigen Dichter ziehn freudig das Land wir hinauf.
Groß ist das Werden umher. Dort von den äußersten Bergen
    Stammen der Jünglinge viel, steigen die Hügel herab.
Quellen rauschen von dort und hundert geschäfftige Bäche,
    Kommen bei Tag und Nacht nieder und bauen das Land.
Aber der Meister pflügt die Mitte des Landes, die Furchen
    Ziehet der Nekarstrom, ziehet den Seegen herab.
Und es kommen mit ihm Italiens Lüfte, die See schikt
    Ihre Wolken, sie schikt prächtige Sonnen mit ihm.
Darum wächset uns auch fast über das Haupt die gewaltge
    Fülle, denn hieher ward, hier in die Ebne das Gut
Reicher den Lieben gebracht, den Landesleuten, doch neidet
    Keiner an Bergen dort ihnen die Gärten, den Wein
Oder das üppige Gras und das Korn und die glühenden Bäume,
    Die am Wege gereiht über den Wanderern stehn.

5.

Aber indeß wir schaun und die mächtige Freude durchwandeln,
    Fliehet der Weg und der Tag uns, wie den Trunkenen, hin.
Denn mit heiligem Laub umkränzt erhebet die Stadt schon
    Die gepriesene, dort leuchtend ihr priesterlich Haupt.
Herrlich steht sie und hält den Rebenstab und die Tanne
    Hoch in die seeligen purpurnen Wolken empor.
Sei uns hold! dem Gast und dem Sohn, o Fürstin der Heimath!
    Glükliches Stutgard, nimm freundlich den Fremdling mir auf!
Immer hast du Gesang mit Flöten und Saiten gebilligt,
    Wie ich glaub' und des Lieds kindlich Geschwäz und der Mühn

4.

Thus remembering the powerful ones, and the fate that raises hearts,
    Bereft of deeds ourselves and not heavy, yet gazed on by Aether
And pious like the ancients, the joyous poets
    Reared by gods, we joyfully roam through the land.
Great is the growth all around. From the outermost mountains,
    Their native home, many youths descend through the hills.
Springs well up in those ranges, and a hundred busy streams
    Rush down day and night and build up the land.
But the master, the River Neckar, plows down the center,
    Draws out the furrows, draws the blessing down.
And Italian breezes come with him, the sea sends
    Its clouds and it sends him magnificent suns.
That's why, overwhelming, the fullness grows up to our heads,
    For here the goods were brought down with more richness,
Down to the plain to the dear ones, the people of this land,
    Yet none in the mountains has envy of gardens and wine of the
        valley,
Or the lush and tall grass and the wheat, or the trees all aglow
    That, lining the roads, cover the wanderers' way.

5.

But, as we gaze there and walk through such powerful joy,
    The road and the day flee before us as if we were drunk.
For already the city, crowned with holy leaves and praised,
    Luminous there she raises her priesterly head.
She stands in magnificence and holds up the grape staff
    And fir tree aloft in the red and blest clouds.
Be gracious to us, the guest and son, O queen of the homeland!
    Happy Stuttgart, welcome with gladness this stranger for me!
You've always approved of the hymns made with flute and with strings,
    I believe, and the childish chatter of song, and the sweet

Süße Vergessenheit bei gegenwärtigem Geiste,
　　Drum erfreuest du auch gerne den Sängern das Herz.
Aber ihr, ihr Größeren auch, ihr Frohen, die allzeit
　　Leben und walten, erkannt, oder gewaltiger auch,
Wenn ihr wirket und schafft in heiliger Nacht und allein herrscht
　　Und allmächtig empor ziehet ein ahnendes Volk,
Bis die Jünglinge sich der Väter droben erinnern,
　　Mündig und hell vor euch steht der besonnene Mensch—

6.

Engel des Vaterlands! o ihr, vor denen das Auge,
　　Sei's auch stark und das Knie bricht dem vereinzelten Mann,
Daß er halten sich muß an die Freund' und bitten die Theuern,
　　Daß sie tragen mit ihm all die beglükende Last,
Habt, o Gütige, Dank für den und alle die Andern,
　　Die mein Leben, mein Gut unter den Sterblichen sind.
Aber die Nacht kommt! laß uns eilen, zu feiern das Herbstfest
　　Heut noch! voll ist das Herz, aber das Leben ist kurz,
Und was uns der himmlische Tag zu sagen geboten,
　　Das zu nennen, mein Schmidt! reichen wir beide nicht aus.
Trefliche bring' ich dir und das Freudenfeuer wird hoch auf
　　Schlagen und heiliger soll sprechen das kühnere Wort.
Siehe! da ist es rein! und des Gottes freundliche Gaaben
　　Die wir theilen, sie sind zwischen den Liebenden nur.
Anderes nicht—o kommt! o macht es wahr! denn allein ja
　　Bin ich und niemand nimmt mir von der Stirne den Traum?
Kommt und reicht, ihr Lieben, die Hand! das möge genug seyn,
　　Aber die größere Lust sparen dem Enkel wir auf.

Forgetting of toil, the oblivion come to a presence-filled mind,
  That's why you gladly bring joy to the singers' hearts too.
But you, you greater ones, you joyful ones who live
  And preside for all time whether known, or, more powerfully yet,
When you work and create in holy night and rule above
  And all-powerfully draw up a people who guess at your signs,
Until the younger ones remember their fathers on high,
  And before you stands, mature and bright, thoughtful man—

6.

You angels of the fatherland, O you before whom a man by himself
  Will find his eyes failing no matter how strong, and his knees broken,
And he'll need all his friends for support and must ask
  For his dear ones to help him to carry his burden of joy,
Accept my thanks, O kind ones, for him and for everyone else
  Who make up my life and my wealth among mortals.
But night comes on—let's hurry to mark now the feast of this fall
  Yet today! The heart is full but life is short,
And that which the heavenly day has commanded to say
  And to name, my Schmidt, you and I cannot possibly give.
I'll bring you some excellent men, and high the bonfire will
  Climb and more sacredly speak the bolder word.
Look—there it's pure! And the god's friendly gifts
  That we share come only for lovers.
Nothing else will—O come, O make it true! For I'm alone
  In the end, and will no one take then the dream from my brow?
Come and give me your hands, O dear friends, that will suffice,
  But the pleasure that's greater we'll save for the son of our son.

Der Gang aufs Land.

An Landauer.

Komm! ins Offene, Freund! zwar glänzt ein Weniges heute
   Nur herunter und eng schließet der Himmel uns ein.
Weder die Berge sind noch aufgegangen des Waldes
   Gipfel nach Wunsch und leer ruht von Gesange die Luft.
Trüb ists heut, es schlummern die Gäng' und die Gassen und fast will
   Mir es scheinen, es sei, als in der bleiernen Zeit.
Dennoch gelinget der Wunsch, Rechtglaubige zweifeln an Einer
   Stunde nicht und der Lust bleibe geweihet der Tag.
Denn nicht wenig erfreut, was wir vom Himmel gewonnen,
   Wenn ers weigert und doch gönnet den Kindern zulezt.
Nur daß solcher Reden und auch der Schritt und der Mühe
   Werth der Gewinn und ganz wahr das Ergözliche sei.
Darum hoff ich sogar, es werde, wenn das Gewünschte
   Wir beginnen und erst unsere Zunge gelöst,
Und gefunden das Wort, und aufgegangen das Herz ist,
   Und von trunkener Stirn' höher Besinnen entspringt,
Mit der unsern zugleich des Himmels Blüthe beginnen,
   Und dem offenen Blik offen der Leuchtende seyn.

Denn nicht Mächtiges ists, zum Leben aber gehört es,
   Was wir wollen und scheint schiklich und freudig zugleich.
Aber kommen doch auch der seegenbringenden Schwalben
   Immer einige noch, ehe der Sommer ins Land.
Nemlich droben zu weihn bei guter Rede den Boden,
   Wo den Gästen das Haus baut der verständige Wirth;
Daß sie kosten und schaun das Schönste, die Fülle des Landes,
   Daß, wie das Herz es wünscht, offen, dem Geiste gemäß
Mahl und Tanz und Gesang und Stutgards Freude gekrönt sei,
   Deßhalb wollen wir heut wünschend den Hügel hinauf.
Mög' ein Besseres noch das menschenfreundliche Mailicht
   Drüber sprechen, von selbst bildsamen Gästen erklärt,

The Walk in the Country

To Landauer

Come, friend, and into the open! True, the sun's hardly
    Shining today, and the sky hems us in.
And neither have the mountains or treetops appeared
    As we wished, and the air rests empty of song.
It's so cloudy today, the pathways and alleys are dozing,
    And it almost seems to me we're in an age of lead.
Yet our wish is fulfilled, true believers don't doubt
    For a moment, and may the day still remain dedicated to joy.
For the sun that we've gained gives tremendous delight
    When the sky, withholding this prize, grants it at last to us children.
Only may this great gain be worth all our talking and effort
    And steps, and the pleasure truly be real.
And therefore I hope, when we start on our walk,
    And our tongues have been loosened, and the word
Is found and hearts opened, and exalted thoughts spring
    From drunken brows, I hope that, together with ours,
The flower of heaven will bloom, and the wide-open
    View will open to him who shines down.

For what we want's not beyond us, but belonging
    To life appears both proper and joyous,
Yet some swallows come too, bringing their blessings into the country,
    There's always a few before summer arrives.
For up there to give a fine speech and hallow the ground
    Where the practical host has built up an inn for the guests,
That they might see and enjoy the country's wide fullness,
    This most beautiful sight, and that, open as the heart desires, and fit
For the spirit, the meal and dance and song and Stuttgart's joy might be
        crowned—
    That's why we're climbing the hill so full of desire today.
And may the light of benevolent May express something
    Still better, clear in itself to impressionable guests.

Oder, wie sonst, wenns andern gefällt, denn alt ist die Sitte,
   Und es schauen so oft lächelnd die Götter auf uns,
Möge der Zimmermann vom Gipfel des Daches den Spruch thun,
   Wir, so gut es gelang, haben das Unsre gethan.

Aber schön ist der Ort, wenn in Feiertagen des Frühlings
   Aufgegangen das Thal, wenn mit dem Nekar herab,
Weiden grünend und Wald und all die grünenden Bäume
   Zahllos, blühend weiß, wallen in wiegender Luft,
Aber mit Wölkchen bedekt an Bergen herunter der Weinstok
   Dämmert und wächst und erwarmt unter dem sonnigen Duft.
Schöner freilich muß es werden, wenn
       Liebende in den

        entgegentönt

Or, as it used to be done, if it pleases the others, for the custom
    Is old and so often the gods will look smiling upon us,
May the carpenter shout out the adage from up on the roof;
    We, as best as we could, have given our due.

Beautiful though is the place when the valley unfolds
    On holidays during the spring, when, following the Neckar down,
The meadows of green and the woods and all of the trees that are
        greening,
    Countless and blooming in white, flow in the cradling breezes,
But down on the mountain all covered in cloudlets the grapevine is
        dawning
    And growing and warming there under the sunlight-strewn haze.
Yet this must become more beautiful still when
                lovers in the

                call to each other

Brod und Wein.

An
Heinze.

1.

Rings um ruhet die Stadt; still wird die erleuchtete Gasse,
    Und, mit Fakeln geschmükt, rauschen die Wagen hinweg.
Satt gehn heim von Freuden des Tags zu ruhen die Menschen,
    Und Gewinn und Verlust wäget ein sinniges Haupt
Wohlzufrieden zu Haus; leer steht von Trauben und Blumen,
    Und von Werken der Hand ruht der geschäfftige Markt.
Aber das Saitenspiel tönt fern aus Gärten; vieleicht, daß
    Dort ein Liebendes spielt oder ein einsamer Mann
Ferner Freunde gedenkt und der Jugendzeit; und die Brunnen,
    Immerquillend und frisch rauschen an duftendem Beet.
Still in dämmriger Luft ertönen geläutete Gloken,
    Und der Stunden gedenk rufet ein Wächter die Zahl.
Jezt auch kommet ein Wehn und regt die Gipfel des Hains auf,
    Sieh! und das Schattenbild unserer Erde, der Mond
Kommet geheim nun auch; die Schwärmerische, die Nacht kommt,
    Voll mit Sternen und wohl wenig bekümmert um uns,
Glänzt die Erstaunende dort, die Fremdlingin unter den Menschen
    Über Gebirgeshöhn traurig und prächtig herauf.

2.

Wunderbar ist die Gunst der Hocherhabnen und niemand
    Weiß von wannen und was einem geschiehet von ihr.
So bewegt sie die Welt und die hoffende Seele der Menschen,
    Selbst kein Weiser versteht, was sie bereitet, denn so
Will es der oberste Gott, der sehr dich liebet, und darum
    Ist noch lieber, wie sie, dir der besonnene Tag.

Bread and Wine

To

Heinze

1.

Calm has fallen over the town; the street grows still in the lamplight,
   And, adorned with torches, the carriages hasten away.
The people, replete with the pleasures of day, go home to rest,
   And they carefully reckon their profit and loss
Well-pleased by their hearth; the busy market is calm now and empty
   Of grapes and of flowers, and works made by hand.
But the music of strings sounds afar in the gardens;
   Perhaps a lover is playing, or a lonely man thinking
Of faraway friends and his youth; and the fountains,
   Always flowing and fresh, rush by the beds of sweet-smelling flowers.
The ringing of bells sounds softly through the early evening air,
   And minding the hour a watchman calls out the time.
Now a wind comes and rustles the treetops—
   And look! The shadow-image of our earth, the moon,
Steals into view; night, the enraptured dreamer, arrives
   Full of stars and seems unconcerned with our lives,
She shines there, the astounding one, this stranger amidst men,
   And rises over mountaintops resplendent and sad.

2.

Wonderful is the goodwill of exalted night, and no one
   Knows what she'll give or from where it comes to him.
Thus she moves the world and our hoping souls;
   Not even the wise understand what she's planned, for this
Is the will of the highest god who loves you so dearly, and that's why
   The enlightened day is dearer to you than her.

Aber zuweilen liebt auch klares Auge den Schatten
    Und versuchet zu Lust, eh' es die Noth ist, den Schlaf,
Oder es blikt auch gern ein treuer Mann in die Nacht hin,
    Ja, es ziemet sich ihr Kränze zu weihn und Gesang,
Weil den Irrenden sie geheiliget ist und den Todten,
    Selber aber besteht, ewig, in freiestem Geist.
Aber sie muß uns auch, daß in der zaudernden Weile,
    Daß im Finstern für uns einiges Haltbare sei,
Uns die Vergessenheit und das Heiligtrunkene gönnen,
    Gönnen das strömende Wort, das, wie die Liebenden, sei,
Schlummerlos und vollern Pokal und kühneres Leben,
    Heilig Gedächtniß auch, wachend zu bleiben bei Nacht.

3.

Auch verbergen umsonst das Herz im Busen, umsonst nur
    Halten den Muth noch wir, Meister und Knaben, denn wer
Möcht' es hindern und wer möcht' uns die Freude verbieten?
    Göttliches Feuer auch treibet, bei Tag und bei Nacht,
Aufzubrechen. So komm! daß wir das Offene schauen,
    Daß ein Eigenes wir suchen, so weit es auch ist.
Fest bleibt Eins; es sei um Mittag oder es gehe
    Bis in die Mitternacht, immer bestehet ein Maas,
Allen gemein, doch jeglichem auch ist eignes beschieden,
    Dahin gehet und kommt jeder, wohin er es kann.
Drum! und spotten des Spotts mag gern frohlokkender Wahnsinn
    Wenn er in heiliger Nacht plözlich die Sänger ergreift.
Drum an den Isthmos komm! dorthin, wo das offene Meer rauscht
    Am Parnaß und der Schnee delphische Felsen umglänzt,
Dort ins Land des Olymps, dort auf die Höhe Cithärons,
    Unter die Fichten dort, unter die Trauben, von wo
Thebe drunten und Ismenos rauscht, im Lande des Kadmos,
    Dorther kommt und zurük deutet der kommende Gott.

But at times a clear eye loves even the shadows
    And takes pleasure in sleep before its proper time,
Or a loyal man too enjoys gazing into night.
    Yes, it's fitting to dedicate garlands and song to her,
For to the mad and astray she is sacred, and to the dead;
    She herself though remains, eternal, in the freest of spirits.
But, that in the wavering moment and in darkness
    We may have something solid to hold to,
She must also grant us oblivion, and holy drunkenness,
    And grant that the streaming word like lovers be
Ever-sleepless, and our goblet fuller, and life bolder,
    And holy memory too, to stay wakeful through the night.

3.

And in vain we hide our hearts in our breasts, in vain
    We check our courage, masters and pupils, for who
Would hinder it, and who would forbid us such joy?
    Heavenly fire drives us too, day and night,
To set out. So come! Come behold the open
    And search for what's ours, however distant it may be.
One thing is certain: whether it's noon
    Or deep in the night there's always a measure
Common to all, yet for each his own way is determined,
    And everyone aims there, approaching as far as they can.
So then! And jubilant madness gladly scorns those who scorn it
    When it suddenly seizes the singers in holy night.
So then, come to the Isthmus! There where the open sea
    Roars near Parnassus and the snow shines on the Delphian cliffs,
There in the land of Olympus, there on the heights of the Cithaeron,
    Under the pine trees there midst the grapes, from there
Rush Thebe and the Ismenus down in the land of Cadmus,
    From there he comes and points back, the coming god.

Seeliges Griechenland! du Haus der Himmlischen alle,
  Also ist wahr, was einst wir in der Jugend gehört?
Festlicher Saal! der Boden ist Meer! und Tische die Berge
  Wahrlich zu einzigem Brauche vor Alters gebaut!
Aber die Thronen, wo? die Tempel, und wo die Gefäße,
  Wo mit Nectar gefüllt, Göttern zu Lust der Gesang?
Wo, wo leuchten sie denn, die fernhintreffenden Sprüche?
  Delphi schlummert und wo tönet das große Geschik?
Wo ist das schnelle? wo brichts, allgegenwärtigen Glüks voll
  Donnernd aus heiterer Luft über die Augen herein?
Vater Aether! so riefs und flog von Zunge zu Zunge
  Tausendfach, es ertrug keiner das Leben allein;
Ausgetheilet erfreut solch Gut und getauschet, mit Fremden,
  Wirds ein Jubel, es wächst schlafend des Wortes Gewalt
Vater! heiter! und hallt, so weit es gehet, das uralt
  Zeichen, von Eltern geerbt, treffend und schaffend hinab.
Denn so kehren die Himmlischen ein, tiefschütternd gelangt so
  Aus den Schatten herab unter die Menschen ihr Tag.

Unempfunden kommen sie erst, es streben entgegen
  Ihnen die Kinder, zu hell kommet, zu blendend das Glük,
Und es scheut sie der Mensch, kaum weiß zu sagen ein Halbgott
  Wer mit Nahmen sie sind, die mit den Gaaben ihm nahn.
Aber der Muth von ihnen ist groß, es füllen das Herz ihm
  Ihre Freuden und kaum weiß er zu brauchen das Gut,
Schafft, verschwendet und fast ward ihm Unheiliges heilig,
  Das er mit seegnender Hand thörig und gütig berührt.
Möglichst dulden die Himmlischen diß; dann aber in Wahrheit
  Kommen sie selbst und gewohnt werden die Menschen des Glüks
Und des Tags und zu schaun die Offenbaren, das Antliz
  Derer, welche schon längst Eines und Alles genannt

4.

Blessèd Greece! You house to all of the gods,
    Is it true what we once learned in our youth?
Festive hall! Your floor is a sea and your tables are mountains,
    Built eons before us for one single use!
But where are the thrones? And the temples, and where are the vessels,
    Where is the song filled with nectar that gives gods delight?
Where, where do they shine, the far-striking oracles?
    Delphi slumbers, and where does the great destiny sound?
Where is the quick one? Where does it break on our eyes
    Full of all-present joy, thundering from clear air above?
Father Aether! someone called, and it flew from tongue to tongue
    Thousandfold, for no one could bear life alone;
Such wealth when shared becomes joy, and traded with strangers
    Elation; sleeping, the word's power grows:
Father! Clarity! The ancient sign, passed down from our parents,
    Echoes as far as it can, hitting its mark and creating.
For thus the heavenly enter, and thus deeply shaking
    Down from the shadows to men comes their day.

5.

They arrive unperceived at first, and the children
    Rush toward them, but the joy is too bright, too blinding,
And man shies away, even a demigod hardly knows
    What to call them, they who approach him with gifts.
But great is the courage they bring, their joys fill
    His heart, he hardly knows what to make of this wealth;
He fiddles around and he wastes it, almost thinking the unholy holy,
    That which he kindly and foolishly touches with his blessing hand.
The heavenly bear this as much as they can; but they
    Themselves then come in truth, and men grow accustomed to joy
And the day and beholding those manifest, the faces of those
    Who were named long ago the One and the All, and who

Tief die verschwiegene Brust mit freier Genüge gefüllet,
  Und zuerst und allein alles Verlangen beglükt;
So ist der Mensch; wenn da ist das Gut, und es sorget mit Gaaben
  Selber ein Gott für ihn, kennet und sieht er es nicht.
Tragen muß er, zuvor; nun aber nennt er sein Liebstes,
  Nun, nun müssen dafür Worte, wie Blumen, entstehn.

6.

Und nun denkt er zu ehren in Ernst die seeligen Götter,
  Wirklich und wahrhaft muß alles verkünden ihr Lob.
Nichts darf schauen das Licht, was nicht den Hohen gefället,
  Vor den Aether gebührt müßigversuchendes nicht.
Drum in der Gegenwart der Himmlischen würdig zu stehen,
  Richten in herrlichen Ordnungen Völker sich auf
Untereinander und baun die schönen Tempel und Städte
  Vest und edel, sie gehn über Gestaden empor—
Aber wo sind sie? wo blühn die Bekannten, die Kronen des Festes?
  Thebe welkt und Athen; rauschen die Waffen nicht mehr
In Olympia, nicht die goldnen Wagen des Kampfspiels,
  Und bekränzen sich denn nimmer die Schiffe Korinths?
Warum schweigen auch sie, die alten heilgen Theater?
  Warum freuet sich denn nicht der geweihete Tanz?
Warum zeichnet, wie sonst, die Stirne des Mannes ein Gott nicht,
  Drükt den Stempel, wie sonst, nicht dem Getroffenen auf?
Oder er kam auch selbst und nahm des Menschen Gestalt an
  Und vollendet und schloß tröstend das himmlische Fest.

7.

Aber Freund! wir kommen zu spät. Zwar leben die Götter
  Aber über dem Haupt droben in anderer Welt.
Endlos wirken sie da und scheinens wenig zu achten,
  Ob wir leben, so sehr schonen die Himmlischen uns.

Filled the silent breasts deeply with contentment so free,
    And were first and alone to satisfy every desire.
Thus is man; when the wealth is there, and a god himself
    Provides him with gifts, he won't see it and remains unaware.
First he must bear it; now, though, he names what is dearest,
    Now he needs words, words that bloom forth like flowers.

6.

And now he thinks to honor the blessèd gods in earnest,
    All must proclaim their praise in truth and in deed,
Nothing may look on the light that displeases the high ones,
    The Aether deserves no idle attempts.
That's why, to stand worthy in the presence of heaven,
    Nations rise up in marvelous order
And among them build beautiful temples and cities,
    Strong and noble they tower above the shores—but where are they?
Where do the famous ones bloom, the wreaths of celebration?
    Thebes has faded and Athens; the weapons no longer clash
In Olympia, nor the golden chariots in competition,
    And will the ships of Corinth be wreathed never more?
And the theaters, ancient and holy, why are they silent?
    Why does the consecrated dance no longer feel joy?
Why won't a god inscribe a man's brow as before,
    Press his stamp, as before, upon him who is struck?
Or the god himself came and took on human form
    And, consoling, fulfilled and ended the heavenly feast.

7.

But, friend, we come too late. It's true the gods live,
    But they live above us in another world.
They move without end and it seems to matter little
    To them if we live, that's how much the gods want to spare us.

Denn nicht immer vermag ein schwaches Gefäß sie zu fassen,
 Nur zu Zeiten erträgt göttliche Fülle der Mensch.
Traum von ihnen ist drauf das Leben. Aber das Irrsaal
 Hilft, wie Schlummer und stark machet die Noth und die Nacht,
Biß daß Helden genug in der ehernen Wiege gewachsen,
 Herzen an Kraft, wie sonst, ähnlich den Himmlischen sind.
Donnernd kommen sie drauf. Indessen dünket mir öfters
 Besser zu schlafen, wie so ohne Genossen zu seyn,
So zu harren und was zu thun indeß und zu sagen,
 Weiß ich nicht und wozu Dichter in dürftiger Zeit?
Aber sie sind, sagst du, wie des Weingotts heilige Priester,
 Welche von Lande zu Land zogen in heiliger Nacht.

8.

Nemlich, als vor einiger Zeit, uns dünket sie lange,
 Aufwärts stiegen sie all, welche das Leben beglükt,
Als der Vater gewandt sein Angesicht von den Menschen,
 Und das Trauern mit Recht über der Erde begann,
Als erschienen zu lezt ein stiller Genius, himmlisch
 Tröstend, welcher des Tags Ende verkündet' und schwand,
Ließ zum Zeichen, daß einst er da gewesen und wieder
 Käme, der himmlische Chor einige Gaaben zurük,
Derer menschlich, wie sonst, wir uns zu freuen vermöchten,
 Denn zur Freude mit Geist, wurde das Größre zu groß
Unter den Menschen und noch, noch fehlen die Starken zu höchsten
 Freuden, aber es lebt stille noch einiger Dank.
Brod ist der Erde Frucht, doch ists vom Lichte geseegnet,
 Und vom donnernden Gott kommet die Freude des Weins.
Darum denken wir auch dabei der Himmlischen, die sonst
 Da gewesen und die kehren in richtiger Zeit,
Darum singen sie auch mit Ernst die Sänger den Weingott
 Und nicht eitel erdacht tönet dem Alten das Lob.

For a weak vessel is not always able to hold them,
  Man can only bear heavenly fullness at times.
Life becomes then a dream of them. But our bewilderment
  Helps, like sleep, and need and night make us strong
Until enough heroes have grown in cradles of iron,
  And hearts in their strength have become like the gods, as before.
Then thundering they come. Meanwhile I've often thought
  It better to sleep than to be without friends,
Always waiting, and what to do or say in the meanwhile
  I don't know, and what are poets for in these meager times?
But they are, you say, like the holy priests of the wine god,
  Who roamed from land to land through holy night.

8.

Yes, some time ago, to us it seems ages before,
  They all rose on high, they who made life happy,
When the Father turned his face from mankind,
  And mourning, rightly, spread over Earth,
When finally the calm genius appeared, divinely
  Consoling, he who proclaimed the day's end and departed,
Then the heavenly choir, leaving a sign that once
  They were here and again would return, left us some gifts
In which we can find, as before, some joy that is human,
  Since for joy in spirit what was great became too great
Among men, and still there's no one with strength enough
  For the highest joy, but some gratitude still lives on in silence.
Bread is the fruit of the earth yet is blest by the light,
  And from the thundering god comes the joy of wine.
That's why in those things we remember the gods, who
  Once were here and will return when the time is right,
That's why they, serious, sing of the wine god, the singers,
  And the praise they hymn to the ancient one isn't conceived in vain.

9.

Ja! sie sagen mit Recht, er söhne den Tag mit der Nacht aus
    Führe des Himmels Gestirn ewig hinunter, hinauf,
Allzeit froh, wie das Laub der immergrünenden Fichte,
    Das er liebt und der Kranz, den er von Epheu gewählt,
Weil er bleibet und selbst die Spur der entflohenen Götter
    Götterlosen hinab unter das Finstere bringt.
Was der Alten Gesang von Kindern Gottes geweissagt,
    Siehe! wir sind es, wir; Frucht von Hesperien ists!
Wunderbar und genau ists als an Menschen erfüllet,
    Glaube, wer es geprüft! aber so vieles geschieht
Keines wirket, denn wir sind herzlos, Schatten, bis unser
    Vater Aether erkannt jeden und allen gehört.
Aber indessen kommt als Fakelschwinger des Höchsten
    Sohn, der Syrier, unter die Schatten herab.
Seelige Weise sehns; ein Lächeln aus der gefangnen
    Seele leuchtet, dem Licht thauet ihr Auge noch auf.
Sanfter träumet und schläft in Armen der Erde der Titan,
    Selbst der neidische, selbst Cerberus trinket und schläft.

9.

Yes, they are right to say he reconciles day with night,
   That he leads the stars of heaven around in their timeless turn,
· Always glad, like the green that he loves
   Of the evergreen pine and the wreath of ivy he chose
Because it endures and brings to the godless down
   In the darkness the trace of the gods who have fled.
What the songs of the ancients foretold of god's children,
   Look! We are it, we, the fruit of Hesperia!
It's a wonder and near, as if fulfilled now in men.
   Whoever has seen it, believe! But so much happens,
And nothing succeeds because we are heartless, shadows until our
   Father Aether is known and belongs to us all.
But meanwhile, down among the shadows comes
   The son of the highest, the Syrian, as torchbearer.
Blessèd wise men see it; a smile shines forth from their
   Imprisoned souls, their eyes thaw in the light.
The Titan dreams more softly and sleeps in the arms of the earth,
   Even the envious one, even Cerberus drinks now and sleeps.

Heimkunft.

an

die Verwandten.

1.

Drinn in den Alpen ists noch helle Nacht und die Wolke,
    Freudiges dichtend, sie dekt drinnen das gähnende Thal.
Dahin, dorthin toset und stürzt die scherzende Bergluft,
    Schroff durch Tannen herab glänzet und schwindet ein Stral.
Langsam eilt und kämpft das freudigschauernde Chaos,
    Jung an Gestalt, doch stark, feiert es liebenden Streit
Unter den Felsen, es gährt und wankt in den ewigen Schranken,
    Denn bacchantischer zieht drinnen der Morgen herauf.
Denn es wächst unendlicher dort das Jahr und die heilgen
    Stunden, die Tage, sie sind kühner geordnet, gemischt.
Dennoch merket die Zeit der Gewittervogel und zwischen
    Bergen, hoch in der Luft weilt er und rufet den Tag.
Jezt auch wachet und schaut in der Tiefe drinnen das Dörflein
    Furchtlos, Hohem vertraut, unter den Gipfeln hinauf.
Wachstum ahnend, denn schon, wie Blize, fallen die alten
    Wasserquellen, der Grund unter den Stürzenden dampft,
Echo tönet umher, und die unermeßliche Werkstatt
    Reget bei Tag und Nacht, Gaaben versendend, den Arm.

2.

Ruhig glänzen indeß die silbernen Höhen darüber,
    Voll mit Rosen ist schon droben der leuchtende Schnee.
Und noch höher hinauf wohnt über dem Lichte der reine
    Seelige Gott vom Spiel heiliger Stralen erfreut.
Stille wohnt er allein und hell erscheinet sein Antliz,
    Der ätherische scheint Leben zu geben geneigt,

Homecoming

to

my relatives

1.

There in the Alps the lambent night lingers and the cloud,
 Composing its joy, covers the wide-yawning valley inside.
The playful mountain breeze rushes and falls this way and that,
 A ray, quickly flashing, beams through firs and is gone.
Trembling with joy this chaos slowly hurries and struggles,
 Young in its figure yet strong, it celebrates the loving strife
Among rocks, it seethes and it reels in its timeless bounds,
 For more bacchantically the morning arises within.
For the year grows more endlessly there and the holy
 Hours, the days, they're more boldly ordered, mixed.
Yet the thunderbird marks out the time, and, high in the air
 Between mountains, soaring he calls out the day.
The village awakens now too in the depths and, familiar with heights,
 Gazes out without fear up from under the peaks.
It senses growth, for already like lightning the ancient
 Sources of water crash down, the ground full of steam where they fall,
Echo sounds all around, and the immeasurable workshop
 Stirs its arm day and night giving gifts.

2.

Meanwhile the silvery heights gleam calmly above,
 The glistening snow is filled already with roses.
And higher up over the light the pure and blessèd
 God lives gladdened by the play of holy rays.
Silent he lives there alone, and bright is his face,
 He seems, the aetherial, inclined to give life,

Freude zu schaffen, mit uns, wie oft, wenn, kundig des Maases,
    Kundig der Athmenden auch zögernd und schonend der Gott
Wohlgediegenes Glük den Städten und Häußern und milde
    Reegen, zu öffnen das Land, brütende Wolken, und euch,
Trauteste Lüfte dann, euch, sanfte Frühlinge, sendet,
    Und mit langsamer Hand Traurige wieder erfreut,
Wenn er die Zeiten erneut, der Schöpferische, die stillen
    Herzen der alternden Menschen erfrischt und ergreifft,
Und hinab in die Tiefe wirkt, und öffnet und aufhellt,
    Wie ers liebet, und jezt wieder ein Leben beginnt,
Anmuth blühet, wie einst, und gegenwärtiger Geist kömmt,
    Und ein freudiger Muth wieder die Fittige schwellt.

3.

Vieles sprach ich zu ihm, denn, was auch Dichtende sinnen
    Oder singen, es gilt meistens den Engeln und ihm;
Vieles bat ich, zu lieb dem Vaterlande, damit nicht
    Ungebeten uns einst plözlich befiele der Geist;
Vieles für euch auch, die im Vaterlande besorgt sind,
    Denen der heilige Dank lächelnd die Flüchtlinge bringt,
Landesleute! für euch, indessen wiegte der See mich,
    Und der Ruderer saß ruhig und lobte die Fahrt.
Weit in des Sees Ebene wars Ein freudiges Wallen
    Unter den Seegeln und jezt blühet und hellet die Stadt
Dort in der Frühe sich auf, wohl her von schattigen Alpen
    Kommt geleitet und ruht nun in dem Hafen das Schiff.
Warm ist das Ufer hier und freundlich offene Thale,
    Schön von Pfaden erhellt grünen und schimmern mich an.
Gärten stehen gesellt und die glänzende Knospe beginnt schon,
    Und des Vogels Gesang ladet den Wanderer ein.
Alles scheinet vertraut, der vorübereilende Gruß auch
    Scheint von Freunden, es scheint jegliche Miene verwandt.

To create with us joy, as often, knowing the measure well,
   And knowing well those who breathe, hesitant, the god spares us,
Sends pure fortune well-formed to cities and houses, and mild rain
   To open the land, ominous clouds, and you,
Most intimate breezes, and you, soft springtimes,
   And with deliberate hands he gladdens the sad ones again
When renewing the seasons, the creator refreshes and seizes
   The hearts fallen silent of men growing old
And works into depths and opens and brightens
   Just as he loves to, and life begins now anew,
Grace blooms as before, and the present spirit comes,
   And a joyful courage expands its wings once again.

3.

I said many things to him, for what the poets imagine
   Or sing applies for the most to the angels and him;
I asked for much for the sake of my country,
   That the spirit not suddenly seize us unbidden;
And much for all you who are anxious there in our country,
   To whom holy gratitude brings fugitives back with a smile,
My countrymen, for you! Meanwhile I've been softly rocked
   By the lake and the boatman sat calmly, praising the trip.
But on the plains of those waters it was one joyous swirling
   Under the sails, and there in the daybreak the town
Is blooming now and bright, from under the shadowy Alps
   The boat now comes guided to rest in the harbor,
Warm are the shores here and friendly the wide-open valleys
   Beautifully brightened by paths, they glimmer to me full of green.
Gardens are gathered together and gleaming buds are beginning
   To open, and the song of the bird invites the wanderer home.
All seems familiar, people hurry by and give greetings
   And seem to be friends, all of the faces seem related by blood.

4.

Freilich wohl! das Geburtsland ists, der Boden der Heimath,
Was du suchest, es ist nahe, begegnet dir schon.
Und umsonst nicht steht, wie ein Sohn, am wellenumrauschten
Thor' und siehet und sucht liebende Nahmen für dich,
Mit Gesang ein wandernder Mann, glükseeliges Lindau!
Eine der gastlichen Pforten des Landes ist diß,
Reizend hinauszugehn in die vielversprechende Ferne,
Dort, wo die Wunder sind, dort, wo das göttliche Wild
Hoch in die Ebnen herab der Rhein die verwegene Bahn bricht,
Und aus Felsen hervor ziehet das jauchzende Thal,
Dort hinein, durchs helle Gebirg, nach Komo zu wandern,
Oder hinab, wie der Tag wandelt, den offenen See;
Aber reizender mir bist du, geweihete Pforte!
Heimzugehn, wo bekannt blühende Wege mir sind,
Dort zu besuchen das Land und die schönen Thale des Nekars,
Und die Wälder, das Grün heiliger Bäume, wo gern
Sich die Eiche gesellt mit stillen Birken und Buchen,
Und in Bergen ein Ort freundlich gefangen mich nimmt.

5.

Dort empfangen sie mich. O Stimme der Stadt, der Mutter!
O du triffest, du regst Langegelerntes mir auf!
Dennoch sind sie es noch! noch blühet die Sonn' und die Freud' euch,
O ihr Liebsten! und fast heller im Auge, wie sonst.
Ja! das Alte noch ists! Es gedeihet und reifet, doch keines
Was da lebet und liebt, lässet die Treue zurük.
Aber das Beste, der Fund, der unter des heiligen Friedens
Bogen lieget, er ist Jungen und Alten gespart.
Thörig red ich. Es ist die Freude. Doch morgen und künftig
Wenn wir gehen und schaun draußen das lebende Feld
Unter den Blüthen des Baums, in den Feiertagen des Frühlings
Red' und hoff' ich mit euch vieles, ihr Lieben! davon.

4.

Why of course! It's your native land, the soil of your homeland,
   What you search for is near, will encounter you soon.
And a wandering man doesn't stand there in vain like a son
   At your gates lapped with waves, searching for names
Of love for you with his song, O blissful Lindau!
   This is one of the welcoming gates of the country,
Tempting to leave through her out to the promising distance,
   There where the miracles happen, there where that godly wild beast
The Rhine hurtles down its reckless path from the heights to the plains,
   And beyond the rocks the valley expands in delight;
To wander there through the sunlit mountains toward Como,
   Or to drift on the water as the sun moves through day;
But you tempt me more, hallowed gate,
   To go home where the blossoming paths are known to me,
And to visit my land and the beautiful vales of the Neckar,
   And the woods, the green of holy trees, where oaks
Gladly gather with silent birches and beeches,
   And a place in the mountains holds me captive in kindness.

5.

They welcome me there. O voice of my town, of my mother,
   You strike and stir up what I learned long ago!
Yet they're still here! The sun and the joy still bloom in your
   Eyes, my dearest ones, almost brighter than ever before.
Yes, it's still what it was! It flourishes, ripens, and nothing
   That lives there and loves ever abandons its faith.
But the best, the treasure lying under the rainbow of holy
   Peace, is saved for the young and the old.
I speak like a fool. Because of my joy. But, tomorrow and later,
   When walking out under the blossoms of trees we take in
The field full of life on the feast days of spring,
   O dear friends, I'll speak and hope much of these things with you.

Vieles hab' ich gehört vom großen Vater und habe
　　Lange geschwiegen von ihm, welcher die wandernde Zeit
Droben in Höhen erfrischt, und waltet über Gebirgen
　　Der gewähret uns bald himmlische Gaaben und ruft
Hellern Gesang und schikt viel gute Geister. O säumt nicht,
　　Kommt, Erhaltenden ihr! Engel des Jahres! und ihr,

6.

Engel des Haußes, kommt! in die Adern alle des Lebens,
　　Alle freuend zugleich, theile das Himmlische sich!
Adle! verjünge! damit nichts Menschlichgutes, damit nicht
　　Eine Stunde des Tags ohne die Frohen und auch
Solche Freude, wie jezt, wenn Liebende wieder sich finden,
　　Wie es gehört für sie, schiklich geheiliget sei.
Wenn wir seegnen das Mahl, wen darf ich nennen und wenn wir
　　Ruhn vom Leben des Tags, saget, wie bring' ich den Dank?
Nenn' ich den Hohen dabei? Unschikliches liebet ein Gott nicht,
　　Ihn zu fassen, ist fast unsere Freude zu klein.
Schweigen müssen wir oft; es fehlen heilige Nahmen,
　　Herzen schlagen und doch bleibet die Rede zurük?
Aber ein Saitenspiel leiht jeder Stunde die Töne,
　　Und erfreuet vielleicht Himmlische, welche sich nahn.
Das bereitet und so ist auch beinahe die Sorge
　　Schon befriediget, die unter das Freudige kam.
Sorgen, wie diese, muß, gern oder nicht, in der Seele
　　Tragen ein Sänger und oft, aber die anderen nicht.

Much I have heard from the Father, the great one, and for long
    I've not spoken of him, who from his heights renews
Ever-moving time and rules over mountains,
    Who'll soon grant us heavenly gifts and call
Forth more resplendent song and send many good spirits. Don't tarry,
    Come, you who preserve! Angels of the year! And you,

6.

Angels of the house, come! Enter all of life's veins,
    Gladdening all together, let the heavenly be shared!
And made noble and younger! So that no human good, so that no
    Hour of the day be bereft of the joyful ones, and also that
Such joy as now, as when lovers find each other
    Again as they should, be properly hallowed.
When we bless the meal, whom should I name, and when we
    Rest from the life of the day, tell me, how should I bring forth my
        thanks?
Should I name then the high one? A god doesn't love what's unsuited
    to him,
    To grasp him our joy is almost too small.
We must often fall silent; we lack holy names,
    Hearts pound and yet words shy away?
But the lyre lends each hour its music
    And perhaps will bring joy to the gods who approach.
Prepare this, and so will the care
    That came amidst joy be nearly assuaged.
Gladly or not, a singer needs often to bear such cares
    In his soul, but other kinds not.

Brod und Wein.

An

Heinze.

[Zweite Fassung]

1.

Rings um ruhet die Stadt; still wird die erleuchtete Gasse,
    Und, mit Fakeln geschmükt, rauschen die Wagen hinweg.
Satt gehn heim von Freuden des Tags zu ruhen die Menschen,
    Und Gewinn und Verlust wäget ein sinniges Haupt
Wohlzufrieden zu Haus; leer steht von Trauben und Blumen,
    Und von Werken der Hand ruht der geschäfftige Markt.
Aber das Saitenspiel tönt fern aus Gärten; vieleicht, daß
    Dort ein Liebendes spielt oder ein einsamer Mann
Ferner Freunde gedenkt und der Jugendzeit; und die Brunnen,
    Immerquillend und frisch rauschen an duftendem Beet.
Still in dämmriger Luft ertönen geläutete Gloken,
    Und der Stunden gedenk rufet ein Wächter die Zahl.
Jezt auch kommet ein Wehn und regt die Gipfel des Hains auf,
    Sieh! und das Ebenbild unserer Erde, der Mond
Kommet geheim nun auch; die Schwärmerische, die Nacht kommt,
    Voll mit Sternen und wohl wenig bekümmert um uns,
Glänzt die Erstaunende dort, die Fremdlingin unter den Menschen
    Über Gebirgeshöhn traurig und prächtig herauf.

2.

Wunderbar ist die Gunst der Hocherhabnen und niemand
    Weiß von wannen und was einem geschiehet von ihr.
So bewegt sie die Welt und die hoffende Seele der Menschen,
    Selbst kein Weiser versteht, was sie bereitet, denn so

Bread and Wine

To

Heinze

[second version]

1.

Calm has fallen over the town; the street grows still in the lamplight,
    And, adorned with torches, the carriages hasten away.
The people, replete with the pleasures of day, go home to rest,
    And they carefully reckon their profit and loss
Well-pleased by their hearth; the busy market is calm now and empty
    Of grapes and of flowers, and works made by hand.
But the music of strings sounds afar in the gardens;
    Perhaps a lover is playing, or a lonely man thinking
Of faraway friends and his youth; and the fountains,
    Always flowing and fresh, rush by the beds of sweet-smelling flowers.
The ringing of bells sounds softly through the early evening air,
    And minding the hour a watchman calls out the time.
Now a wind comes and rustles the treetops—
    And look! The perfect image of our earth, the moon,
Steals into view; night, the enraptured dreamer, arrives
    Full of stars and seems unconcerned with our lives,
She shines there, the astounding one, this stranger amidst men,
    And rises over mountaintops resplendent and sad.

2.

Wonderful is the goodwill of exalted night, and no one
    Knows what she'll give or from where it comes to him.
Thus she moves the world and our hoping souls;
    Not even the wise understand what she's planned, for this

Will es der oberste Gott, der sehr dich liebet, und darum
    Ist noch lieber, wie sie, dir der besonnene Tag.
Aber zuweilen liebt auch klares Auge den Schatten
    Und versuchet zu Lust, eh' es die Noth ist, den Schlaf,
Oder es blikt auch gern ein treuer Mann in die Nacht hin,
    Ja, es ziemet sich ihr Kränze zu weihn und Gesang,
Weil den Irrenden sie geheiliget ist und den Todten,
    Selber aber besteht, ewig, in freiestem Geist.
Aber sie muß uns auch, daß in der zaudernden Weile,
    Daß im Finstern für uns einiges Haltbare sei,
Uns die Vergessenheit und das Heiligtrunkene gönnen,
    Gönnen das strömende Wort, das, wie die Liebenden, sei,
Schlummerlos und vollern Pokal und kühneres Leben,
    Heilig Gedächtniß auch, wachend zu bleiben bei Nacht.

3.

Auch verbergen umsonst das Herz im Busen, umsonst nur
    Halten den Muth noch wir, Meister und Knaben, denn wer
Möcht' es hindern und wer würd uns die Freude verbieten?
    Herrliches Zeichen auch singen, bei Tag und bei Nacht,
Witterungen. So komm! daß wir das Offene schauen,
    Daß ein Lebendiges wir suchen, so weit es auch ist.
Fest bleibt Eins; es sei um Mittag oder es gehe
    Bis in die Mitternacht, immer bestehet ein Maas,
Allen gemein, doch jeglichem auch ist eignes beschieden,
    Dahin gehet und kommt jeder, wohin er es kann.
Drum! und spotten des Spotts mag gern frohlokkender Wahnsinn
    Wenn er in heiliger Nacht plözlich die Sänger ergreift.
Drum an den Isthmos komm! dorthin, wo das offene Meer rauscht
    Am Parnaß und der Schnee delphische Felsen umglänzt,
Dort ins Land des Olymps, dort auf die Höhe Cithärons,
    Unter die Fichten dort, unter die Trauben, von wo
Thebe drunten und Ismenos rauscht, im Lande des Kadmos,
    Dorther kommt und da lachet verpflanzet, der Gott.

Is the will of the highest god who loves you so dearly, and that's why
    The enlightened day is dearer to you than her.
But at times a clear eye loves even the shadows
    And takes pleasure in sleep before its proper time,
Or a loyal man too enjoys gazing into night.
    Yes, it's fitting to dedicate garlands and song to her,
For to the mad and astray she is sacred, and to the dead;
    She herself though remains, eternal, in the freest of spirits.
But, that in the wavering moment and in darkness
    We may have something solid to hold to,
She must also grant us oblivion, and holy drunkenness,
    And grant that the streaming word like lovers be
Ever-sleepless, and our goblet fuller, and life bolder,
    And holy memory too, to stay wakeful through the night.

3.

And in vain we hide our hearts in our breasts, in vain
    We check our courage, masters and pupils, for who
Would hinder it, and who would forbid us such joy?
    A wondrous sign all weathers sing too day and night.
So come! Come behold the open and search
    For something alive, however distant it may be.
One thing is certain: whether it's noon
    Or deep in the night there's always a measure
Common to all, yet for each his own way is determined,
    And everyone aims there, approaching as far as they can.
So then! And jubilant madness gladly scorns those who scorn it
    When it suddenly seizes the singers in holy night.
So then, come to the Isthmus! There where the open sea
    Roars near Parnassus and the snow shines on the Delphian cliffs,
There in the land of Olympus, there on the heights of the Cithaeron,
    Under the pine trees there midst the grapes, from there
Rush Thebe and the Ismenus down in the land of Cadmus,
    From there he comes and laughs transplanted, the god.

Seeliges Griechenland! du Haus der Himmlischen alle,
    Also ist wahr, was einst wir in der Jugend gehört?
Festlicher Saal! der Boden ist Meer! und Tische die Berge
    Wahrlich zu einzigem Brauche vor Alters gebaut!
Aber die Thronen, wo? Geseze der Erd, und die Schritte,
    Wo mit Nectar gefüllt, schreitend in Winkeln Gesang?
Wo bedeuten sie denn, die bäurisch sinnigen Sprüche?
    Schaal ist Delphi, begreifts besser, erfüllet es sich
Daß es wahr wird, denn wo brichts allgegenwärtigen Glüks voll
    Donnernd aus heiterer Luft über die Augen herein?
Vater Aether verzehrt und strebt, wie Flammen, zur Erde,
    Tausendfach kommet der Gott. Unt liegt wie Rosen, der Grund
Himmlischen ungeschikt, vergänglich, aber wie Flammen
    Wirket von oben, und prüft Leben, verzehrend, uns aus.
Die aber deuten dort und da und heben die Häupter
    Menschen aber, gesellt, theilen das blühende Gut.
Das Verzehrende. So komt Himmlisches, tiefschütternd gelangt so
    Aus den Schatten herab unter die Menschen sein Tag.

Unempfunden kommt es zuerst, es streben entgegen
    Diesem die Kinder. Fast triffet den Rükken das Glük,
Denn es scheut sie der Mensch. Darum auch siehet mit Augen
    Kaum ein Halbgott; und ist Feuer um diesen, und Schlaf.
Ihnen aber ist groß der Muth, voll füllen das Herz ihm
    Diese, aber er sieht kaum, in den Gluthen, das Gut,
Schafft, verschwendet und fast ward ihm Gränze die Erde,
    Aber zu ruhn, reißt hin ewig in Nacht das Geschik.
Selbst bevestigen das die Himmlischen aber wo anders
    Die nichts irrt und gewohnt werden die Menschen des Glüks

Blessèd Greece! You house to all of the gods,
    Is it true what we once learned in our youth?
Festive hall! Your floor is a sea and your tables are mountains,
    Built eons before us for one single use!
But where are the thrones? And the laws of the earth, and the steps,
    Where is the nectar-filled song stepping in turns?
Where then do they mean something, the clever peasant sayings?
    A shell is Delphi, grasps it better, fulfills itself
So it turns true, for where does it break on our eyes
    Full of all-present joy, thundering from clear air above?
Father Aether consumes and strives like flames down to Earth,
    The god comes thousandfold. Below the ground lies like roses,
Awkward to the gods and unsent, fleeting, but like flames
    From above life affects us and tests us, consuming.
People though point and interpret here and there and raise
    Their heads, but, gathered, they share of the blossoming good.
The consuming. Thus comes what's heavenly, and thus deeply shaking
    Down from the shadows to men comes its day.

It arrives unperceived at first, and the children
    Rush toward it. The joy almost meets with their backs,
For man shies away. Thus even a demigod hardly sees
    With his eyes; and there's fire around him, and sleep.
But to them the courage is great, they fill his heart full,
    But he hardly sees the good in the embers,
He fiddles around and he wastes it, and the earth becomes almost a
        border to him,
    But, to rest, fate tears forever away in the night.
The heavenly fortify this themselves but somewhere else
    Where nothing confuses them, and men grow accustomed to joy

Und des Tags und zu schaun die Offenbaren, das Antliz
    Derer, welche schon längst Eines und Alles genannt
Tief die verschwiegene Brust mit freier Genüge gefüllet,
    Und zuerst und allein alles Verlangen beglükt;
Lang und schwer ist das Wort von dieser Ankunft aber
    Weiß ist der Augenblik. Diener der Himmlischen sind
Aber, kundig der Erd, ihr Schritt ist gegen den Abgrund
    Jugendlich menschlicher, doch das in den Tiefen ist alt.

6.

Nun behalten sie die Seeligen und die Geister,
    Alles wahrhaft muß kündigen deren ihr Lob.
Nichts darf schauen das Licht, was nicht den Hohen gefället,
    Vor den Aether gebührt Müßigversuchendes nicht.
Drum in der Gegenwart deß eine Weile zu stehen,
    Richten in Tuskischen Ordnungen Völker sich auf
Untereinander und baun die schönen Tempel und Städte
    Je nach Gegenden, gehn über den Küsten empor—
Aber wo sind sie? wo blühn die Bekannten, die Kronen des Festes?
    Thebe welkt und Athen; rauschen die Waffen nicht mehr
In Olympia, nicht die goldnen Wagen des Kampfspiels,
    Und bekränzen sich denn nimmer die Schiffe Korinths?
Warum schweigen auch sie, die heilgen Handlungen, damals,
    Warum freuet sich denn nicht der geweihete Tanz?
Warum zeichnet, wie sonst, die Stirne des Mannes ein Gott nicht,
    Drükt den Stempel, wie sonst, nicht dem Getroffenen auf?
Aber er kam dann selbst und nahm des Menschen Gestalt an
        ein Aergerniß aber ist Tempel und Bild,

7.

Narben gleichbar zu Ephesus. Auch Geistiges leidet,
    Himmlischer Gegenwart, zündet wie Feuer, zulezt.

And the day and beholding those manifest, the faces of those
    Who were named long ago the One and the All, and who
Filled the silent breasts deeply with contentment so free,
    And were first and alone to satisfy every desire.
The word of this arrival is long and hard but
    The moment is white. Servants of the gods
Know well though the earth, their step toward the chasm
    Is more humanly youthful, yet old is the one in the depths.

6.

Now they remember the blest and the spirits,
    All must proclaim of them their praise in truth,
Nothing may look on the light that displeases the high ones,
    The Aether deserves no idle attempts.
That's why, to stand for a while in his presence,
    The nations rise up in Tuscan arrangements and among them
Build beautiful temples and cities unique to their regions,
    They tower above the coasts—but where are they?
Where do the famous ones bloom, the wreaths of celebration?
    Thebes has faded and Athens; the weapons no longer clash
In Olympia, nor the golden chariots in competition,
    And will the ships of Corinth be wreathed never more?
Why did the holy actions, too, grow silent back then,
    Why does the consecrated dance no longer feel joy?
Why won't a god inscribe a man's brow as before,
    Press his stamp, as before, upon him who is struck?
But then the god came himself and took on human form
                    but temple and image are an offense,

7.

Scars comparable to Ephesus. The spiritual suffers as well
    Of heavenly presence, ignites like fire in the end.

Eine Versuchung ist es. Versuch, wenn Himmlische da sind
    Sich sein Grab sinnt, doch klug mit den Geistern, der Geist.
Auch die Geister, denn immer hält den Gott ein Gebet auf,
    Die auch leiden, so oft diesen die Erde berührt.
Nimmer von ihnen ist grün und die süßen Pfade der Heimath
    Regeln; Gebäuden gleich stehen die Bäum und Gebüsch
Nimmer, und goldnes Obst, und eingerichtet die Wälder,
    Nur zu Zeiten erträgt eigenen Schatten der Mensch.
Aber Herzen an Kraft, wie auf weißer Haide Blümlein,
    Da es dürr ist; das Grün aber ernähret das Roß
Und den Wolf, in der Wildniß, aber des Todes denkt Einer
    Kaum, und der Jugend Haus fassen die Seher nicht mehr.
Aber doch etwas gilt, allein. Die Regel, die Erde.
    Eine Klarheit, die Nacht. Das und das Ruhige kennt
Ein Verständiger wohl, ein Fürstlicherer, und zeiget
    Göttliches, ihrs auch sei lang, wie der Himmel und tief.

8.

Nemlich, als vor einiger Zeit, uns dünket sie lange,
    Aufwärts stiegen sie all, welche das Leben beglükt,
Als der Vater gewandt sein Angesicht von den Menschen,
    Und das Trauern mit Recht über der Erde begann,
Und erschienen zu lezt ein stiller Genius, himmlisch
    Tröstend, welcher des Tags Ende verkündet' und schwand,
Ließ zum Zeichen, daß einst er da gewesen und wieder
    Käme, der himmlische Chor einige Gaaben zurük,
Derer menschlich, wie sonst, wir uns zu freuen vermöchten,
    Aber, wie Waagen bricht, fast, eh es kommet, das Schiksaal
Auseinander beinah, daß sich krümmt der Verstand
    Vor Erkenntnis, auch lebt, aber es sieget der Dank.
Brod ist der Erde Frucht, doch ists vom Lichte gesegnet,
    Und vom donnernden Gott kommet die Freude des Weins.

It's a temptation. A trial, when the gods are there
    The spirit thinks of its grave yet is clever with spirits.
The spirits too, for a prayer always holds back the god,
    They suffer too, as often as the earth touches him.
It's no longer green from them, and the sweet paths of the homeland
    Are no longer rules; the trees and the bushes stand
No longer like buildings, and golden fruit, and the forests arranged,
    Only at times does man bear his own shadow.
But like a tiny withered flower upon a heath of white,
    So too are hearts in their strength; the green though nurtures the
        steed
And the wolf in the wild, but one hardly thinks about
    Death, and the seers can no longer grasp the house of youth.
But still something matters, alone. The rule, the earth.
    A clarity, the night. A sensible man, a more princely man,
Knows that well and what's calm and points out
    The divine, theirs may also be long like the heavens and deep.

8.

Yes, some time ago, to us it seems ages before,
    They all rose on high, they who made life happy,
When the Father turned his face from mankind,
    And mourning, rightly, spread over Earth,
And finally the calm genius appeared, divinely
    Consoling, he who proclaimed the day's end and departed,
Then the heavenly choir, leaving a sign that once
    They were here and again would return, left us some gifts
In which we can find, as before, some joy that is human,
    But, like the chariot, Fate breaks nearly apart almost before it
Arrives, such that understanding convulses before
    Knowledge and lives, but gratitude conquers.
Bread is the fruit of the earth yet is blest by the light,
    And from the thundering god comes the joy of wine.

Darum denken wir auch dabei der Himmlischen, die sonst
    Da gewesen und die kehren in richtiger Zeit,
Darum singen sie auch mit Ernst die Sänger den Herbstgeist
    Und nicht eitel erdacht tönet dem Alten das Lob.

9.

Ja! sie sagen mit Recht, er söhne den Tag mit der Nacht aus
    Führe des Himmels Gestirn ewig hinunter, hinauf,
Allzeit froh, wie das Laub der immergrünenden Fichte,
    Das er liebt und der Kranz, den er von Epheu gewählt,
Weil er bleibet. Vergnügt ist nemlich der in der Wildniß
    Auch. Und süßer Schlaf bleibet und Bienen und Mahl.
Was der Alten Gesang von Kindern Gottes geweissagt,
    Siehe! wir sind es, wir; Frucht von Hesperien ists!
Wunderbar und genau ists als an Menschen erfüllet,
    Glaube, wer es geprüft! nemlich zu Hauß ist der Geist
Nicht im Anfang, nicht an der Quell. Ihn zehret die Heimath.
    Kolonien liebt, und tapfer Vergessen der Geist.
Unsre Blumen erfreuen und die Schatten unserer Wälder
    Den Verschmachteten. Fast wär die Beseeler verbrandt.
Seelige Weise sehns; ein Lächeln aus der gefangnen
    Seele leuchtet, dem Licht thauet ihr Auge noch auf.
So lang währt' es. Aber es ruhn die Augen der Erde,
    Die allwissenden auch schlafen die Hunde der Nacht.

That's why in those things we remember the gods, who
   Once were here and will return when the time is right,
That's why they, serious, sing of the spirit of autumn, the singers,
   And the praise they hymn to the ancient one isn't conceived in vain.

9.

Yes, they are right to say he reconciles day with night,
   That he leads the stars of heaven around in their timeless turn,
Always glad, like the green that he loves
   Of the evergreen pine and the wreath of ivy he chose
Because it endures. For he's satisfied too in the wild.
   And sweet sleep remains and bees and repast.
What the songs of the ancients foretold of god's children,
   Look! We are it, we, the fruit of Hesperia!
It's a wonder and near, as if fulfilled now in men.
   Whoever has seen it, believe! For the spirit's not at home
In the beginning, is not at the source. The homeland gnaws at him.
   The spirit loves colonies and brave forgetting.
Our flowers and the shade of our forests gladden
   Him pining away. The ensouler would almost burn up.
Blessèd wise men see it; a smile shines forth from their
   Imprisoned souls, their eyes thaw in the light.
It lasted so long. But the eyes of the earth are at rest,
   The all-knowing ones, even the dogs of the night are asleep.

IV

Nightsongs

Chiron.

Wo bist du, Nachdenkliches! das immer muß
  Zur Seite gehn, zu Zeiten, wo bist du, Licht?
    Wohl ist das Herz wach, doch mir zürnt, mich
      Hemmt die erstaunende Nacht nun immer.

Sonst nemlich folgt' ich Kräutern des Walds und lauscht'
  Ein waiches Wild am Hügel; und nie umsonst.
    Nie täuschten, auch nicht einmal deine
      Vögel; denn allzubereit fast kamst du,

So Füllen oder Garten dir labend ward
  Ratschlagend, Herzens wegen; wo bist du, Licht?
    Das Herz ist wieder wach, doch herzlos
      Zieht die gewaltige Nacht mich immer.

Ich war's wohl. Und von Krokus und Thymian
  Und Korn gab mir die Erde den ersten Straus.
    Und bei der Sterne Kühle lernt' ich,
      Aber das Nennbare nur. Und bei mir

Das wilde Feld entzaubernd, das traur'ge, zog
  Der Halbgott, Zevs Knecht, ein, der gerade Mann;
    Nun siz' ich still allein, von einer
      Stunde zur anderen, und Gestalten

Aus frischer Erd' und Wolken der Liebe schafft,
  Weil Gift ist zwischen uns, mein Gedanke nun;
    Und ferne lausch' ich hin, ob nicht ein
      Freundlicher Retter vieleicht mir komme.

Dann hör' ich oft den Wagen des Donnerers
  Am Mittag, wenn er naht, der bekannteste,
    Wenn ihm das Haus bebt und der Boden
      Reiniget sich, und die Quaal Echo wird.

Chiron

Where are you, O thought-provoking god, who must always
   Move aside at times, where are you, light?
      Yes, my heart's awake, but astounding night
        Is angry, she always hinders me.

For I used to look for forest herbs, and on the hill
   Heard gentle deer; and never in vain.
      Never, not once, did your birds deceive me;
        For almost too readily you approached

When foal or garden refreshed you,
   Advising, for the sake of the heart; where are you, light?
      My heart's awake again, but I'm always
        Heartlessly drawn by powerful night.

I really was like that. And Earth gave me the first
   Bouquet of crocus and thyme and wheat,
      And in the cool of the stars I learned much,
        But only what is named. And the demigod,

Zeus' servant, the upright man, moved in with me
   And broke the spell of the sad wild fields;
      Now I sit alone in silence from one
        Hour to the next, and my thoughts

Spin shapes from the virgin soil and clouds
   Of love, since poison is between us;
      And I strain my hearing harder, for perhaps a
        Friendly savior is approaching.

Then I often hear the Thunderer's chariot at noon,
   When he, the most celebrated, draws near,
      When his house quakes and the ground
        Is purified, and my torment echoes.

Den Retter hör' ich dann in der Nacht, ich hör'
　　Ihn tödtend, den Befreier, und drunten voll
　　　　Von üpp'gem Kraut, als in Gesichten
　　　　　　Schau ich die Erd', ein gewaltig Feuer;

Die Tage aber wechseln, wenn einer dann
　　Zusiehet denen, lieblich und bös', ein Schmerz,
　　　　Wenn einer zweigestalt ist, und es
　　　　　　Kennet kein einziger nicht das Beste;

Das aber ist der Stachel des Gottes; nie
　　Kann einer lieben göttliches Unrecht sonst.
　　　　Einheimisch aber ist der Gott dann
　　　　　　Angesichts da, und die Erd' ist anders.

Tag! Tag! Nun wieder athmet ihr recht; nun trinkt,
　　Ihr meiner Bäche Weiden! ein Augenlicht,
　　　　Und rechte Stapfen gehn, und als ein
　　　　　　Herrscher, mit Sporen, und bei dir selber

Örtlich, Irrstern des Tages, erscheinest du,
　　Du auch, o Erde, friedliche Wieg', und du,
　　　　Haus meiner Väter, die unstädtisch
　　　　　　Sind, in den Wolken des Wilds, gegangen.

Nimm nun ein Roß, und harnische dich und nimm
　　Den leichten Speer, o Knabe! Die Wahrsagung
　　　　Zerreißt nicht, und umsonst nicht wartet,
　　　　　　Bis sie erscheinet, Herakles Rükkehr.

I hear the savior then in the night, I hear
  Him killing, the liberator, and down below
    All rank with weeds, I see Earth
      As in a vision, awash in violent fire;

But, when one looks to them, the days change,
  Become good and bad, pain
    If you're divided, and there's
      No one who knows what is best;

But that's the goad of the god; otherwise
  One could never love divine injustice.
    But then the god is visibly present, facing you
      In his native home, and the earth is utterly changed.

Day! Day! Now again you're breathing aright;
  Now drink in the sight, O willows of my streams,
    And sure footsteps mark a path, and like a
      Ruler with spurs you appear

In your own place, wandering star of the day,
  And you, O Earth, peaceful cradle, and you,
    House of my fathers, who, banished from cities,
      Wandered in clouds of wild beasts.

Now mount a horse, arm yourself and take
  Your light spear, O child! The prophecy
    Will not be broken, and Hercules' return
      Doesn't wait for it in vain.

Thränen.

Himmlische Liebe! zärtliche! wenn ich dein
   Vergäße, wenn ich, o ihr geschiklichen,
      Ihr feur'gen, die voll Asche sind und
         Wüst und vereinsamet ohnediß schon,

Ihr lieben Inseln, Augen der Wunderwelt!
   Ihr nemlich geht nun einzig allein mich an,
      Ihr Ufer, wo die abgöttische
         Büßet, doch Himmlischen nur, die Liebe.

Denn allzudankbar haben die Heiligen
   Gedienet dort in Tagen der Schönheit und
      Die zorn'gen Helden; und viel Bäume
         Sind, und die Städte daselbst gestanden,

Sichtbar, gleich einem sinnigen Mann; izt sind
   Die Helden todt, die Inseln der Liebe sind
      Entstellt fast. So muß übervortheilt,
         Albern doch überall seyn die Liebe.

Ihr waichen Thränen, löschet das Augenlicht
   Mir aber nicht ganz aus; ein Gedächtniß doch,
      Damit ich edel sterbe, laßt ihr
         Trügrischen, Diebischen, mir nachleben.

Tears

Heavenly love! Tender one! If I should
    Forget you, if I—O you fated ones,
        So fiery and full of ash, so alone
            And desolate so long before this,

O lovely islands, eyes of the wondrous world!
    You alone are now my concern,
        Your shores where idolatrous love
            Does penance, but only to the gods.

For all too gratefully did the holy ones
    Serve in days of beauty, and
        The furious heroes; and many trees
            And cities stood there once

Visible, like a man lost in thought; the heroes
    Are dead now, the islands of love are
        Almost in ruins. Love is deceived,
            Appears everywhere a fool.

Soft tears, don't darken completely
    The light in my eyes; O that I
        Might die nobly, O deceitful ones, O thieves,
            Leave a memory to outlast me.

An die Hofnung.

O Hofnung! holde! gütiggeschäfftige!
   Die du das Haus der Trauernden nicht verschmähst,
     Und gerne dienend, Edle! zwischen
       Sterblichen waltest und Himmelsmächten,

Wo bist du? wenig lebt' ich; doch athmet kalt
   Mein Abend schon. Und stille, den Schatten gleich,
     Bin ich schon hier; und schon gesanglos
       Schlummert das schaudernde Herz im Busen.

Im grünen Thale, dort, wo der frische Quell
   Vom Berge täglich rauscht, und die liebliche
     Zeitlose mir am Herbsttag aufblüht,
       Dort, in der Stille, du Holde, will ich

Dich suchen, oder wenn in der Mitternacht
   Das unsichtbare Leben im Haine wallt,
     Und über mir die immerfrohen
       Blumen, die blühenden Sterne glänzen,

O du des Aethers Tochter! erscheine dann
   Aus deines Vaters Gärten, und darfst du nicht,
     Ein Geist der Erde, kommen, schrök', o
       Schröke mit anderem nur das Herz mir.

To Hope

O hope! So dear, so busy with kindness!
    You who won't scorn the mourner's home,
        And, O noble one, gladly you serve us,
            Creating bonds between mortals and heavenly powers,

Where are you? I haven't lived long, but already
    The chill breath of evening comes on. And I'm already
        As silent as the shades here; and already my shuddering
            Heart sleeps in my breast without song.

In the verdant valley, there where the fresh spring
    Plunges from mountains each day, and the lovely
        Crocus opens in autumn light for me,
            There, I'll look for you, dear one, there

In the stillness, or when in the night
    All unseen life is astir in the woods,
        And the ever-joyful flowers overhead,
            The blooming stars, are shining,

O daughter of Aether, then come forth
    From your father's gardens, and if you may
        Not appear a spirit of the earth, then
            Frighten, O frighten my heart with something else!

Vulkan.

Jezt komm und hülle, freundlicher Feuergeist,
 Den zarten Sinn der Frauen in Wolken ein,
  In goldne Träum' und schüze sie, die
   Blühende Ruhe der Immerguten.

Dem Manne laß sein Sinnen, und sein Geschäfft,
 Und seiner Kerze Schein, und den künftgen Tag
  Gefallen, laß des Unmuths ihm, der
   Häßlichen Sorge zu viel nicht werden,

Wenn jezt der immerzürnende Boreas,
 Mein Erbfeind, über Nacht mit dem Frost das Land
  Befällt, und spät, zur Schlummerstunde,
   Spottend der Menschen, sein schröklich Lied singt,

Und unsrer Städte Mauren und unsern Zaun,
 Den fleißig wir gesezt, und den stillen Hain
  Zerreißt, und selber im Gesang die
   Seele mir störet, der Allverderber;

Und rastlos tobend über den sanften Strom
 Sein schwarz Gewölk ausschüttet, daß weit umher
  Das Thal gährt, und, wie fallend Laub, vom
   Berstenden Hügel herab der Fels fällt.

Wohl frömmer ist, denn andre Lebendige,
 Der Mensch; doch zürnt es draußen, gehöret der
  Auch eigner sich, und sinnt und ruht in
   Sicherer Hütte, der Freigeborne.

Und immer wohnt der freundlichen Genien
 Noch Einer gerne seegnend mit ihm, und wenn
  Sie zürnten all', die ungelehrgen
   Geniuskräfte, doch liebt die Liebe.

Vulcan

Come now, friendly spirit of fire, and enwrap
   The women's delicate minds in clouds,
      In golden dreams, and protect the
         Blossoming peace of these ever-kindly souls.

Let man be content with his thoughts,
   His daily work and his candle's light and all his
      Tomorrows, and don't let vexations
         And hateful cares overwhelm him

When the ever-raging Boreas,
   My arch-foe, assails the land with frost
      In the night, and, late, when all are asleep,
         Mocking at men he sings his dreaded song

And tears down our city walls and all the fences
   That we, working hard, had built up, and the peaceful
      Groves, and even unsettles my soul
         In the middle of song, this one who ruins all;

And raging restless over the gentle stream
   He pours out his blackened clouds, and all around
      The valley seethes, and the boulders tumble
         Like falling leaves down from the crumbling hills.

Human beings are surely more devout than other
   Living things; yet when it's raging outside they
      Tend more to themselves and, pensive,
         Rest safely in their huts, the free-born ones.

And from among the friendly spirits there's always one
   Who lives with them and gives his blessing,
      And however much they'd rage in fury, those unruly
         Spirit powers, love would still be love.

Blödigkeit.

Sind denn dir nicht bekannt viele Lebendigen?
   Geht auf Wahrem dein Fuß nicht, wie auf Teppichen?
      Drum, mein Genius! tritt nur
         Baar ins Leben, und sorge nicht!

Was geschiehet, es sei alles gelegen dir!
   Sei zur Freude gereimt, oder was könnte denn
      Dich belaidigen, Herz, was
         Da begegnen, wohin du sollst?

Denn, seit Himmlischen gleich Menschen, ein einsam Wild
   Und die Himmlischen selbst führet, der Einkehr zu,
      Der Gesang und der Fürsten
         Chor, nach Arten, so waren auch

Wir, die Zungen des Volks, gerne bei Lebenden,
   Wo sich vieles gesellt, freudig und jedem gleich,
      Jedem offen, so ist ja
         Unser Vater, des Himmels Gott,

Der den denkenden Tag Armen und Reichen gönnt,
   Der, zur Wende der Zeit, uns die Entschlafenden
      Aufgerichtet an goldnen
         Gängelbanden, wie Kinder, hält.

Gut auch sind und geschikt einem zu etwas wir,
   Wenn wir kommen, mit Kunst, und von den Himmlischen
      Einen bringen. Doch selber
         Bringen schikliche Hände wir.

Timidity

Aren't many living creatures known to you?
   Don't your feet tread the truth as they do on soft carpet?
      So then, my genius, just step
         Boldly into life without care!

Whatever happens, may it all be a boon to you!
   Rhyme yourself with joy, or what could
      Offend you, heart, what could
         Affront you there on your way?

For ever since the gods became like men, lonely deer,
   And the song and the choir of princes,
      Each in its way, brought the gods
         Back to communion, so too were

We, the tongues of the people, glad to find ourselves among the living
   Where many companions are gathered in joy, each equal to each,
      Open to each, and thus indeed is
         Our father, the god of the sky,

Who grants the pensive day to poor and to rich,
   Who holds us upright at the turning of time,
      Us sleeping ones, on golden
         Leading strings, like children.

We too are good, sent to serve someone, and useful
   For something when we bring forth one of the gods
      With our art. Yet we ourselves
         Bring our skillful and suitable hands.

Ganymed.

Was schläfst du, Bergsohn, liegest in Unmuth, schief,
Und frierst am kahlen Ufer, Gedultiger!
    Denkst nicht der Gnade, du, wenn's an den
        Tischen die Himmlischen sonst gedürstet?

Kennst drunten du vom Vater die Boten nicht,
Nicht in der Kluft der Lüfte geschärfter Spiel?
    Trift nicht das Wort dich, das voll alten
        Geists ein gewanderter Mann dir sendet?

Schon tönet's aber ihm in der Brust. Tief quillt's,
Wie damals, als hoch oben im Fels er schlief,
    Ihm auf. Im Zorne reinigt aber
        Sich der Gefesselte nun, nun eilt er

Der Linkische; der spottet der Schlaken nun,
Und nimmt und bricht und wirft die Zerbrochenen
    Zorntrunken, spielend, dort und da zum
        Schauenden Ufer und bei des Fremdlings

Besondrer Stimme stehen die Heerden auf,
Es regen sich die Wälder, es hört tief Land
    Den Stromgeist fern, und schaudernd regt im
        Nabel der Erde der Geist sich wieder.

Der Frühling kömmt. Und jedes, in seiner Art,
Blüht. Der ist aber ferne; nicht mehr dabei.
    Irr gieng er nun; denn allzugut sind
        Genien; himmlisch Gespräch ist sein nun.

Ganymede

Why do you sleep, mountain son, and lie crooked, disgruntled,
  And freeze on the barren banks, O patient one?
    Don't you remember the manifest grace when
      The gods suffered thirst at the tables?

Don't you recognize your father's messengers below,
  Or the whetted play of winds in the gorge?
    Aren't you struck by the word,
      Full of ancient breath, sent by a much-traveled man to you?

But now it resounds in his breast. It surges up
  From the depths, as when he slept up high
    On the cliff. But in anger
      The fettered one now purifies himself, now hastens,

The clumsy one; he mocks his rocky fetters now
  And takes and breaks and throws the broken pieces down,
    Drunk on rage, playing, here and there on
      The banks that observe him, and at the stranger's

Peculiar voice the herds rise to their feet,
  The forests stir, and deep in the country
    The river spirit is heard, and in the
      Navel of Earth the spirit shudders again.

Spring is coming. And everything blooms in its
  Way. But he is far distant; no longer here.
    He went astray; for the guardians of place are
      Far too good; now it's for him to speak with the gods.

Hälfte des Lebens.

Mit gelben Birnen hänget
Und voll mit wilden Rosen
Das Land in den See,
Ihr holden Schwäne,
Und trunken von Küssen
Tunkt ihr das Haupt
Ins heilignüchterne Wasser.

Weh mir, wo nehm' ich, wenn
Es Winter ist, die Blumen, und wo
Den Sonnenschein,
Und Schatten der Erde?
Die Mauern stehn
Sprachlos und kalt, im Winde
Klirren die Fahnen.

Lebensalter.

Ihr Städte des Euphrats!
Ihr Gassen von Palmyra!
Ihr Säulenwälder in der Eb'ne der Wüste,
Was seid ihr?
Euch hat die Kronen,
Dieweil ihr über die Gränze
Der Othmenden seid gegangen,
Von Himmlischen der Rauchdampf und
Hinweg das Feuer genommen;
Jezt aber siz' ich unter Wolken (deren
Ein jedes eine Ruh' hat eigen) unter
Wohleingerichteten Eichen, auf
Der Heide des Rehs, und fremd
Erscheinen und gestorben mir
Der Seeligen Geister.

Half of Life

With yellow pears,
And full of wild roses,
The land hangs in the lake,
O dear inclining swans,
And drunk with kisses
You dip your heads
In the holy, sober water.

Ah, where in the winter will
I come upon flowers, and where
The sun's light,
And shadows of the earth?
The walls stand
Speechless and cold, in the wind
The weathervanes clatter.

Ages of Life

You cities of the Euphrates!
You streets of Palmyra!
You forests of columns in the desert plains,
What are you?
Your crowns,
As you crossed
The bounds of those breathing,
Were taken away by the heavenly
Vapor of smoke and the fire;
Now though I sit under clouds (each
Has its own calm) amidst
A pleasant stand of oaks on
The heath where deer gather, and strange
They appear, dead to me,
The spirits of the blest.

Der Winkel von Hahrdt.

Hinunter sinket der Wald,
Und Knospen ähnlich, hängen
Einwärts die Blätter, denen
Blüht unten auf ein Grund,
Nicht gar unmündig.
Da nemlich ist Ulrich
Gegangen; oft sinnt, über den Fußtritt,
Ein groß Schiksaal
Bereit, an übrigem Orte.

The Shelter at Hardt

The forest slopes down,
And the leaves turned inward
Hang like buds, below
A ground blooms up toward them,
Not at all speechless.
For Ulrich walked
There; a great destiny
Often ponders over his footprint,
Ready, on the site that remains.

APPENDIXES

German Editions of Hölderlin

A good number of Hölderlin's texts are known to us only through his handwritten drafts and fair copies; Hölderlin did not himself see a large portion of his poems into print.[1] The state of these handwritten manuscripts is far from unequivocal; multiple layers of revision, handwriting that is at times difficult to decipher, and numerous unfinished poems and revisions often make it difficult to determine what "the poem" in question actually is. Furthermore, in some cases the published versions of poems Hölderlin himself saw into print vary from Hölderlin's own fair copies. The texts of Hölderlin's poems are consequently not always a settled matter.

For several decades the standard edition of Hölderlin's works was Friedrich Beissner's historical-critical *Stuttgarter Hölderlin-Ausgabe* (known as the *Grosse Stuttgarter Ausgabe*, or *GSA*), which was published between 1943 and 1985 (the poems being published by 1951). Beissner produced, in addition to an edition of "reading texts" (i.e., the poems by themselves), a large critical apparatus that noted all variants, revisions, and versions of a poem, and situated the poems in the context of the manuscripts and Hölderlin's life. In 1975, however, D. E. Sattler—a graphic designer by trade and complete outsider to the German academic world—challenged the *GSA* in the so-called "trial volume" of the *Frankfurter Hölderlin–Ausgabe* (*FHA*). Sattler accused Beissner of making out of Hölderlin a tidy classical poet with finished, polished texts and thereby ignoring the truth of Hölderlin's texts—that is, that many are unfinished, fragmentary, and equivocal.[2] One of Sattler's major criticisms was that Beissner separated the "reading texts" of the poems in the *GSA* from the critical apparatus, making it difficult to read the variants as texts in themselves and thus creating the illusion that the texts were somehow decided once and for all. Sattler, in contrast, chose to interweave his "emended" and "constituted" texts within his critical apparatus, which includes facsimiles of the handwritten manuscripts and intricate typographical reproductions of the manuscripts in an (at times bewildering) array of different fonts. The result of this editing model is often a plethora of texts of each poem, some obviously drafts, some perhaps more like different versions, but, in the end, a more accurate presentation of the state of Hölderlin's texts and his constant revisions. The *FHA*'s reception has been quite controversial, but whatever one thinks about its presentation of multiple texts, its great advantage is that its facsimiles of the handwritten manuscripts and corresponding typographical reproductions give patient readers a chance to discover for themselves the handwritten basis (or lack thereof) for an editorial decision.

Michael Knaupp's 1992 revision of Günther Mieth's *GSA*-based three-volume study edition of Hölderlin also presents some textual variants different from the *FHA* and *GSA* texts, though Knaupp, who worked with Sattler on some volumes of the *FHA*, for the most part follows the *FHA*.

I have used all three editions (the *GSA*, *FHA*, and Knaupp) in determining the German texts for this book. In general, there are not significant differences between most of the *GSA* and *FHA* texts—though very few are identical. In the case of most differences, I've decided the issue in favor of the text as it appears in the handwritten drafts and fair copies (which often have different punctuation and spellings than the original published versions of the poems). When there are no handwritten copies of a poem, I've followed the critical editions in emending the obvious spelling variants of the versions of the poems as they were first printed. I've not noted the spelling or punctuation differences unless they are significant. Where there are significant differences between the *FHA* and *GSA*, I give reasons for my choice of text in the notes to the poem. I have followed tradition in using the word "version" to differentiate multiple texts of a poem, though strictly speaking this is probably not accurate, as "version" implies something more finished than a draft or revision actually is. Spaces in the text reflect spaces Hölderlin left in the manuscripts.

NOTES TO APPENDIX A

1. Of the seventy-nine poems translated in this book (excluding those in Appendix C), Hölderlin himself saw forty-six into print. He could not have taken part in the publication of any poem published after 1806.

2. D. E. Sattler, ed., Friedrich Hölderlin, *Sämtliche Werke: Frankfurter Ausgabe* (Frankfurt am Main, 1975), Einleitung: 16–17.

Meter in Hölderlin

Hölderlin uses precise meters in his odes and elegies. German, like English, is a stressed language, and meter therefore is counted in stressed and unstressed syllables. The German meters borrowed and adapted from Greek models, therefore, do not follow the Greek long and short syllables (i.e., duration), but must use stressed (indicated below by "—") and unstressed (indicated below by "∪") syllables instead. I have chosen not to reproduce the meters exactly, as I was unable to do so without making large sacrifices in syntax and word choice. Furthermore, achieving the right meter would often have meant padding lines with extra words, a strategy that cannot maintain the directness of Hölderlin's language. When I did try to reproduce the meter precisely, the results always seemed to lose the force and pathos of the original, and these losses never seemed worth the formal gains. That said, I have not ignored meter completely, but tried for approximations. The hexameters, because of their length and flexibility, were easier to approximate. In the case of the odes, I could only sometimes achieve hints of the original.

Hölderlin uses the following meters in the poems included in this book:

Hexameter—A line consisting of a combination of six dactyls (— ∪ ∪, as in "heavenly") and troches (— ∪, as in "pious").

Elegiac distichs—This couplet indents its second line and is used in the elegies and elegiac fragments. The first line consists of six feet of dactyls and spondees, with the dactyl providing the predominant rhythm. The second line is a pentameter with two stresses in the middle, surrounded by dactyls and spondees. A typical second line might take the form

$$— \cup — \cup \cup — \mid — \cup \cup — \cup \cup —$$

The caesura in the pentameter is always in the middle of the two middle stressed syllables. If I was able, without mutilating the English syntax or adding words not in the original, I included double stresses in the second line of the elegiac distichs, as in

Breath, and a rustling song, over this happy pair's bliss.

Alcaic ode—Adapted from the Greek poet Alcaeus of Lesbos via Horace, the Alcaic ode was naturalized in the German language by Klopstock in the eighteenth century (in contrast to the English tradition, which has only a smattering of isolated attempts at this form). The scansion of each verse is as follows:

$$\cup — \cup — \cup — \cup \cup — \cup —$$
$$\cup — \cup — \cup — \cup \cup — \cup —$$
$$\cup — \cup — \cup — \cup — \cup$$
$$— \cup \cup — \cup \cup — \cup — \cup$$

The first two lines are the same, the third line a regular iambic, and the fourth, by beginning with two dactyls, creates an impression of a hurrying, falling end, or even of breaking waves. Because in the Alcaic ode a stressed syllable never follows another stressed syllable, I have tried not to let this happen often in the translations. I have also tried as much as possible to have at least one dactyl near the beginning of each fourth line.

Asclepiadic ode—This form was also adapted from Alcaeus via Horace and Klopstock. The scansion is:

$$— \cup — \cup \cup — \mid — \cup \cup — \cup —$$
$$— \cup — \cup \cup — \mid — \cup \cup — \cup —$$
$$— \cup — \cup \cup — \cup$$
$$— \cup — \cup \cup — \cup —$$

The predominance of stressed syllables at the beginning of the feet as well as the frequent occurrence of a stress following a stress—in contrast to the Alcaic ode—lends an entirely different feel to the Asclepiadic ode. The meter here is less fluid and more halting or congested.

Notes to the Poems

The following notes situate the poems chronologically, justify my choice of
German text when appropriate, translate significant variants and versions of
the poems, and provide annotations of various terms, allusions, and par-
allels. I have tried to provide a selection of what I consider the more signifi-
cant variants; the compilation here is by no means exhaustive. Because
Hölderlin constantly revised his work, even after its publication, the variants
presented here are not merely curiosities but an important part of the texts.

The poems appear, for the most part, in the order in which they were writ-
ten (and not when they were published). This order is often tenuous, as the
evidence for the creation date of a number of poems is scanty. When a group
of poems appeared together in a journal published during Hölderlin's life-
time, I've ordered them according to the order they appeared in print.

Many of the notes are derived from the commentaries of D. E. Sattler,
Friedrich Beissner, Günter Mieth, Michael Knaupp, and Jochen Schmidt (all
editors of various Hölderlin editions); the *Dictionary of Classical Mythology* by
J. E. Zimmerman; and the *Classical Dictionary* by John Lemprière. I have put
their names in parentheses after a note when this is the case. Quotes from the
Bible are taken from the King James version.

Poems from the Early Frankfurt Period

The Oaks

The first draft of this hexameter poem was probably begun in
early 1796 (on the possibility that this poem represents Hölderlin's
attempt to break with Schiller, see the Introduction). Most com-
mentators have the final version in Schiller's hands in June of 1797,
along with "To the Aether" and "The Wanderer," but Sattler, cit-
ing several letters between Schiller and Hölderlin, places it with
Schiller already in July of 1796. Schiller published "The Oaks" in

his journal *Die Horen* in 1797. Hölderlin later copied the published version of the poem in a notebook, probably in 1799, and began (perhaps later in 1801) to rework the ending for a collection of his poems that never materialized. In this reworking he wrote under the title that the poem was "to be used as a proemium," that is, as a preamble or introduction, perhaps for the collection of poems, and began a revised ending (see variants below).

Titans—The sons and daughters of Uranus (heaven) and Gaia (earth) in Greek mythology. Cronus, the youngest Titan, led a war of his siblings against their parents, after which the Titans' offspring, led by Zeus, dethroned Cronus.

Or so set on love—Compare the last stanza of "Empedocles."

VARIANTS

[line 17]—*wie gern würd' ich unter euch wohnen* (how gladly I'd dwell there among you) was changed in the later revision to *wie gerne würd ich zum Eichbaum* (how gladly I'd become an oak).

[lines 14–17]—These lines were bracketed in the later revision and under them written:

O daß mir nie nicht altere, daß der Freuden
daß der Gedanken unter den Menschen, der Lebens-
zeichen keins mir unwerth werde, daß ich seiner mich schämte,
denn alle brauchet das Herz, damit es Unaus-
sprechliches nenne.

O that my heart may never grow old, that the joys,
that the thoughts among men, the signs
of life, that none of these become unworthy to me, that I not be
               ashamed of what belongs to my heart,
for the heart needs everything that it
might name what can't be expressed.

To the Aether

Probably begun in the summer of 1796, this hexameter poem was submitted with "The Wanderer" (not included in this book) to

Schiller on June 20, 1797. Hölderlin asked Schiller to write if the poems were accepted for the *Musen-Almanach für 1798*, as he "couldn't calmly wait" for the journal to come out to discover his "fate." On June 27, Schiller sent the two poems to Goethe without naming their author, asking for his opinion. Goethe responded the next day that

> the two poems you sent me [. . .], toward which I'm not entirely unfavorably disposed, will certainly find a friendly audience. [. . .] The other poem ["To the Aether"] seems more natural-historical than poetic, and reminds one of those paintings in which all the animals gather around Adam in Paradise. Both poems express a gentle striving that resolves itself in contentment. The poet has a clear view of nature, but he only seems to have come to it through tradition. A few lively images surprise the reader [. . .] Some specific expressions and in some places the meter could still use a little work. [. . .] I would say that both poems contain good ingredients for making a poet, but they do not make a poet by themselves.

Schiller responded that he

> found much of my former likeness in these poems, and that's not the first time that the author has reminded me of myself. He has an intense subjectivity combined with a certain philosophical spirit and pensiveness. His condition is dangerous, for it's so hard to get through to such natures. But meanwhile I think these newer pieces are the beginning of a certain improvement compared to his previous work; for, in short, it's Hölderlin, whom you met at my house several years ago.

Schiller ended up publishing the poems in his *Musen-Almanach für 1798*. Because there are deviations from the text published in the *Musen-Almanach* and a fair copy Hölderlin wrote down after sending the manuscript to Schiller, who must have lightly edited the poem, I have followed the *FHA* in using the fair copy as the basis for the text. But since we no longer have lines 1–22 of the fair copy, these lines are based on a list, compiled by Gustav Schlesier (who was researching for a biography of Hölderlin in the 1840s), of variations between the fair copy and the *Musen-Almanach* version. Lines 23–52 are based on the fair copy itself.

Aether—An important concept in Hölderlin's poetry, the Aether is an all-encompassing, elemental force that unites all living beings and engenders a longing in them to return to the All (Schmidt). In Greek myth it was the upper region of the sky, and in classical science it was considered the fifth element.

blessèd boy—Ganymede, a beautiful boy who was brought to Olympus by an eagle to be cupbearer to the gods.

[*and, smiling, the sovereigns . . .*]

This fragment of elegiac distichs, first published in 1922, has been variously titled by editors "To Diotima," "To a Tree," and "On a Tree." None of these titles exist in the manuscript, so, following the *FHA*, I've used the first half-line as the title. The fragment comes to us through a handwritten copy of Christoph Theodor Schwab, who published a selection of Hölderlin's poems in 1846. Because Schwab is known to have written imitations of Hölderlin, Sattler has characterized the authenticity of the fragment as "questionable," even though it does not contain "Schwab's usual breaks in style";[1] Knaupp goes further and states that one can assume that Schwab reworked a draft of Hölderlin's to create the poem.[2] Beissner, on the other hand, states that the authenticity of the fragment is "not to be doubted."[3] Sattler places its origin as early as the summer of 1796, while Beissner has it in 1797.

my girl—Both Beissner and Knaupp remark that this phrase sounds odd today, especially in an elegy. Beissner points out that Hölderlin used it often in his novel *Hyperion* as a form of pathos-filled address to Diotima.

To Diotima (*"Beautiful creature . . ."*)

Composed probably in early 1797, first published in 1896. The *FHA* puts this and the following poem under the heading "Diotima."

Compare, for example, their similar last lines. Written in elegiac distichs.

Diotima—A priestess in Plato's *Symposium*, Diotima taught Socrates that love, the child of lack and plenty, holds the world together and is a messenger between the gods and mortals. Though by the time of this poem Hölderlin had already met his real-life Diotima in the person of Susette Gontard, he had addressed Diotima in his poetry before their meeting.

Diotima ("You favorite of the heavenly muse . . .")
Composed right after "To Diotima" ("Beautiful creature . . ."). First published in 1826.

You favorite of the heavenly muse, you who once reconciled the elements—Allusion to Urania, the muse of cosmic harmony (Schmidt).
only—This is a translation of the last word of the last line (*nur*), which replaces the last word *nun* (now) in "To Diotima" ("Beautiful creature . . .") above.

Leisure
Beissner and Knaupp place this poem in early 1797, but Sattler sees it in the summer of 1796. First published in its entirety in 1922.

For the most part I've followed the *FHA* text's punctuation and exclusion of the last "words" in line 41. The *GSA* emends what is clearly just a "W" in the manuscript to *Wald da* (woods there). I did not follow Sattler in line 40 where he reads *unsterbliches* (immortal), the first few letters of which are clearly crossed out, in place of *erzählendes* (narrative), which, though underlined, is written above.

look to the mountain—The Große Feldberg, a mountain near Frankfurt (Knaupp).
villages lie at rest—Compare the first stanzas of "Bread and Wine" and "Evening Fantasy" (Beissner).

[lines 28–33]—Compare lines 3–8 in "The nations were silent, they slumbered . . ."

one womb—Compare Pindar's Sixth Nemean: "There is one race of men, / one race of gods, / yet from one mother we both take our breath"⁴ (Beissner).

VARIANTS

[lines 39–40]—*read / To the end a storied page of human life* replaces the crossed-out *von Attikas Schiksaal / Ein unsterbliches Blatt zu gutem Ende gelesen* (read to the end the immortal story of Attica's fate).

[line 41]—Above this line in the handwritten draft is another line in parentheses, perhaps indicating deletion: *Dann ist mein Abendgebet: sei wie dir dünket, o Schiksaal* (Then my evening prayer: be as you imagine yourself, O Fate).

[*The nations were silent, they slumbered . . .*]

This poem, written in blank verse and dealing with the War of the First Coalition (1793–1797), has been dated from 1796 to early 1799. The *FHA* adds *zahllos* (countless) to modify "stars," but this word is clearly crossed out in the manuscript. The large space between the second stanza and the last three lines reflects the space Hölderlin left between those lines in the manuscript. First published in 1921.

[lines 3–8]—Compare lines 28–33 in "Leisure."

shakes the ancient cities / Like trees of ripened fruit—Compare Nahum 3:12: "All thy strong holds shall be like fig trees with the firstripe figs: if they be shaken, they shall even fall into the mouth of the eater"(Beissner).

golden fruits sparkle—Compare lines 31–32 of "Man" and line 29 of "The Neckar" (Beissner).

for you—Probably refers to Napoleon (Beissner). Hölderlin wrote several drafts of poems on Napoleon. Compare this earlier sketch for an ode written in 1797 and first published in 1896:

Buonaparte.

Heilige Gefäße sind die Dichter,
  Worinn des Lebens Wein, der Geist
    Der Helden sich aufbewahrt,

Aber der Geist dieses Jünglings
  Der schnelle müßt' er es nicht zersprengen
    Wo es ihn fassen wollte, das Gefäß
      Der Dichter laß ihn unberührt
        wie den Geist der Natur,
          An solchem Stoffe
            wird zum Knaben
              der Meister
            Er kann im Gedichte
              nicht leben und bleiben
                Er lebt und bleibt
                  in der Welt.

Buonaparte

The poets are holy vessels
  In which the wine of life, the spirit
    Of heroes, is kept.

But the spirit of this youth,
  The quick, won't it burst apart
    The vessel that tries to hold it
      The poet leaves him untouched,
        like the spirit of nature,
          Such stuff
            turns masters
              into unskilled boys.
            He can't live
              and remain in a poem
                He lives and remains
                  in the world.

"To the Universally Known," another draft of a Napoleon poem,
has been variously dated from the end of 1797 to the summer of

1800. It was first published in 1911. Earlier titles were "Buonaparte" and "Dem Allgenannten" ("To the Universally Named"). The draft continues in an even more fragmentary nature beyond what I have translated below.

Dem Allbekannten.

Hexameter.

Frei wie die Schwalben, ist der Gesang, sie fliegen und wandern
Fröhlich von Land zu Land, und ferne suchet den Sommer
Sich das heilge Geschlecht, denn heilig war es den Vätern
Und nun sing ich den Fremdling, ihn,

Diß neide mir keiner der andern, gleichst du dem Ernsten
Oder gleichst du ihm nicht, laß jezt in Ruhe mich sprechen
Denn der Herrliche selbst er gönnet gerne mein Spiel mir.
Fragen möcht' ich, woher er ist? am Rheine der Deutschen
Wuchs er nicht auf wenn schon nicht arm an Männern das Land ist,
Das bescheidene Land, und an allernährender Sonne
Schön auch da der Genius reift,

To the Universally Known

Hexameter

Song is free like the swallows who fly and wander
In joy from land to land, the holy race
Looks in the distance for summer, for it was holy to the fathers,
And now I'll sing the stranger, him

None of the others envies me this, and whether you resemble the
Serious one or not, let me speak now in peace,
For the glorious one himself gladly grants me my song.

I'd like to ask where he's from. He didn't grow up
On the Rhine of the Germans, though that land isn't lacking in men,
The modest land, and the all-nourishing sun
Beautifully ripens the genius there too,

VARIANTS

[line 12]—Above this line in an earlier draft of "The nations were silent, they slumbered . . ." stand the lines:

Fünf Sommer leuchtete das große Leben
Ein unaufhörlich Wetter unter uns.

For five summers magnificent life,
An unending storm, glowed under us.

To Diotima ("Come and look at the joy . . .")

Probably composed in the spring of 1797, this uncompleted poem in the so-called Archilochian meter (the alternation between a hexameter and half of a pentameter) is the only instance of this meter in Hölderlin. The poem was first published in 1908.

loving quarrel—Beissner points out the similarity to the end of Hölderlin's novel *Hyperion*: "'Like lovers' quarrels are the dissonances of the world. Reconciliation is there, even in the midst of strife, and all things that are parted find one another again.'"[5] See also line 6 of "Homecoming" and the related note (the German *Streit* [quarrel] can also be translated as "strife").

The Shorter Odes

Hölderlin sent the following fourteen poems (through "Home") in two packages to Christian Ludwig Neuffer in the summer of 1798; Neuffer published them in his *Taschenbuch für Frauenzimmer von Bildung auf das Jahr 1799*. Their order below follows the order in which they were published in the *Taschenbuch* and is not necessarily the order in which they were conceived.

Neuffer, a close friend of Hölderlin's from their days at the Tübingen seminary, was the subject of this 1797 draft (first published in 1922):

An Neuffer

Brüderlich Herz! ich komme zu dir, wie der thauende Morgen
    Schließe du, wie der Kelch zärtlicher Blumen dich auf
Einen Himmel empfängst du, der Freude goldene Wolke
    Rieselt in eilenden freundlichen Tönen herab.
Freund! ich kenne mich nicht, ich kenne nimmer den Menschen,
    Und es schämet der Geist aller Gedanken sich nun.
Fassen wollt' er auch sie, wie er faßt die Dinge der Erde
    Fassen
Aber ein Schwindel ergriff ihn süß, und die ewige Veste
    Seiner Gedanken stürzt'

To Neuffer

Brotherly heart, I'm coming to you like the opening morning,
    Open your heart like a tender flower's cup,
You're receiving a heaven, a golden cloud of joy
    Gently falls down, rushing in amiable tones.
Friend! I don't know myself, I know that man no longer,
    And my mind's now ashamed of all of its thoughts.
It wanted to grasp her, too, like it grasps the things of this earth,
    To grasp
But a swoon gripped it sweetly, its timeless firmament
    Of thoughts tumbled

Seven of Hölderlin's contributions to Neuffer's journal were attributed to the pseudonym Hillmar: "To Her Genius," "Farewell," "The Lovers," "Home," "Good Faith," "Her Recovery," and "The Unpardonable." In a review of the journal, A. W. von Schlegel singled out Hölderlin's poems for being "full of spirit and soul."

It's possible some of these shorter odes were written in reaction to advice Hölderlin received from Goethe and Schiller. In a letter to Schiller of August 23, 1797, Goethe writes of meeting with Hölderlin in which he advised him to "write short poems

and for each one to choose a subject of human interest." Simi-
larly, Schiller had written Hölderlin earlier advising him to avoid
philosophizing in his poetry (see the notes to "To the Young
Poets" below). Many of the poems here were later expanded into
longer odes.

The Unpardonable

Asclepiadic. See the expanded version "Love."

Then and Now

Alcaic.

The Lovers

Asclepiadic. Later expanded into "Der Abschied" ("The Farewell,"
not translated here).

To the Germans [two stanzas]

Asclepiadic. Compare the later fourteen-stanza expansion under
the same title.

Her Recovery [three stanzas]

Asclepiadic. Compare the later six-stanza expansion under the same
title.

To the Young Poets

Asclepiadic. For the German text I've followed the *GSA*, which
keeps the metrically correct version of the second line. The *FHA*
uses Schlesier's list of variants (see the note to "To the Aether"
above) that has this line in a slightly different but metrically incor-
rect form.

Don't describe or teach!—Compare the short epigram "Descriptive
Poetry," written perhaps at the end of 1796:

Wißt! Apoll ist der Gott der Zeitungsschreiber geworden
Und sein Mann ist, wer ihm treulich das Factum erzählt.

Breaking news! Apollo's now the god of newspapermen,
  And he who loyally states all the facts is his man.

Mieth surmises that "Descriptive Poetry" and "To the Young Poets" could be polemics against Schiller, who had commented on some poems Hölderlin had sent him that arrived too late for inclusion in his *Musen-Almanach*. Schiller wrote in a letter to Hölderlin on November 24, 1796 that he should

> Flee, where possible, philosophical subject matter, for it's the most ungrateful, and the best often consume themselves struggling with it; stay nearer the world of the senses, and you will thus be in less danger of losing your sobriety in enthusiasm or going astray in artificial expression.

VARIANTS

[line 3]—Schlesier notes that this line read in the fair copy *Bald zu göttlicher Stille* ([Will ripen] soon to divine stillness), which is metrically incorrect. Beissner conjectures the metrical improvement may stem from Neuffer.

The Course of Life [one stanza]

Asclepiadic. Compare the later four-stanza expansion under the same title.

life's arc—A reference to the Greek wordplay of βίος (life) and βιός (a bow) found in Heraclitus' fragment 48: "The name of the bow is bios [life], its function death"[6] (Schmidt).

To Her Genius

This short poem in elegiac distichs is the only poem in this group sent to Neuffer that is not an ode.

Phidias—The Athenian sculptor who created the Zeus statue in Olympia and the Athena in the Parthenon.

Brevity

Asclepiadic. Compare "Socrates and Alcibiades," which has a similar form of statement and reply (Beissner).

To the Fates

Mieth points out that this Alcaic ode evidently unsettled Hölderlin's mother, for in a letter to her on July 8, 1799, Hölderlin writes about this ode that "The little poem should not have alarmed you, dear mother! It means nothing more than how much I desire some quiet time in which I can fulfill what nature seems to have destined for me."

Similar in theme is the following fragment of elegiac distichs, probably written some time in the beginning of 1799 and first published in 1922:

[Hört' ich die Warnenden izt . . .]

Hört' ich die Warnenden izt, sie lächelten meiner und dächten,
  Früher anheim uns fiel, weil er uns scheute, der Thor.
Und sie achtetens keinen Gewinn,

Singt, o singet mir nur, unglükweissagend, ihr Furchtbarn
  Schiksaalsgötter das Lied immer und immer ums Ohr
Euer bin ich zu lezt, ich weiß es, doch will zuvor ich
  Mir gehören und mir Leben erbeuten und Ruhm.

[If I could hear the warning ones now . . .]

If I could hear the warning ones now they'd smile at me and think,
  He fell to us sooner, the fool, because he shunned us.
And they'd think it no gain,

Sing, O sing to me foretelling doom, you terrible
  Gods of fate, forever and ever the song in my ear.
I'm yours in the end, I know it, yet before that I want to
  Belong to myself and seize for myself life and some fame.

divine right—Compare line 38 of "Chiron."
Orcus—The Roman name for Hades, the Greek lord of the underworld.

[line 1]—An earlier draft has *Furchtbaren* (terrible ones) for *Gewaltigen* (powerful ones/gods).

[line 2]—An earlier draft has *reinem* (pure) for *reifem* (ripened).

Apology

Asclepiadic.

Good Faith

Asclepiadic.

Diotima *("You fall silent . . .") [two stanzas]*

This two-stanza Alcaic ode was later expanded to six stanzas. Knaupp points out that the first letter in the first three lines of each stanza is *D*, and the first letters of each of the fourth lines is *S* and *G*. He sees in the *D*s an allusion to the Latin "Dat, Dicat, Dedicat" (Gives, Devotes, Dedicates), which appeared on the title page of Hölderlin's first family register and which is commonly abbreviated as D. D. D.; and in the *S* and *G* a hidden dedication to Susette Gontard.

time steals by—The German word I've translated as "steals by" is *eilt*, which is normally rendered as "hurries" or "hastens." In the six-stanza version of the poem, however, Hölderlin changes *eilt* by adding an "h" to make it *heilt* (heals). "Steals" offers a way to keep this intertextual rhymed play relatively painlessly, though the phrase's connotation of surreptitiousness is not quite right.

Home *[two stanzas]*

Alcaic. Compare the later six-stanza expansion under the same title.

Human Applause

This Asclepiadic ode, like the "The Sanctimonious Poets," was sent to Neuffer in the summer of 1798 but not published in the 1799 issue of the *Taschenbuch für Frauenzimmer von Bildung.* It was published instead the following year.

masters—The German *gewaltsam* means "violent, forcible," so an alternative translation might be simply "the powerful."

The Sanctimonious Poets
Alcaic. First published in the *Taschenbuch für Frauenzimmer von Bildung auf das Jahr 1800*. I owe the first phrase of the second verse to Michael Hamburger's version of the poem.

Thunderer—Zeus.
Sea God—Poseidon.

The following three poems and "Man" were sent to Schiller in June of 1798 for publication in the 1799 issue of his *Musen-Almanach*. Schiller only accepted "Socrates and Alcibiades" and "To Our Great Poets." Hölderlin also sent a fifth poem, "Vanini," which is not included in this book.

Socrates and Alcibiades
Asclepiadic. "Brevity" has a similar structure of statement and response (Beissner).

Alcibiades—Athenian statesman and commander who was a student
   of Socrates; he is the youth in the first stanza. In Plato's *Sympo-
   sium*, Alcibiades gives a speech in praise of Socrates.
youth—Youth often represents in Hölderlin an "unbroken unity of
   all life" and is thus a "revelation of the [. . .] One and All"
   (Schmidt). See, for example, "When I was a boy . . ." and
   "Home."

VARIANTS
[line 6]—An earlier draft has *nur der gereifte Geist* (only the matured
   spirit) recognizing the nobility of youth.
[line 7]—In an earlier draft *der Weiseste wendet / Fromm* (the wisest
   turns devoutly) to beauty.

To Our Great Poets

Alcaic. Compare the later expansion "The Poet's Calling."

Bacchus went forth from Indus—One school of thought believes that Bacchus (the Roman name for Dionysius, the Greek god of wine) was a foreign god who "invaded" the Greek religion from India.

To the Sun God

Alcaic. Compare "Sunset," a shortened version of "To the Sun God." First published in 1846.

god-fearing peoples—The mythical Hyperboreans, with whom the sun god Apollo lived in winter (Knaupp).

Sunset

Alcaic. Compare the earlier "To the Sun God." This poem and "Voice of the People" may have been sent to Neuffer in the summer of 1799. First published in the *Taschenbuch für Frauenzimmer von Bildung auf das Jahr 1800.*

Voice of the People [two stanzas]

Alcaic. Compare the eighteen-stanza expansion of this poem under the same title. First published in the *Taschenbuch für Frauenzimmer von Bildung auf das Jahr 1800.*

Later Odes; Elegies and Elegiac Fragments

[When I was a boy . . .]

First published in 1874 in its complete form, this poem, according to Mieth and Beissner, was probably written in 1797 or 1798. Sattler thinks it was written much earlier, perhaps 1795 or 1796.

Helios—The god of the sun.

Endymion—The son of Zeus and Calyce. Luna made love to Endymion in his dreams. Endymion then asked Zeus for perpetual youth, sleep, and immortality so he could dream of Luna for eternity.

Luna—Also known as Artemis, the sister of Apollo and goddess of the moon.

[*Hyperion's Song of Fate*]

Probably composed in the late summer or fall of 1798, this poem is taken from the second volume of Hölderlin's novel *Hyperion* (1799). The poem is untitled in the novel, but it is referred to by the character Hyperion as his "song of fate."

Hyperion—The son of heaven and earth, and the father of the sun. Hyperion also often refers to the sun itself (Zimmerman).

one hour to the next—Compare line 20 in "The Blind Singer."

rock to rock—See line 17 of the eighteen-stanza "Voice of the People."

Achilles

This poem in elegiac distichs, written probably in late 1798 or early 1799, was first published by Schwab in 1846. Sattler claims that the last four lines were not composed in verse form by Hölderlin but by Schwab himself,[7] a possibility that Beissner does not exclude (the last four lines have come down only through the Schwab edition and exist in no copy of the poem in Hölderlin's hand). As evidence for this thesis, Sattler quotes Schwab's introduction to his 1846 Hölderlin edition:

> Nowhere have I dared to add one word that was not itself in the papers; only once did I make an exception to this rule, in a lyric poem where I encountered a complete prose draft, the versified execution of which was not brought to completion; I allowed myself here a few small transpositions to create the verse and harmonize the whole. The critics will discover these [changes].

Sattler claims that this must refer to "Achilles" and consequently has struck the last four lines of Schwab's version (Beissner keeps them in the *GSA*) and places the prose draft of them after line 24.

Achilles—The great Achaean warrior in the *Iliad*.

your belovèd—Patroclus, Achilles' beloved friend who was killed by the Trojan warrior Hector. Achilles mourned by his ship for Patroclus before reentering the war.

like mist—Compare the *Iliad*, Book I, line 359: "And lightly she emerged like a mist from the grey water"[8] (Beissner).

VARIANTS

Prose draft included in the *FHA* after line 24:

und stärkt mir das Herz, damit
ich nicht ganz verstumme, daß ich
leb, und eine kurze Zeit
mit frommen Gesang noch Himm-
lischen danke, für Freuden
vergangener Jugend, und
dann nimmt gütig zu
euch den Einsamen auf.

and strengthen my heart that
I not fade into silence completely, that I may
live and for a short time
still give thanks in pious song to you heav-
enly ones for the joys
of past youth, and
then may you kindly receive
this one who's alone.

The ending suspected to have been versified by Schwab and included in the *GSA*:

Daß ich lebe und euch, ihr hohen himmlischen Mächte,
    Noch am fliehenden Tag danke mit frommem Gesang,
Danke für voriges Gut, für Freuden vergangener Jugend,
    Und dann nehmet zu euch gütig den Einsamen auf.

That I may live and still on the fleeing day
    Give thanks in pious song to you high heavenly powers;

Thanks for the good that has been, for joys of past youth;
And then may you kindly receive this one who's alone.

[*Time was the gods walked with men . . .*]

This fragment, written sometime around March of 1799 and first published in 1911, is the middle (hence the "4") of a larger elegy that has not been preserved. I have followed Sattler in including later pencil corrections as part of the text.

Apollo—The Greek god of the sun, fine arts, music, and poetry.
healing and inspiring like you—The "you" here is Diotima (Susette Gontard), who is referred to in the third person at the end of the stanza (Beissner).
better times—Compare line 27 of "Rousseau" and line 16 of "Love."
In future—The space after this phrase corresponds to the missing word at the end of the corresponding German line. Beissner added *Jahren* (years) here, but it's not in the manuscript.

VARIANTS
[line 2]—An earlier version reads *versöhnend* (reconciling) for *begeist-ernd* (inspiring).
[line 10]—The *GSA* adds *Jahren* (years) here, but it's not in the manuscript.
[lines 11–13]—The "you" and "your" in lines 11–12 are from pencil revisions; the *GSA* reads "they" and their." All of line 13 is left off in the *GSA*.
[line 15]—An earlier version reads *Sank die Menge, doch sie fanden zu den Göttern die Bahn.* (The crowd sank, but they found the way to the gods.)

Man

Alcaic. First published in this form in 1891, "Man" was sent to Schiller in June of 1798 for publication in his *Musen-Almanach* but wasn't accepted. I've placed it here because of its length.

[lines 31–32]—Compare lines 20–22 of "The nations were silent, they slumbered . . ." and line 29 of "The Neckar" (Beissner).

The Temperamental Ones
Sent to Neuffer in July of 1799, this Asclepiadic ode was first published in his *Taschenbuch für Frauenzimmer von Bildung auf das Jahr 1800*.

Dying for the Fatherland
A reworking of the earlier version of the poem called "The Battle" (see the variants below), this Alcaic ode was sent to Neuffer in July 1799 and was published in his *Taschenbuch für Frauenzimmer von Bildung auf das Jahr 1800*.

"Dying for the Fatherland," along with the ode "Song of the German" (not translated here), were the two most quoted Hölderlin poems in the Nazi era. Although used by the Nazis as a call for a defense of the eastern front, the poems were also used by Germans in exile as appeals to the "other" or "better" Germany.

fatherland—In Hölderlin's time the word *Vaterland* did not have the racist, xenophobic, and violent connotations it has today. For Hölderlin, the fatherland was the place of one's birth, characterized by "[l]ove of what is close at hand and nostalgia for the warmth of childhood."9 Hölderlin was not narrowly nationalistic; on the contrary, hatred of the other and the smallness of those who could not see past their own little corner of the earth—"lack of elasticity," as Hölderlin put it in a letter to his brother on January 1, 1799—were inimical to his vision of a communal life in which, as Adorno writes, "love of what is close at hand would be freed of all enmity." Further, Schmidt points out that the poem has allusions to the "Marseillaise": "cutthroat foe" and "songs of the fatherland"; young revolutionaries who prevail, because of their spirit, over experienced royalist troops who don't believe in their cause (the first two stanzas); and to the ideals of the French Revolution ("brotherhood"). There is no good way for the translator to solve the problem of this word's evolution. The German reader, too, must take the historical context into account.

VARIANTS
This earlier draft is not included in the *GSA* as a separate poem; it was first published as such in 1970 by Mieth.

Die Schlacht.

O Morgenroth der Deutschen, o Schlacht! du kömmst
   Flammst heute blutend über den Völkern auf,
      Denn länger dulden sie nicht mehr, sind
         Länger die Kinder nicht mehr, die Deutschen.

Du kömmst, o Schlacht! schon woogen die Jünglinge
   Hinab von ihren Hügeln, hinab ins Thal
      Wo kek herauf die Würger dringen,
         Sicher der Kunst und des Arms! doch schröklich

Kömmt über sie die Seele der Neulinge,
   Denn die Gerechten schlagen wie Zauberer
      Und ihre Vaterlandsgesänge
         Lähmen die Knie den Ehrelosen.

O nimmt mich, nimmt auch mich in die Reihen auf
   Damit ich einst nicht sterbe gemeinen Tods!
      Umsonst zu sterben, lieb ich nicht, doch
         Lieb' ich zu fallen am Opferhügel,

Fürs Vaterland! zu bluten des Herzens Blut
   Fürs Vaterland und bald ists geschehn! hab ichs
      Doch schon als Knabe, mirs geweissagt
         Da wie zuerst vom Heroentode

Die heitergroßen Worte mein Herz vernahm,
   Nun aber wall' ich nieder ins Schattenreich,
      Zu euch, ihr Alten komm' ich, die mich leben
         Die mich zu sterben gelehrt, hinunter.

Ach! oft im Leben dürstet' ich, euch zu schaun
   Ihr Helden und Dichter aus gold'ner Zeit!
      Gastfreundlich grüßt ihr den geringen
         Fremdling und brüderlich ists hier unten

Und Siegesboten kommen herab; die Schlacht
   Ist unser; o nun freue der Jugend dich
      Mein Vaterland, denn herrlich hubst du
         Heute sie an und sie wird einst reifen.

The Battle

O dawn of Germans, O battle! You're coming today,
   You're bursting out in bloody flames over the nations,
      For they won't bear it anymore, no
         Longer are they children, the Germans.

You've come, O battle! The youths are already flowing
   Down from their hills and into the valley
      Where the cut-throat foe is boldly poised,
         Sure of its art and its arms, but ferociously

The recruits' young souls descend down upon them,
   For the righteous slay as if in a spell,
      And the songs of their fatherland
         Weaken the knees of those without honor.

O enlist me, enlist me too in the ranks
   So I won't die some paltry death!
      I don't want to die in vain,
         I'd rather fall on the field, a sacrifice

For the fatherland! To bleed my heart's
   Own blood for the fatherland, and now it will happen!
      I foretold this as a boy
         When my heart first heard

The glorious echoes of the hero's death,
   But now I'm floating down to the world of shades,
      To you, O ancient ones, I'm coming down,
         You who taught me how to live and die.

How often, alive, I longed to gaze upon you,
   O heroes and poets from the golden age!
      Welcoming, you greet this lowly
         Stranger into the brotherhood down here,

And messengers of victory arrive; the battle's
  Ours; O rejoice now in your youths,
    My fatherland, for gloriously today
      You raised them up, and one day they will ripen.

The Time-Spirit

This Alcaic ode was first published in Neuffer's *Taschenbuch für Frauenzimmer von Bildung auf das Jahr 1800*.

The Time-Spirit—The word *Zeitgeist* has become too much a part of English-speaking pop culture to leave untranslated. Richard Sieburth has pointed out that "Time-Spirit," as opposed to the more idiomatic "spirit of the times," is the nineteenth-century translation of the German term by writers such as Emerson and Carlyle.

timidly—The German *blöd* today means predominantly "stupid" or "silly," but in the eighteenth century, in addition to "timid," it could also mean "weak-sighted."

confronted in the mild breeze with a god—Compare Genesis 3:8: "And they heard the voice of the Lord God walking in the Garden in the cool of the day."

Evening Fantasy

Probably written in the summer of 1799, this Alcaic ode was first published in the *Brittischer Damenkalender und Taschenbuch für das Jahr 1800*.

The peaceful village—Compare the opening of "Bread and Wine" and the end of the second stanza in "Leisure" (Beissner).

[line 5]—Compare the boatmen in the two odes titled "Home."

In the Morning

Probably written some time in the summer of 1799; first published in the *Brittischer Damenkalender*. The draft title of this Alcaic ode was "Morning Fantasy" and was thus clearly conceived as a companion piece to "Evening Fantasy."

[lines 16–20]—An earlier draft of the last lines reads:

> Könnt ich empor, wie die Morgenwinde
>
> Mit dir, mit dir! doch lächelst des Sängers du
> Des Übermüth'gen, daß er dir gleichen möcht'
> Und wandelst schweigend mir, indeß ich
> Sinne nach Nahmen für dich, vorüber!

> If I could, like the morning winds, I'd go up
>
> With you, with you! But you smile at the singer,
> At the presumption of one who'd be like you,
> And, as you wander in silence above me
> I think of names for you.

The Main

Probably written some time in the summer of 1799, possibly before "Evening Fantasy" and "In the Morning"; first published in the *Brittischer Damenkalender*. This Alcaic ode was later reworked into "The Neckar."

The Main—A river in Germany.

Sunium—A famous cape at the end of Attica, on which a temple to Poseidon stands.

Olympieion—The temple to Zeus in Athens.

Ionia—The Greek coastal area of Asia Minor.

Five Epigrams

The following five epigrams were probably written in late summer of 1799 as Hölderlin made plans for his journal *Iduna*, which never saw the light of day (the publisher had asked that writers with name recognition like Goethe and Schiller contribute to the journal, and Hölderlin was unable to get their support). "Sophocles," "The Angry Poet," and "The Jokers" were first published in 1826 (the titles of the latter two given by the editor Gustav Schwab), "Root of All Evil" in 1896, and "Προς εαυτον," written on a different manuscript and probably earlier than the other four, in 1916.

Προς εαυτον—Greek for "to himself" (no diacritical marks in
  manuscript).
his letter / Kills, but his spirit brings spirits to life—Compare 2 Corinthians
  3:6: "for the letter killeth, but the spirit giveth life" (Beissner).
Root of All Evil—Compare Timothy 6:10: "For the love of money is
  the root of all evil" (Beissner).
that there be only one and one only—Perhaps a reference to Fichte's con-
  cept of the absolute I, of which Hölderlin was an early critic.
  But the epigram also finds echo in Hölderlin's politics. In a letter
  to his friend Isaac Sinclair in December of 1798, for example,
  Hölderlin wrote that "[i]t is also good, and even the first condi-
  tion of all life and organization, that there be no monarchical
  power in heaven or on earth. Absolute monarchy abolishes itself
  everywhere because it is without an object." And in a letter to his
  brother on June 4, 1799: "*Not that they [people] are the way they are, but
  that they maintain that that which they are is the only way [to be] and do not
  want to acknowledge anything else, that is the evil. I am an enemy of*
  egoism, despotism, and misanthropy [. . .]"

What Is Mine

This Alcaic ode was written in the fall of 1799. Originally titled "Am
Herbsttag" ("On an Autumn Day"), it was first published in 1846.

I was once—That is, he was once a happy man.
lasting resting place—Knaupp points out that this may be an allusion
  to Paul's letter to the Hebrews, 13:14: "For here we have no con-
  tinuing city, but we seek one to come." In German "continuing
  city" is *bleibende Stadt*, and in the poem the German phrase is *blei-
  bende Stätte* (literally: lasting place).

VARIANTS
[line 27]—In an earlier draft *Tageslichte* (daylight) reads *großen Göttern*
  (the great gods).
[line 28]—In an earlier draft *Armer* (pauper) reads *Fremder*
  (stranger).

[Each day I walk . . .]

The Alcaic ode was probably composed sometime in the spring of 1800, soon after Hölderlin left the Gontard household. First published in 1846.

forest's green—"Green" here should be understood as an adjective and not a noun. The line is missing one syllable. Hölderlin's handwritten draft has no extra space between "green" and "in" for another word, but the *FHA* has inserted one. Beissner adds *Laub* (leaves, foliage). I've followed Knaupp and left it as it seems to appear in the handwritten draft.

blissful face—Susette Gontard.

departs and returns—Compare the end of Hölderlin's novel *Hyperion*: "The arteries depart and return to the heart and all is one single, eternal, glowing life" (Beissner).

[Go now and set, O beautiful sun . . .]

Written on an envelope, this Alcaic draft was composed in the first half of 1800 while Hölderlin was still in Homburg. First published in 1846 under the title "Am Abend" ("In the Evening").

The following four poems follow the order in which they appeared in *Aglaia: Jahrbuch für Frauenzimmer auf 1801*, though most were begun (and in some cases finished) considerably earlier—perhaps even before some of the earlier shorter odes.

The Gods

This Alcaic ode was written by June 1800 at the latest (the *FHA* has it as early as 1797–98).

Heidelberg

This Asclepiadic ode was begun in early summer 1798 at the latest and perhaps finished in 1800. A later revision, perhaps in 1803–04, changes the beginning of the fourth stanza (see variants).

bridge—The Alte Neckarbrücke (also known as the Karl-Theodor-Brücke), a bridge that spans the Neckar in Heidelberg.

soar and vault [. . .] *Spanning*—The German verb here is *sich schwingen*, which can be said of birds (that they soar) and bridges (that they span).

gods—Earlier drafts name Apollo as the god who visited the poet.

streets / Joyfully rest below gardens—The gardens were installed on the ruins of the destroyed city in 1689, so the streets lie below them (Schmidt).

VARIANTS

[lines 10–12]—An earlier draft reads:

> Da ich müßig und still über die Brüke gieng
>   Ein vertriebener Wandrer
>   Der vor Menschen und Büchern floh.

> I went idly and silently over the bridge,
>   A banished wanderer
>   Who fled before people and books.

[lines 13–16]—I follow here the *GSA* reconstruction of the later revision to this stanza, including the emended "*ward*."

> Aber ferne vom Ort, wo er geboren [ward]
>   Zog die dunkle die Lust, welche den Halbgott treibt,
>   Liebend unterzugehen
>   Dir den deinen, den Strom hinab.

> But far from the site of his birth
>   The dark one, the desire that drives the demigod
>   To perish going down to you and yours
>   While loving, draws the river down.

The Neckar

This Alcaic ode is a reworking of "The Main."

Neckar—A river in Hölderlin's native Swabia.

Pactolus—A river in Lydia known in antiquity for its wealth of gold. Midas washed himself in the river after he had received the golden touch.

Smyrna—Port city in Asia Minor (today's Izmir).

Ilium—Troy.

Sunium—See the notes to "The Main."

Olympieion—See the notes to "The Main."

orange grove—Compare lines 31–32 of "Man" and lines 20–22 of "The nations were silent, they slumbered . . ."

mastic tree—An evergreen shrub whose resin was especially valued in antiquity.

VARIANTS

[line 21]—The *FHA* reads *Götterbilder* (images of gods) for *Gottesbilder* (images of god) in the manuscript.

Empedocles

This Alcaic ode, begun in 1797, was written around the same time as "Buonaparte" (see the notes to "The peoples were silent, they slumbered . . ."). It is unclear when it was completed.

Empedocles—A Greek philosopher, politician, poet, and healer (5th century B.C.E.) who allegedly claimed divinity because of his knowledge and, according to legend, committed suicide by throwing himself into the Aetna volcano. Hölderlin tried several times to write a tragedy of the philosopher's life, but he never succeeded.

the whim of the queen once melted / Pearls in wine—According to Pliny, Cleopatra, in order to win a wager with Antony that she could consume 10 million sesterces in one meal, dissolved a pearl worth that amount in wine and then drank the mixture. Compare line 32 of "Stuttgart."

And if love no longer held me in its grasp—Compare the end of "The Oaks."

To the Germans *[fourteen stanzas]*

This incomplete Asclepiadic ode, an expansion of the earlier two-stanza "To the Germans," was probably conceived in late summer of 1800 (the *GSA* places it nearer the turn of the century); the first twelve stanzas were first published in 1846. After the last verse translated here, there is a confusion of lines in the handwritten manuscript. The *FHA* sees the last three fragmentary lines, which I've included in the text, as key words for a later expansion. A very rough draft of lines stands around these key words.

fatherland—see the note to "Dying for the Fatherland."
Pindus and Helicon, / And Parnassus—Greek mountains (mountain chain in the case of Pindus) sacred to Apollo and the Muses. Parnassus, one of the highest mountains in Greece, was also sacred to Dionysius.
judge—Refers to a female judge.

VARIANTS
I follow here the *FHA* reconstruction of the draft conclusion, though Sattler leaves the "key words" out.

Aber ihr!
    Helle Morgen und ihr Stunden der Nacht! wie oft,
       O wie
                          Richterin!
    Wenn er ihn sah,
    Nachwelt! hab ich
       den Wagen deines Triumphs
und die Beute gesehn,
       Und die Wilden in goldenen Ketten,
Und es sangen die Priester des Friedens
       dem liebenden Volk und seinem
          Genius Wonnegesang! in den Hainen
          des Frühlings!

But you!
    Bright morning and you hours of the night! How often,
       O how
                     judge!

When he saw him,
    Afterworld! I've seen
        the chariot of your triumph
and the booty,
    And the beasts in golden chains,
    And the priests of peace sang
        to the loving people and their
            genius a song of rapture! In the groves
            of spring!

Rousseau

This incomplete draft is a reworking in Alcaic meter of the Asclep-
iadic "To the Germans." It was first published in 1911.

You have lived!—Compare Horace Book III, Ode 29, lines 41–43:
    "mastery / over himself shall be his who daily / can say: 'I have
    lived [. . .]'"[10] (Beissner).
ed you too—The *ge* in German signals the beginning of a past parti-
    ciple, which in conjunction with the auxiliary *hast* would yield a
    past tense here, so I have used the ending of the simple past in
    English ("ed").
rays from a better time—Compare line 8 of "Time was the gods walked
    with men . . ." and line 16 of "Love."
their soul—The *ihre* (their or her/its) in *ihre Seele* (their soul) in the
    German can also refer grammatically to *die Sprache* (language).
    Compare the similar construction in line 28 of "Love."
human spirit—The German for this phrase (*Des Menschen Geist*) is am-
    biguous—it might also be read as "the spirit of the man," that
    is, of Rousseau.
completion—The German *Vollendung*, literally "full ending," also has
    the sense of "perfection."

VARIANTS
[line 6]—In an earlier draft *Ihm zeigt ein Gott ins Freie* (A god has
    shown them [into] the open) reads *Ihm eilt der Geist ins Freie* (Their
    spirit hastened into the open).
[line 17]—The *FHA* reads here *So eile denn zufrieden* (so hasten then
    content).

[line 28]—In an earlier draft *gefunden* (found) reads *gestillet* (stilled).
[line 29]—The *FHA* strikes *verstanden* (understood).

The following five poems follow the order in which they appear in Hölderlin's Homburg papers, except for "Her Recovery," which appears after an earlier draft of "The Course of Life" in his Stuttgart notebooks. The Homburg versions of these odes are fair copies with minor revisions that were probably undertaken after the summer of 1801.

Home *[six stanzas]*

An expansion of the two-stanza Alcaic ode of the same title, this poem was written in the summer of 1800 and first published in the *Würtembergisches Taschenbuch auf das Jahr 1806 für Freunde und Freundinnen des Vaterlands*. It is unknown whether Hölderlin saw this poem into print.

VARIANTS
[lines 23–24]—In an earlier draft the last two lines read:
  Drum bleib' mirs nur, bis mit der theuern
    Haabe das friedliche Land mich aufnimmt.

  So let it be for me until the peaceful country
    Takes me up with my costly possessions.

Love

Expanded from the two-stanza Asclepiadic ode "The Unpardonable" in the summer of 1800. Hölderlin attempted to revise the fair copy with pencil in 1803–04; Sattler tries to incorporate these revisions into his constituted text of the poem, but since they are so incomplete he can only take up a few minor changes. I have thus gone with Beissner's text, save for a few commas he seems to have added. The poem was first published in 1826.

O grateful ones—One of the few instances of irony in Hölderlin (Beissner).
cares—Compare line 8 of "Vulcan" (Beissner).

sign of the better times—Compare line 8 of "Time was the gods walked with men . . ." and line 27 of "Rousseau" (Beissner).

their soul—The *ihre* (their or her/its) in *ihre Seele* (their soul) can also refer grammatically to *die Sprache* (language). Compare the similar construction in line 30 of "Rousseau."

people's voice—The German word here is *Laut*, which usually means "sound" or "tone."

VARIANTS

[line 6]—An earlier version reads *Da die Tochter der Nacht* (Since the daughter of night) in place of *Da die knechtische jezt* (Now that we're slaves).

The Course of Life *[four stanzas]*

This expansion of the two-stanza Asclepiadic ode of the same title was composed in the summer of 1800, and the fair copy produced then was probably reworked in the fall of 1801. The fair copy without the revisions was first published in 1826, and the version with the revisions (which is the version I've translated) in 1914.

our arc does not return—Compare Heraclitus, fragment 51: "They do not comprehend how, in differing, it [the universe] agrees with itself—a backward-turning connection, like that of a bow and a lyre"[11] (Beissner). *Bogen* in German can mean both "arc" and "bow."

Upward or down—Heraclitus, fragment 60: "The path up and down is one and the same"[12] (Schmidt).

Let man test everything—Compare 1 Thessalonians 5:21: "but test everything, hold fast to what is good"[13] (Beissner).

set out—Compare line 41 of "Bread and Wine."

VARIANTS

[line 5]—An earlier draft reads *lezter Nacht* (the last night) for *heil'ger Nacht* (the holy night).

[lines 7–8]—An earlier draft reads *Weht ein lebender Othem / Nicht im untersten Orkus auch?* (Doesn't a living breath / Blow in deepest hell too?) for *Herrscht im schiefsten Orkus / Nicht ein Grades* (Doesn't

a straightness [...] / prevail [...] / in the crookedest bend of hell). The fair copy before the revision has *nüchternen Orkus* (sober hell) and *liebender Othem* (loving breath).

Her Recovery *[five stanzas]*

The text for this Asclepiadic ode, an expansion of the earlier ode of the same title, was probably composed in the summer of 1800 in response to an illness of Susette Gontard. First published in 1914, the manuscript is more convoluted than most and the ending is quite unclear. Hölderlin reworked the last fair copy but never completed it. I've followed the *GSA* in using the underlying fair copy as the basis for the text.

VARIANTS

[lines 12–16]—The reworking of the concluding stanzas begins with the last line of the third stanza:

Seine Blume den Tagsgott an,

Neugeborene, sei unter den Hoffenden
   Sei nun freudiges Licht unserer dämmernden
      Kranken Erde willkommen
         Bei den Weinenden, Götterkind!

His flower gleams to the god of day,

You newly born one, be among the hoping ones,
   Be now welcome, joyful light, to our
      Sick and twilit Earth, be welcome
         Among the weeping ones, child of gods!

Diotima *("You fall silent . . .")* *[six stanzas]*

An expansion of the two-stanza Alcaic ode of the same title, composed perhaps in the summer of 1800 with the expansion of the other shorter odes, or perhaps finished and sent to Neuffer already in 1798, as the *FHA* surmises. It was first published in 1826, but without the fifth stanza. The basis for the text is a fair copy; the subsequent beginnings of a penciled-in reworking of this fair copy in 1803–04 (after Susette Gontard's death) have not been incorporated in the text translated here. The most significant revisions are to the second stanza (see variants).

Those royal ones—The Greeks, especially the Athenians (Beissner).
Remembering still their source in resounding hearts—Compare lines 3 and 9
    in "The Fettered River" and line 42 of "The Poet's Calling."
Tartarus—The lowest region of hell.
time heals—See note to the two-stanza "Diotima."

VARIANTS
[lines 5–8]—The second stanza pencil revision:

    Die Freigebornen, die des Alpheus sich
        Noch jezt, und jenes Lands und Olympias
           Und des Gesanges sich und ihres
               Immerumfangenden Himmels freuen,

    The free-born ones, they who rejoice still
        In Alpheus and that country, and Olympia
           And the song, and their
               Ever-embracing heaven,

Alpheus—A Greek river god.
[line 20]—The later pencil revision replaces the concept of *Natur*
    (nature) with *Leben* (life).

Return to the Homeland

Conceived probably in June of 1800 and first published in the journal *Für Herz und Geist* in 1801; a later revision of this Alcaic ode was probably undertaken in 1803–04.

messengers of Italy—Compare the "Italian breezes" in line 11 of the
    fourth stanza in "Stuttgart."

VARIANTS
[lines 7–10]—These lines were changed in the later revision to:

Und du mein Haus, wo Felder mich und
    Heilige Schriften noch auferzogen!

Wie lang ists her, wie lange! die Alten sind
    Dahin und draußen starben die Völker auch,

    And you my house, where fields and
        Holy writs raised me,

How long it's been, how long! The ancient ones
    Are gone and outside the people died too,

The Poet's Calling

This reworking of the Alcaic "To Our Great Poets," begun probably in the summer of 1800 and finished a year later, was first published in the journal *Flora* in 1802.

Bacchus—Compare "Bread and Wine."

nourish themselves and work—The German is *sich wehren*, which would normally mean "defend/protect themselves." Beissner points out, however, that in the Swabian dialect this word meant "to work" in the sense of working and improving a household.

recently the thunder—The French Revolution and the revolutionary wars (Mieth).

He remembers his origin—Compare line 9 of the six-stanza "Diotima" ("You fall silent . . .") and lines 3 and 9 of "The Fettered River."

when the exalted / One works in their fields—Apollo, as punishment for killing Gaia's son, the dragon Python, had to work for nine years as a cowherd for King Admetus.

Count and name all the stars—Compare Psalm 147: "He telleth the number of stars; he calleth them all by their names" (Schmidt).

VARIANTS

[lines 53–64]—In place of the last three stanzas stand these two in an earlier draft:

Anbetungswürdig aber und ewigfroh,
  Lebst du Natur, den Deinen und einig sind
    Im Glanze deines Lichts, in deinem
      Geiste die Sterblichen, die dich lieben;

Wohin sie gehn, die goldene Wolke folgt,
  Erheiternd, und befruchtend, beschirmend auch
    Und keiner Würden brauchts, und keiner
      Waffen, so lange der Gott uns nah bleibt.

But, Nature, to your kin you live worthy of worship
  And always in gladness, and the mortals
    Who love you live united
      In the brightness of your light, in your spirit;

Wherever they go the golden cloud follows,
  Brightening, enriching, sheltering too,
    And no ranks are needed and no weapons,
      So long as the god remains near us.

In an even earlier draft, the final phrase read *so lange der Gott nicht fehlet* (so long as the god isn't absent). Beissner and Schmidt, in light of the above two stanzas, interpret the last line "till God's absence has helped" as ironic. This seems improbable. One of Hölderlin's central concerns was the absence of the gods and the poet's relationship to the people and the divine in light of this fact. For Hölderin, the task of the poet was to awaken the hearts of human beings to the traces of the divine through the holy word. It's hard to believe that Hölderlin would play ironically with this idea, especially given that he hardly ever uses irony. In contrast to Beissner, I take the last line to mean that only when we truly experience the absence of the gods will we begin to be able to relate to the divine. In this way the absence of the gods can help us, for only the painful experience of their absence can awaken us to our need of them.

Voice of the People [second version; eighteen stanzas]
This expansion of the one-stanza Alcaic ode of the same title was probably begun in 1800 (the "first version") and finished in 1801 (the

"second version," translated here) for publication in the journal *Flora* (1802). The first version doesn't include the Xanthus legend, and the last three stanzas are significantly different (see variants).

For mortal beings forget themselves, and once they've / Wandered their allotted paths—Compare Pindar's Seventh Isthmian, lines 17–18 ("for mortals forget / what doesn't reach the highest peak of song") and lines 40–42 ("Daily I pursue undisturbed / a pleasant course till I reach my alloted span of old age").

From rock to rock—Compare line 23 of "Hyperion's Song of Fate."

art that's long—Compare the Latin saying *ars longa, vita brevis* (art is long, life is short).

Xanthus—A Lycian city in Asia Minor that was besieged by the Persians in the sixth century B.C.E. Rather than face capture, the men, according to Herodotus, "collected their women, children, slaves and other property and shut them up in the citadel, set fire to it and burnt it to the ground. Then having sworn to do or die, they marched out to meet the enemy and were killed to a man."[14] This was the legend the Xanthians knew in Roman times when the Roman general Brutus, in 42 B.C.E., besieged the town with his army. Rather than surrender, the Xanthians again destroyed themselves. According to Plutarch, "the Lycians were of a sudden possessed with a strange and incredible desperation; such a frenzy as cannot be better expressed than by calling it a violent appetite to die . . ."[15] They proceeded to set their city ablaze and leapt into the fire or fell on swords rather than accept the distraught Brutus' offer of aid.

one to interpret the holy lore—Compare Pindar's Second Olympian, line 85: "but the crowd need interpreters"[16] (Schmidt).

VARIANTS

[lines 41–52]—The final three stanzas of the earlier fair copy are quite different than the later version:

Nicht, o ihr Theuern, ohne die Wonnen all
    Des Lebens giengt ihr unter, ein Festtag ward
        Noch Einer euch zuvor, und dem gleich
            Haben die Anderen keins gefunden.

Doch sicherer ists und größer und ihrer mehr
   Die Allen Alles ist, der Mutter werth,
      In Eile zögernd, mit des Adlers
         Lust die geschwungnere Bahn zu wandeln.

Drum weil sie fromm ist, ehre den Göttern ich
   Zu lieb des Volkes Stimme, die ruhige,
      Doch um der Götter und der Menschen
         Willen, sie ruhe zu gern nicht immer.

Not without the blissful joys of life
   Did you perish going down, O dear ones,
      There was a celebration day before you,
         And the others have found no day like that.

Yet it's more certain and greater and more than she
   Who is all to all, of value to mothers,
      Hesitating in her rush, with the eagle's desire
         To soar the winding way.

Therefore since she's devout I honor the gods
   For the sake of her the people's voice, the calm and rested one,
      Yet for the sake of the gods and men
         May she not always rest too gladly.

The Poet's Courage [*second version*]
The first version of this Asclepiadic ode was probably begun in fall
of 1800, and the second version was finished in late 1800, early 1801.
Walter Benjamin uses this later version in his essay "Two Poems by
Friedrich Hölderlin," but mistakenly refers to it as the earlier ver-
sion. This second version was first published in 1885. The poem was
later reworked into "Timidity."

sun god—Apollo, also the god of the Muses and poets.
equable mind—Literal translation of Horace's "aequam memento" in
   Book II, Ode 3 (Beissner).

Dichtermuth.

[Erste Fassung]

Sind denn dir nicht verwandt alle Lebendigen?
    Nährt zum Dienste denn nicht selber die Parze dich?
        Drum! so wandle nur wehrlos
            Fort durchs Leben und sorge nicht!

Was geschiehet, es sei alles geseegnet dir
    Sei zur Freude gewandt! oder was könnte denn
        Dich belaidigen, Herz, was
            Da begegnen, wohin du sollst?

Denn, wie still am Gestad, oder in silberner
    Fernhintönender Fluth, oder auf schweigenden
        Wassertiefen der leichte
            Schwimmer wandelt, so sind auch wir,

Wir, die Dichter des Volks gerne, wo Lebendes
    Um uns athmet und wallt, freudig, und jedem hold;
        Jedem trauend; wie sängen
            Sonst wir jedem den eignen Gott?

Wenn die Wooge denn auch einen der Muthigen
    Wo er treulich getraut, schmeichlend hinunterzieht,
        Und die Stimme des Sängers
            Nun in blauender Halle schweigt;

Freudig starb er und noch klagen die Einsamen,
    Seine Haine, den Fall ihres Geliebtesten
        Öfters tönet der Jungfrau
            Vom Gezweige sein freundlich Lied.

Wenn des Abends vorbei Einer der Unsern kömmt,
    Wo der Bruder ihm sank, denket er manches wohl
        An der warnenden Stelle,
            Schweigt und gehet gerüsteter.

The Poet's Courage

[first version]

Aren't all living creatures kin to you?
    Doesn't fate herself raise you to serve her ends?
        So then wander defenseless
            Through life without care!

Whatever happens, may it all be a blessing to you,
    Be well-versed in joy! Or what could
        Offend you, heart, what could
            Affront you there on your way?

For as the nimble swimmer quietly moves
    By the shore, or through the silver and far-sounding
        Tide, or over the silent
            And watery depths, so do we, too,

The poets of the people, gladly abide
    Where life surges and breathes all around us,
        And we're joyful, fondly inclined to all and trusting;
            How else would we sing to each his own god?

If a wave though, flattering, pulls down one of the brave
    Where he'd loyally given his trust,
        And the voice of the singer grows
            Silent now in the hall turning blue;

Gladly he died, and his lonely groves
    Still mourn the fall of their most beloved;
        Through the branches his friendly song
            Often sounds to a virgin.

When, in the evening, one of our kin passes the place
    Where his brother sank down, he thinks hard
        At this site of warning, grows silent,
            And goes on more fully prepared.

more fully prepared—The German can also mean "more armed."

The Fettered River

This Alcaic ode, originally titled "Der Eisgang" ("The Ice Floe") was probably written in late 1800, early 1801; it was first published in 1826. Compare the reworked version "Ganymede."

you don't heed the origin—Compare line 9 of the six-stanza "Diotima" ("You fall silent . . .") and line 42 of "The Poet's Calling."

Son of the Ocean, the friend to the Titans—The Ocean was referred to as "the friend to the Titans," although Hesiod refers to him as one of the Titans himself. Oceanus is the father of all rivers and waters.

broken pieces—The chains, that is, the broken pieces of ice (Beissner).

arms of his father—The Ocean.

The Blind Singer

Originally titled "Täglich Gebet" ("Daily Prayer"), this Alcaic ode was composed, according to Beissner and Mieth, in the summer of 1801, but Sattler thinks late 1800 more probable; it was first published in 1826. See the later reworked version "Chiron."

Ελυσεν αινον αχος απ' ομματων Αρης.—Sophocles' *Ajax* line 706 (lacking diacritical marks in Hölderlin's version), which in John Moore's translation runs "The harsh god has taken / His siege of grief from our eyes." Hölderlin himself had translated this play, sticking close to the Greek word order for this line. His translation, translated into English, might go something like "Lifted the terrible grief from our eyes did Ares."

where are you, light?—Compare "To the Sun God," "Sunset," and "To Hope."

but night enthralls—Compare the opening stanza of "Bread and Wine."

wings / Of heaven—The birds of heaven (Beissner). Compare line 5 of "Stuttgart."

from one / Hour to the next—Compare "Hyperion's Song of Fate."

Thunderer—Zeus.

Stuttgart

This elegy was begun in September of 1800 at the earliest and re-
vised in 1804. It was first published in Seckendorf's *Musenalmanach
für das Jahr 1807* as "Die Herbstfeier" ("The Autumn Festival"), but
without Hölderlin's knowledge. As with the elegies "Bread and
Wine" and "Homecoming," I've followed the *GSA* in using the last
fair copy of the poem, even though this manuscript contains some
later revisions. Most of these made it into the 1807 publication, and
I've included the most significant in the variants below. It's just as
possible these changes represent Hölderlin's final intentions; the
FHA uses them in its final version of the poem.

Siegfried Schmidt—Schmidt was a friend of Hölderlin's when Hölderlin
   lived in Homburg.
hall—Compare the third line of the fourth stanza in "Bread and
   Wine" (Beissner).
bound wings—Compare line 17 of "The Blind Singer" (Beissner).
realm of song—Compare line 4 of "The Walk in the Country."
holy staffs—The thyrsus, a staff of ivy and grapes tipped with a pine
   cone, was used by Dionysius' followers.
communal god—The wine god.
pearls—See line 5 of "Empedocles."
Barbarossa—Frederick I of the Staufer dynasty, Herzog of Swabia,
   crowned king of Germany in Frankfurt in 1152, and later Holy
   Roman Emperor.
Christoph—Herzog of Württemberg from 1550 to 1568.
Conradin—Last of the Staufers, killed in 1268.
Italian breezes—Compare line 1 of "Return to the Homeland" (Beissner).
guest [. . .] stranger—Hölderlin's friend Schmidt.
bright—In the sense of light and clear.
angels of the fatherland—Compare the first line of the sixth stanza in
   "Homecoming."

VARIANTS
The most significant of the later revisions occur in the third and
   fourth stanzas:

[line 44]—*gestaltenden* (forming) for *gefühlteren* (more strongly felt).

[line 51]—*So arm ist des Volks Mund* (Thus is the mouth of the people poor) for *wie du fielst, so fallen Starke* (Strong ones fall as you did).

[line 53]—*fürstlich* (princely) for *heilig* (holy).

[line 54]—*Reich in Tagen des Herbsts* (Rich in days of the fall) for *Und in Tagen des Herbsts* (And on days in the fall).

[line 55]—*ernstunmündigen* (literally, seriously minor, that is, serious and under age) for *herzerhebenden* (that raises hearts).

[lines 56–59]—

> Schlank auch selber, und jung, aber vom lauteren Gott
> Auch gleich Rossen dahin, wie die Alten, die göttlicherzognen
> Dichter, heimischen Lichts, ziehen das Land wir hinauf.
> Wirtemberg ists. Dort von den uralt deutsamen Bergen

> Lithe ourselves too, and young, but by the purer god
> And like horses we're led there, like the ancients, the poets
> Reared by gods, of the native light, we roam through the land.
> It's Wirtemberg. There from the primordial, meaning-filled mountains

[line 62]—*biegen* (bend/curve) for *bauen* (build).

[lines 65–66]—*die See schikt / Ungeheures, sie schikt krankende Sonnen mit ihm* (the sea sends / Him monstrous things, it sends him suffering suns) for *die See schikt / Ihre Wolken, sie schikt prächtige Sonnen mit ihm* (the sea sends / Its clouds and it sends him magnificent suns).

[line 84]—*des Fürsten* (the prince's) for *den Sängern* (the singers').

[line 88]—*gemütliches Volk* (a comfortable/cozy/snug/homey people) for *ahnendes Volk* (a divining people, a people who guess at signs).

The Walk in the Country

Beissner has Hölderlin writing the first draft of this elegiac fragment in 1800, but Sattler places it in the spring of 1801 because of its content and style, and also because one of its drafts was written in close proximity to drafts of "Homecoming," which can be dated to the spring of 1801 with some certainty.

Because of the numerous drafts and the incomplete nature of the only fair copy, it is not at all clear how the text should be edited.

Beissner, Sattler, and Knaupp have come up with quite different texts. They all begin with the fair copy, which has a piece torn from the top where the title was written. The descenders of three barely discernible letters (decoded as "ast") lead them all to think the title of the fair copy was "Das Gasthaus" ("The Guest House"), but only Knaupp uses this title. Beissner and Sattler retain "The Walk in the Country" from an earlier draft.

Beissner stops his version in the *GSA* after the last full line in the fair copy; Knaupp includes the fragmentary elements of the fair copy as well as lines from an earlier draft that did not make it into the fair copy (see the variants below); Sattler includes all these elements and, between the end of the fair copy and the material Knaupp includes from the earlier draft, inserts from yet another draft some very fragmentary lines (which are really just notes). I've followed Beissner, for the most part, but have decided to include, following Knaupp and Sattler, the fragmentary lines of the fair copy. I have not followed Knaupp and Sattler in using the material from the earlier draft, nor Sattler in inserting the fragmentary notes between the end of the fair copy and these lines.

Different sections of the poem have been published at various times. The first eighteen lines were first published in 1826; lines 19–34 in 1896; lines 35–40 in 1951; and the fragmentary lines in 1976.

Landauer—Christian Landauer, a Stuttgart businessman and friend of Hölderlin.
empty of song—Compare line 5 of "Stuttgart."
adage—This poem deals with a roofing or "topping out" ceremony for an inn, celebrated when the roof was put on a new building. Traditionally, the head carpenter would give a blessing from on top of the just completed roof.

VARIANTS
These lines occur at the end of an earlier draft:

Aber fraget mich eins, was sollen Götter im Gasthaus?

Dem antwortet, sie sind, wie Liebende, feierlich seelig,
    Wohnen bräutlich sie erst nur in den Tempeln allein
Aber so lang ein Kleineres noch nach jenen genannt ist,
    Werden sie nimmer und nimmer die Himmlischen uns
Denn entweder es herrscht ihr Höchstes blinde gehorcht dann
    Anderes
Oder sie leben in Streit, der bleibt nicht oder es schwindet
    Wie beim trunkenen Mahl, alles
Diß auch verbeut sich selbst, auch Götter bindet ein Schiksaal
    Denn die Lebenden all bindet des Lebens Gesez.

[am Rand]
    Singen wollt ich leichten Gesang, doch nimmer gelingt mirs,
        Denn es machet mein Glük nimmer die Rede mir leicht.

But someone asks me, why are gods in the guest house?

I answered him, they are festively blessed like lovers,
    At first they live as brides only in temples alone,
But, so long as a trifle's still named after them,
    For us they'll never be gods,
For either you highest one rules blindly obeyed, then
    Another
Or they live in strife that doesn't remain, or it fades
    As at a drunken feast, all
This too cannot be, a fate binds gods too
    For the law of life binds all those alive.

[written sideways on the edge of the paper]
    I wanted to sing a light and nimble song, but I never was able,
        For my happiness never makes speaking easy for me.

Bread and Wine

Begun as early as the summer of 1800 before "The Walk in the Country," this elegy, originally titled "Der Weingott" ("The Wine God"), is one of Hölderlin's more famous poems. The fair copy on which the German text is based, completed perhaps as early as spring of 1801 or even in 1802, is full of revisions to the last five stanzas. Most German editions have not published the revisions and have used only the fair copy underlying them; this is the basis of this first version translated here (the status of this version is controversial—see the notes to the "second version" below). The first stanza of this "first version" was first published in 1807 under the title "Die Nacht" ("The Night"), and the poem was first published in its entirety in 1896.

Heinze—Hölderlin met and became friends with Wilhelm Heinze (1749–1803) in 1796. Heinze's novel *Ardinghello und die glückseligen Inseln* had a strong influence on Hölderlin.

[stanza 1]—Compare "Evening Fantasy" and "Leisure" (Beissner).

set out—The same verb is used in the last line of the four-stanza "The Course of Life."

Isthmus—The Isthmus of Corinth (Beissner).

Parnassus—Mountain near Corinth that was holy to Apollo and Dionysius. Delphi lay on its southern slope.

Delphian—Of the oracle of Delphi, Apollo's oracle; believed to be the center ("navel") of the earth.

Olympus—The mountain Olympus.

Cithaeron—A mountain range between Attica and Boetia.

Thebe—Daughter of the river god Asopus and the nymph Metope.

Ismenus—River near Thebes, the traditional birthplace of Dionysus.

Cadmus—Founder of Thebes.

the coming god—Dionysus.

Festive hall—See line 3 of "Stuttgart."

far-striking—A common attribute of Apollo in Homer (Mieth).

Clarity!—The German word is *heiter*, which can mean clear, serene, cheerful, bright, fair (weather).

in truth—In the German this word stands at the end of the ninth line of the fifth stanza—the precise midpoint of the poem. It's the only use of the word "truth" in the poem.

consoling, fulfilled and ended the heavenly feast—First mention of Christ in the poem (Beissner). Appearing at the end of the second triad of stanzas, which describes the end of the reign of the Olympian gods, Christ becomes the last of the Olympians.

how much the gods want to spare us—Rare example of irony in Hölderlin.

wine god—Dionysus.

calm genius—Jesus Christ.

what was great became too great—See line 10 of the sixth stanza in "Homecoming."

pine and the wreath of ivy—The thyrsus (see notes to "Stuttgart").

Hesperia—Western Europe.

son of the highest—Reference to both Christ and Dionysus, who was the son of Zeus.

the Syrian—Jesus Christ.

torchbearer—Reference to Christ as the bringer of light as well as Dionysus, who was often called the "torchbearer" (Mieth).

Titan—Probably a reference to the Titan Typhon, who lived under the earth and caused earthquakes and Mount Aetna to erupt (Mieth).

Cerberus—Three-headed guard dog of Hades who kept the living from entering and the dead from leaving. According to legend, Cerberus peacefully let Dionysus pass when he went to fetch his mother Semele from the underworld.

VARIANTS

Some significant variants from the earlier draft "The Wine God":

[line 32]—*Menschliche* (something human) for *Haltbare* (something solid to hold to).

[lines 41–42]—*daß wir das Unsrige schauen, / Daß wir heiligen, was heilig den Unsrigen ist.* ([Come] behold what's ours, / And hallow what's holy to our kin.)

[line 54]—*Dort is das Sehnen, o dort schauen zu Göttern wir auf.* (There is the longing, O there we gaze up to the gods.)

[lines 69–70]—*so tief, so ewig die Nacht ist, / So vermessen die Noth* (so deep and eternal is night, / So audacious is need) for *so weit es gehet, das uralt / Zeichen, von Eltern geerbt* (The ancient sign, passed down from our parents, / Echoes as far as it can).

[lines 87–89] —

So ist der Mensch; nicht Anderes kanns; es fördert das Andre
    Freundlich und feindlich nur heilige Tiefen heraus;
Denn der Karge verbargs; nun aber nennt er sein Liebstes,

Thus is man; it can be no other way; the other way
    Mines, as a friend and a foe, the holy depths only;
For the bareness concealed it; now, though, he names what is dearest,

[line 150] — *Orkus, Elysium ists* (It's Orcus, Elysium) for *Frucht von Hesperien ists!* (the fruit of Hesperia!).

[lines 155–56] — *als Freudenbote, des Weines / Göttlichgesandter Geist* (as the messenger of joy, the divinely / Sent spirit of wine) for *als Fakelschwinger des Höchsten / Sohn, der Syrier* (the son of the highest, the Syrian, as torchbearer).

Homecoming

Begun in the spring of 1801, this poem was first published in the journal *Flora* in 1802. Perhaps the last elegy Hölderlin wrote, it was inspired by his return home from Switzerland, where he had been working as a house tutor in the town of Hauptwil. The poem follows his return over Lake Constance to the town of Lindau. Hölderlin subsequently made a fair copy of the poem from the *Flora* version to which he then made changes, possibly in the winter of 1803–04. Sattler and Knaupp present both versions of the poem (the *Flora* version and the fair copy with changes). The changes are to the last three stanzas, which I've included in the variants below.

lambent night lingers — The seeming paradox of a bright, radiant night evokes the image of a breaking morning in the mountains when the mountain valleys are still in darkness (Beissner).

Composing — The German word *dichtend* means to create a written work of art, but the word's etymological roots also mean simply to create in the sense of the Greek ποιεῖν.

loving strife — Compare line 6 of "To Diotima" ("Come and look …"). Compare also the Greek philosopher Empedocles' key concepts of love and strife.

thunderbird—The eagle, Zeus' bird.

roses—The reflection of the morning sun in the snow (Mieth).

Lindau—German town bordering Switzerland and Austria. Hölderlin passed through Lindau on entering his native Swabia when he returned from a trip to Switzerland.

Como—Northern Italian town near the Swiss border.

as the sun moves through day—West (the direction the sun moves), i.e., the direction in which one would travel when leaving Lindau's city gates (Beissner).

Neckar—A river in Hölderlin's native Swabia.

its faith—In the sense of "loyalty."

Angels of the house—Compare the first line in the sixth stanza of "Stuttgart."

And made noble and younger—The German appears to be imperative but is subjunctive (Beissner).

our joy is almost too small—Compare line 10 of the eighth stanza in "Bread and Wine" (Beissner).

VARIANTS

Significant later revisions to the last three stanzas:

[line 72]—*Und vielseitig ein Ort* (And the many facets of a place) for *Und in Bergen ein Ort* (and a place in the mountains).

[lines 77–80]—The *FHA* eliminates *das Deutsche* (what's German) from the following on the grounds that the line has one foot too many. Here is Knaupp's reconstruction:

Ja! das Alte noch ists! das Ständige. Viel ist, doch nichts, was
    Liebt und berühmt ist, läßt beinerne Treue zurük.
Blutlos. Aber der Schaz, das Deutsche, der unter des heiligen Friedens
    Bogen lieget, [...]

Yes, it's still what it was! What stays. It is much, yet nothing
    That loves and is famed abandons its faith made of bone.
Bloodless. But the treasure, what's German, lying under the rainbow of holy
    Peace [...]

[line 90]—*Bescheidenen ihr* (you modest ones) for *Erhaltenden ihr* (you who preserve).

[line 91]—*des Jünglings* (of the youth) for *des Haußes* (of the house).

[line 92]—*Daß sie helfen, zugleich gehen die Maase der Last* (So they'll help, and at the same time the measures of burden go).

[line 94]—*Wachen* (those awake) for *Frohen* (joyful ones).

[line 98]—*Tagesgewalt* (violence of day) for *Leben des Tags* (life of the day).

[line 99]—*Lautern* (pure one) for *Hohen* (high one); *Unfürstliches* (un-princely) for *Unschikliches* (unsuited).

[lines 101–2]—These are difficult lines to reconstruct. Knaupp, for example, strikes *Hehlings* (In secret).

> Aber Erfindungen gehn, als wenn Einfälle das Haus hat
> Hehlings. Arm ist der Geist der Deutscher. Geheimerer Sinn.

> But inventions depart as when the house collapses
> In secret. The spirit of Germans is poor. More secret meaning.

But inventions depart as when the house collapses / In secret.—The German is highly ambiguous here. The word for "depart" (*gehen*) might also mean "go" as in "work" or "function." Also, the word I've translated as "collapses" (*Einfälle*) can also mean "insight" or "idea." So an alternate reading of this line might be "But inventions work when the house has insights / In secret."

Bread and Wine [second version]

Sattler thinks the revision of "Bread and Wine" could have been undertaken after Hölderlin finished his Sophocles translations, sometime between 1802 and 1804, when he refashioned a large part of his metrical work. This revised version of "Bread and Wine" was first published as a complete poem in the *FHA* in 1976 (though Mieth included the last five stanzas in the appendix of his 1970 Hölderlin edition). I've followed the *FHA* version, which includes in the seventh stanza a ninth distich not included by Knaupp and Mieth.

Some lines are not perfectly metrical in this second version, and there are also a few gaps: the revision, though far-reaching, was not carried to completion. Some of the laconic and surprising language of this revision seems to foreshadow the language of Hölderlin's later hymns. The syntax is especially strange and difficult.

The *GSA* relegates these revisions to its critical apparatus and does not print them as a continuous reading text. More recent scholarship, including the *FHA*, has challenged the assumption that the underlying fair copy is the "real" or "final" poem (the revisions themselves are written on this fair copy). Wolfram Groddeck, co-editor of the elegy volume of the *FHA*, argues that we have lost a later fair copy based on these revisions. One piece of evidence he summons for this view is the fact that in the first stanza that was published (by Leo von Seckendorf, without Hölderlin's knowledge) on its own in 1807 under the title "The Night" uses the word *Eben-bild* (perfect image), which is the only change in the first stanza of the so-called revised version. Groddeck surmises that Seckendorf used a fair copy Hölderlin made based on the revised fair copy we possess, and that this revised (and final) version was titled "The Night." This reasoning is the basis for the *FHA* construction of the poem that incorporates the later revisions.

In contrast to this view, Bernhard Böschenstein claims that it is impossible to reconstruct a reliable "revised version" of "Bread and Wine" since the revision is incomplete.[17] He argues that Hölderlin had a "heightened experience of the spiritual presence of God during the weeks he spent in Southern France" that was too consuming to endure, and that the revision of "Bread and Wine" is an attempt to bring the poem—composed some two years earlier—in line with this experience. Thus, according to Böschenstein, we find that the revised stanzas move away from the divine presence in the first version by using a "protective language of signs." These revisions cannot be reconciled with many of the unrevised lines (e.g., "jubilant madness" in the third stanza) that manifest the presence of the gods, which in the second version is experienced as too dangerous and is defended against. Any combination of the two texts, Böschenstein therefore argues, must reflect their essential "incomparability." He feels constructed texts like that of the *FHA*, by melding the two texts, do not accurately reproduce the two versions' radically different experiences of the human relationship to the divine.

Fully aware of this tension, I have used the *FHA* text (except for two changes noted by Knaupp), as it seems that translating a revised version of the poem, even if a somewhat artificial construction, is the only reasonable way to present the "Bread and Wine" revisions to the English reader. Nevertheless, I have done this with the knowledge that the reconstruction is in several places highly speculative, and even metrically incorrect. In one particularly bold instance, the *FHA* moves a line several lines lower. This occurs in the seventh stanza, which in the first version has only eight distichs, one short of the full nine. Because Hölderlin marked dots in the revision to count out all nine distichs of this stanza, the *FHA* forms a (highly speculative) ninth distich by taking a relatively unrevised pentameter line ("Only at times . . .") and making it into the second line of a later distich by placing it between two back-to-back hexameters of the revision (these two hexameters next to each other being a glaring formal mistake Hölderlin could not have made). The reader should keep in mind, though, that if Böschenstein is correct, combining the revised and original texts at all—not just editorial decisions like the one described above—may be unfaithful to the spirit of the revision.

(For notes to lines unchanged in the revision, see the notes to the first version above.)

wondrous sign—It's possible to read this as both accusative (an object) and nominative (a subject), that is, as equating the weathers with the sign, or as having the weathers sing the sign.

a measure / Common to all, yet for each his own way is determined—Compare Pindar's Seventh Isthmian, lines 42–43: "For we all die the same. / Yet no fate is alike."

he comes and laughs transplanted, the god.—Dionysius, who came from the Indus to Greece.

stepping in turns—Refers to the performance of the Greek lyric chorus which would turn around at the end of each stanza (Knaupp).

A shell in Delphi—Hölderlin wrote this line's first word originally as *Schaale* (shell, husk) and later crossed out the *e*, possibly for reasons of rhythm (a common poetic practice). This change, though, produces an ambiguity: without the *e* the word becomes *schaal*, which means "lifeless" or "empty." Most commentators think Hölderlin intended to retain the meaning of *Schaale*.

Awkward [. . .] unsent—The German *ungeschikt* usually means awkward, unskilled, or clumsy; but it might also mean unsent (*schicken* being "to send"), or even be a play on *Geschik* (fate, which appears in the fifth stanza), in which case it would mean something like "unfated."

Tuscan—A type of column, stemming from the Etruscans, that has no adornments.

Ephesus—A major city in Roman Asia Minor, Ephesus was the home of Artemis' chief shrine and was also an important city in early Christianity. See Acts 19:23–35 (Knaupp); see also Revelation 2:1.

The spirit loves colonies—It is difficult to discern from the manuscript whether "colonies" is singular or plural.

pining away—*Verschmachten* can also mean "to be dying of thirst" or "to languish."

VARIANTS

[line 108]—An alternative reconstruction of this line adds *In Ephesus* to the beginning of the line: "But in Ephesus temple and image are an offense."

[line 111]—*Eine versuchung ist es. Versuch* (It's a temptation. A trial) is based on Knaupp's reconstruction. The *FHA* regards this line as a second option, which I've chosen because it is written above the revised line the *FHA* uses: *Trunkenheit ists, eigner Art* (It's drunkenness in its own way).

Nightsongs

The following nine poems were published as a group in Friedrich Wilmans' *Taschenbuch für das Jahr 1805*. Hölderlin referred to them as "Nightsongs" in a letter to Wilmans of December 1803, when he probably brought the poems to their final form; they were sent to Wilmans that winter and were the last poems Hölderlin himself saw into print. Perhaps the English poet Edward Young's immensely popular *Night Thoughts* was inspiration for the title. Their order below follows the order in which they were published by Wilmans.

Chiron

This Alcaic ode is a reworking of "The Blind Singer."

Chiron—The only wise and gentle centaur (half man and half horse), Chiron taught mankind the use of medicine and taught music to many heroes, including Achilles. After he was mistakenly shot by Hercules with an arrow dipped in the Hydra's venom ("since poison is between us"), the pain was so great that Chiron longed to die but couldn't because he was immortal. But after Hercules freed Prometheus, Chiron was allowed to die in Prometheus' place. (Prometheus, in refusing to reveal whom he had prophesied would overcome Zeus, was chained to a cliff to be eaten perpetually by vultures unless another god consented to die in his stead.)

thought-provoking—The German *nachdenklich* can also mean "contemplative, thoughtful, pensive."

must always / Move aside at times—The German plays on the similarly sounding *Zur Seite* (beside, aside) and *zu Zeiten* (at times). *Zur Seite* can mean either "move along beside, move sideways" or "move aside, move away." Schmidt points out that the light that must "always" move away "at times" refers to the periodical nature of the change between day and night, but is also, in much of Hölderlin's work, an analogy of humankind's relationship to divine fullness.

astounding night—Compare the characterization of night in "Bread and Wine" (Beissner).

When foal or garden refreshed you—According to Beissner, "the light frequently came to Chiron in his youth when it [the light] found pleasure in the young centaur (the foal) or his preserve (the garden)."

demigod [. . .] upright man—Hercules.

broke the spell of the sad wild fields—Now that humans try to rule nature rather than simply and naively live within it, the fields that used to seem like a garden are now wild fields in need of cultivation (Schmidt).

Thunderer—Zeus.

killing, the liberator—This refers to death, who, if he comes, will free Chiron of his torment.

divine injustice—Compare line 5 of "To the Fates."

Ruler with spurs [. . .] wandering star—The sun.

banished from cities—It is tempting to translate *unstädtisch*, which literally means un-city-like, as "unurban." For Hölderlin, though, *unstädtisch* is a translation of Sophocles' ἄπολις (Beissner), which means, according to Lidell and Scott's *Greek-English Lexicon*, "one without city, state or country, an outlaw."

clouds of wild beasts—Schmidt points out that the Greek word for cloud, νέφος, can be used in the sense of host, crowd, herd, and flock (e.g., a cloud of birds). Beissner points out that according to one version of the Chiron myth, Chiron's mother was Nephele (i.e., cloud).

prophecy—Hermes' account of Prometheus' future is that Zeus' eagle will eat Prometheus' liver until another god dies in Prometheus' stead.

Hercules' return—In the course of one of his labors, Hercules frees Prometheus by killing the eagle eating Prometheus' liver. Chiron awaits Hercules' return with news of this deed.

Tears

The first draft of this Alcaic ode, originally titled "Sapphos Schwanengesang" ("Sappho's Swan Song") and written in a Sapphic meter, was begun probably in February of 1800.

islands—The Greek islands.

the holy ones—The Greeks.

furious heroes—Aias and Achilles (Schmidt).

To Hope

This Alcaic ode is a slightly modified version of the ode "Bitte" ("Request," not translated here) that Hölderlin worked on probably in December of 1800. The main difference from "Request," besides some punctuation, is in line 19 (see variants).

Crocus—The German word for crocus is *Zeitlose*, which literally means "timeless one."

VARIANTS

An earlier version of the beginning of the second stanza reads:

Wo bist du? Himmelsbotin! umsonst erwacht
   Mein Auge mir des Morgens nur mich weht kalt
      Die Zukunft an, [. . .]

Where are you? Messenger from heaven! My eyes
   Awake in vain each morning, only the future blows
      On me cold, [. . .]

[line 19]—In "Bitte" the phrase *Mir sterblich Glük verheißen* ([and if you may / Not] promise me mortal joy) replaces *Ein Geist der Erde, kommen* ([and if you may / Not] appear a spirit of the earth).

[line 20]—In an earlier draft the last line reads *Unsterblichem* (something immortal) for *anderem* (something else).

Vulcan

An earlier draft of this Alcaic ode, "Der Winter" ("The Winter," not translated here), was begun in 1799.

Let man be content—The German here is *Manne*, a male human being, as opposed to *Mensch*, a human being in general.

Vulcan—The Roman name for Hephaestus, the Greek god of fire and blacksmithing.

hateful cares—Compare line 6 of "Love" (Beissner).

Boreas—The north wind in Greek mythology.

[line 1]—In an earlier draft *freundlicher Feuergeist* (friendly spirit of fire) reads *zaubrischer Phantasus* (magical Phantasus). Phantasus was the god of dreams, brother to sleep and death.

Timidity

This Asclepiadic ode is a reworking of "The Poet's Courage."

Timidity—The German also means "shyness." Beissner explains the seeming contradiction between the title and the poem by seeing the poem as an encouragement to the poet who is inhibited by timidity.

boon—The German *gelegen* can mean "suitable, proper," as well as "opportune."

Each in its way—The syntax here is quite difficult. Beissner thinks this phrase refers to the song and the choir, while Schmidt claims it has to refer to the gods and men (i.e., that each are brought to communion according to what they are).

sent [. . .] useful [. . .] suitable—The German here is *geschikt [. . .] schiklich*, a play I was not able to reproduce in English. I have translated *geschikt*, which is both the past participle of the verb *schiken* (to send) and an adjective meaning skillful, with two words: "sent [. . .] useful." Hölderlin may also be playing here on *Geschik*, which can mean both skill and fate.

Ganymede

This Alcaic ode is a reworking of "The Fettered River."

Ganymede—See the last note to "To the Aether."

Full of ancient breath—The German *Geist* is usually rendered as spirit or mind. But etymologically it's rooted in *Gischt*, which is a fermenting foam created in the wine-making process. Because the Latin *spiritus* has the meanings "breath" and "breathing," it seemed appropriate to infuse "the word," which after all comes from human mouths, with an ancient "breath."

Navel of Earth—The center of the earth. Delphi was considered by Greeks to be the ὀμφαλός, navel or middle point, of the earth (Beissner).

Half of Life

This and the last two Nightsongs are written in free verse.

weathervanes—The German *Fahnen* can also mean flag or banner.

Ages of Life

Palmyra—Ancient Syrian city that was sacked by the Romans in 273, leaving only ruins ("forests of columns in the desert plains").

crowns—The capitals of the columns.

Vapor of smoke—Compare Apostles 2:19: "And I will shew wonders in heaven above, and signs in the earth beneath; blood, and fire, and vapour of smoke" (Beissner).

each—Beissner conjectures that the German *deren* (whose, of whose), which I've rendered as "each," is an error introduced by the printer, and that the word might have been originally *darin* (in which).

The Shelter at Hardt

The Shelter at Hardt—Hardt is a small town in southwestern Germany and close to a shelter formed by two giant slabs of sandstone leaning against each other. According to legend, the Protestant Duke Ulrich von Württemberg (1487–1550) hid there to escape his persecutors, and a spider spun a web over the shelter to prevent Ulrich's enemies from entering the next day. Hölderlin grew up in nearby Nürtingen and one of his first poems, lost to us now, was dedicated to the shelter at Hardt.

Not at all speechless.—The period that ends this line is not in the poem as it was first published in Wilmans' *Taschenbuch*. Beissner adds it in the *GSA* because, he argues, it is the ground that is "not at all speechless" since it has witnessed the flight of Ulrich—that is, it has something of which it can speak. Sattler does not add the period in the *FHA* version of the poem, which would change the meaning of the poem dramatically by relating "Not at all speechless" to Ulrich, yielding something like "For Ulrich walked there / Not at all speechless."

1. D. E. Sattler, ed., Friedrich Hölderlin, *Sämtliche Werke: Frankfurter Ausgabe* (Frankfurt am Main, 1976), 6: 75.

2. Michael Knaupp, ed., *Friedrich Hölderlins Sämtliche Werke und Briefe* (Munich, 1993), 3: 89.

3. Friedrich Beissner, ed., Friedrich Hölderlin, *Sämtliche Werke* (Stuttgart, 1947), 1:2: 523.

4. Pindar, *Pindar's Victory Songs* (Baltimore, 1980), 256. Translated by Frank Nisetich.

5. Friedrich Hölderlin, *Hyperion and Selected Poems* (New York, 2002), 133. Translated by Williard R. Trask, adapted by David Schwarz.

6. Jonathan Barnes, ed. and trans., *Early Greek Philosophy* (London, 1987), 115.

7. D. E. Sattler, ed., Friedrich Hölderlin, *Sämtliche Werke: Frankfurter Ausgabe* (Frankfurt am Main, 1976), 6: 123.

8. Homer, *The Iliad* (Chicago, 1967), 68. Translated by Richard Lattimore.

9. Theodor Adorno, "Parataxis," in *Notes to Literature* (New York, 1992), 2: 119. Translated by Shierry Weber Nicholsen.

10. Horace, *The Complete Odes and Epodes* (London, 1983), 163. Translated by W. G. Shepherd.

11. Jonathan Barnes, ed. and trans., *Early Greek Philosophy* (London, 1987), 102.

12. Ibid., 103.

13. New Standard Revised Edition.

14. Herodotus, *The Histories* (London, 1954), 112. Translated by Aubrey de Sélincourt.

15. Plutarch, *The Lives of the Noble Grecians and Romans* (New York, 1977), 1205. Translated by John Dryden, revised by Arthur Hugh Clough.

16. Pindar, *Pindar's Victory Songs* (Baltimore, 1980), 91. Translated by Frank Nisetich.

17. Bernhard Böschenstein, "'Brod und Wein': Von der 'klassischen' Reinschrift zur späten Überarbeitung," in *Von Morgen nach Abend* (Munich, 2006), 26–48.

Table of Expanded Poems

Hölderlin used the poems in the left column as the basis for the later expansion of those in the right column (except in the case of "To the Sun God," which was shortened). The page number follows in brackets.

The Unpardonable [21]	Love [93]
To the Germans [two stanzas] [23]	To the Germans [fourteen stanzas] [85]
	Rousseau [89]
Her Recovery [three stanzas] [23]	Her Recovery [five stanzas] [97]
The Course of Life [one stanza] [25]	The Course of Life [four stanzas] [95]
Diotima ("You fall silent . . .") [two stanzas] [29]	Diotima [six stanzas] [99]
Home [two stanzas] [31]	Home [six stanzas] [91]
To Our Great Poets [35]	The Poet's Calling [103]
To the Sun God [35]	Sunset [37]
Voice of the People [two stanzas] [37]	Voice of the People [eighteen stanzas] [107]
The Main [63]	The Neckar [81]
The Poet's Courage [113]	Timidity [177]
The Fettered River [115]	Ganymede [179]
The Blind Singer [117]	Chiron [167]
Bread and Wine [133]	Bread and Wine [second version] [153]

INDEX OF ENGLISH TITLES

INDEX OF GERMAN TITLES

INDEX OF ENGLISH FIRST LINES

INDEX OF GERMAN FIRST LINES